Lean Six Sigma

A hybrid methodology, Lean Six Sigma (LSS) is designed to accommodate global challenges and constraints by capitalizing on Six Sigma and Lean Thinking. LSS incorporates best practices from programs such as the International Organization for Standardization (ISO), Capability Maturity Model, and Total Quality Management.

International LSS practitioners must understand the dynamics of LSS, along with its cultural aspects and regulations. *Lean Six Sigma: International Standards and Global Guidelines* provides this understanding.

This book assumes that the overall goal of operational excellence is to ensure that organizational tasks and activities are being performed to the best of their process capabilities. It defines continuous improvement as activities that support and empower environments to make flexible decisions that lead to ongoing improvement and effectiveness. Coverage includes:

- New global LSS standards
- International implementation of process improvement programs
- New international LSS applications
- International LSS areas of competency

This book defines many of the terms popularized by process improvement programs, such as center of excellence and business transformation. It documents these practices and explains how to perform future activities in accordance with the recorded practices. Exploring international approaches to LSS, it details the new ISO Standard for Six Sigma and also addresses the role of project management in LSS.

Illustrating the synergies between Lean and Six Sigma and how they partner with other process improvement programs and initiatives, this book is an ideal study guide for those preparing to take the LSS Black Belt certification exam.

This third edition covers important updates, such as:

- How innovation is being integrated
- The way in which Lean leadership is now being accomplished globally
- Newer case studies with specific attention to how Lean and Six Sigma are being monitored in healthcare and government
- Highlighting updated successes and the consideration of diversity and equity issues as they relate to LSS

Lean Six Sigma

International Standards and Global Guidelines

Third Edition

Terra Vanzant Stern, PhD

A PRODUCTIVITY PRESS BOOK

First published 2024
by Routledge
605 Third Avenue, New York, NY 10158

and by Routledge
4 Park Square, Milton Park, Abingdon, Oxon, OX14 4RN

Routledge is an imprint of the Taylor & Francis Group, an informa business

ISBN: 978-1-032-50260-1 (hbk)
ISBN: 978-1-032-50259-5 (pbk)
ISBN: 978-1-003-39764-9 (ebk)

DOI: 10.4324/9781003397649

Typeset in Garamond
by SPi Technologies India Pvt Ltd (Straive)

To all my friends at the International Standard for Lean Six Sigma (ISLSS) organization, American Society of Quality (ASQ), and Project Management Institute (PMI). Your help, support, and knowledge-sharing have been much appreciated.

Contents

Preface xiii
Acknowledgments xv
Author xvi

SECTION I NEW GLOBAL STANDARDS

1 **ISO 13053 International Standard for Six Sigma** **3**
1.1 ISO 13053-1 9
1.2 ISO 13053-2 12

2 **Lean Project Management** **16**
2.1 PMI Certifications 24
2.2 PRINCE2 Certifications 25
2.3 The American Academy of Project Managers 25
2.4 Self-Study 26

3 **Lean Government in the United States** **30**
3.1 Department of Veterans Affairs 32
3.2 Department of Defense 33
3.3 The Department of Homeland Security 33
3.4 The Department of Health and Human Services 34
3.5 International Government Communities 36

SECTION II LEAN SIX SIGMA, OPERATIONAL EXCELLENCE, AND CONTINUOUS IMPROVEMENT

4 **Core Knowledge** **43**
4.1 Define, Measure, Analyze, Improve, and Control 44
4.2 Plan–Do–Check–Act 45

4.3 DMAIC and PDCA........45
4.4 Rapid Improvement or Kaizen Event Models........46
4.5 Discussion........47

5 Lean Six Sigma Basics........48
5.1 Discussion........53

6 Analytical Problem-Solving Tools........54
6.1 Flowcharting........55
6.2 Check Sheets........56
6.3 Cause-and-Effect Diagram........58
6.4 Histogram........59
6.5 Pareto Chart........61
6.6 Scatter Diagram........62
6.7 Control Charts........63
6.8 Discussion........66

7 DMAIC Basics........67
7.1 Overview of DMAIC........68
7.2 Practice Exercises........72

8 Define........73
8.1 Process Mapping........75
8.2 Project Charter........75
8.3 SWOT Analysis........77
8.4 Critical to Quality........77
8.5 SIPOC Diagram........78
8.6 Quality Function Deployment........79
8.7 DMAIC WBS........80
8.8 Affinity Diagram........81
8.9 Kano Model........81
8.10 Discussion........83

9 Measure........84
9.1 Detailed Process Map........87
9.2 Benchmarking........87
9.3 Scorecards........88
9.4 Failure Mode and Effects Analysis........89
9.5 Sigma Calculations........91
9.6 Cp and Pp Indexes........91

9.7 Measurement Systems Analysis 94
9.8 Data Collection Plan 94
9.9 Discussion 96

10 Analyze 97
10.1 Correlation Analysis 100
10.2 The 5 Whys 100
10.3 The Seven Tools for Process Improvement 101
10.4 Statistical Thinking 101
10.5 Statistical Process Control 103
10.6 Stem-and-Leaf Diagram 106
10.7 Type I and Type II Errors 107
10.8 Design of Experiment 108
10.9 Analysis of Variance 109
10.10 Discussion 110

11 Improve 111
11.1 Project Plan 115
11.2 Discussion 117

12 Control 119
12.1 ROI Calculations 121
12.2 Sustainability 121
12.3 5S Plans 123
12.4 Close-Out Activities 125
12.4.1 Sustainability Reduces Cost 126
12.4.2 Sustainability Conserves Resources 126
12.4.3 Sustainability Improves Employee Morale 127
12.4.4 Sustainability Reduces Waste 128
12.4.5 Sustainability Increases Efficiency 128
12.5 Discussion 129

13 Summary of DMAIC 130
13.1 Define 133
13.2 Measure 133
13.3 Analyze 133
13.4 Improve 134
13.5 Control 134
13.6 Discussion 136

SECTION III INTERNATIONAL IMPLEMENTATION OF PROCESS IMPROVEMENT PROGRAMS

14 Additional Lean Six Sigma Tools 139
14.1 Activity Network Diagram 142
14.2 Box Plots 143
14.3 Delphi Technique 144
14.4 Gantt Chart 145
14.5 Matrix Diagram 145
14.6 Program Evaluation and Review Technique 145
14.7 Prioritization Matrix 145
14.8 Quality Function Deployment (Also Called QFD or House of Quality) 146
14.9 Stem-and-Leaf Plot 146
14.10 Discussion 146

15 Quick Start Guide 147
15.1 Discussion 151

16 Leadership Challenge 152
16.1 Discussion 162

17 Change Management 163
17.1 Primarily Process-Centric Change Management Models 164
17.1.1 Plan–Do–Check–Act (PDCA) 164
17.1.2 Awareness, Desire, Knowledge, Ability, and Reinforcement (ADKAR) 165
17.1.3 Kotter's 8 Steps 166
17.1.4 Lewin's 3-Stage Model of Change 166
17.1.5 McKinsey 7-S Model Framework 166
17.1.6 Governance, Structure, and Systems (GSS) Change Management Model 167
17.1.7 Using the Define–Measure–Analyze–Improve–Control (DMAIC) Approach as Change Management Model 168
17.2 Primarily People-Centric Change Management Models 174
17.2.1 Nudge Theory 174
17.2.2 Bridges Change Management Theory 175
17.2.3 Kübler-Ross Model 176
17.3 Discussion 176

18 Training Modules: Using Instructional Systems Design for Lean Six Sigma Training....177
18.1 The ADDIE Model....178
18.1.1 Analysis....178
18.1.2 Design....178
18.1.3 Development....178
18.1.4 Implementation....179
18.1.5 Evaluation....179
18.2 Training Plans....180
18.3 E-Learning....181
18.4 Training Manuals....182
18.5 Adult Learners....182
18.6 Training in Different Cultures....183
18.7 Discussion....185

SECTION IV LEAN SIX SIGMA APPLICATIONS

19 Lean Six Sigma in Healthcare: Medical Facilities....189

20 Lean Six Sigma and the Medical Device Industry....194

21 From Efficiency to Intelligence: Unleashing the Power of Lean Six Sigma in AI....199
21.1 Introduction....199
21.2 What is AI?....199
21.3 The Potential of Combining Lean Six Sigma and AI....200
21.3.1 Streamlining Processes with AI and Lean Six Sigma....201
21.4 Reducing Waste and Increasing Efficiency with AI and Lean Six Sigma....203
21.5 Improving Quality Control with AI and Lean Six Sigma....204
21.6 Enhancing Decision-Making with AI and Lean Six Sigma....205

22 Lean Six Sigma in Innovative Thinking and Design....207
22.1 Malcolm Baldrige National Quality Award....218

SECTION V INTERNATIONAL LEAN SIX SIGMA AREAS OF COMPETENCY AND RESOURCE MATERIALS

Appendix One A Brief History of Lean Six Sigma 223

Appendix Two Pandemic Proofing the Future with Lean Six Sigma 232

Appendix Three Competency Models 236

Lean Six Sigma Green Belt Basic International Competency Model 237

Lean Six Sigma Black Belt Basic International Competency Model 239

Lean Six Sigma Master Black Belt Basic Competency Model 243

Reference Materials 247

Lean Six Sigma Body of Knowledge Outline (SSD Global Version 4.0) 247

Lean Six Sigma Body of Knowledge Narrative (SSD Global Version 5.0) 290

Index 323

Preface

The Importance of Lean Six Sigma in Uncertain Times

Companies across various industries constantly navigate uncertainty due to changing economic, political, and social factors. The ongoing COVID-19 pandemic has further highlighted the need for organizations to be prepared for any unforeseen circumstances and operate agilely. In such times, Lean Six Sigma is more critical than ever, providing a structured and data-driven approach to problem-solving and process improvement.

Lean Six Sigma helps organizations reduce waste, improve efficiency, and enhance customer satisfaction while maintaining quality standards. It combines the Lean methodology of identifying and eliminating waste with the Six Sigma approach of reducing process variability and defects. By implementing Lean Six Sigma, organizations can streamline their operations, optimize resources, and improve their bottom line while adapting to changes in the external environment.

Moreover, Lean Six Sigma can help organizations stay ahead of the competition by fostering a culture of continuous improvement and innovation. In uncertain times, this mindset can be invaluable in staying nimble and responsive to the changing needs of customers and stakeholders.

Before considering the benefits and strategies for implementing Lean Six Sigma in uncertain times, it's essential to understand the principles and methodologies underpinning this problem-solving approach. Having a common understanding of the industry-standard terms and methodologies helps clarify the intent. It makes customizing the process easier.

Key strategies in implementing a successful Lean Six Sigma program depend on a shared understanding of the vocabulary. Other essential methods include:

1. Developing a clear understanding of your organization's needs and priorities: In uncertain times, organizations may need to pivot quickly to adapt to changing circumstances.
2. Thoroughly understanding your organization's needs and priorities will help ensure that your Lean Six Sigma efforts are aligned with your organization's goals.
3. Creating a comprehensive implementation plan: A comprehensive plan will help ensure that your Lean Six Sigma efforts are focused and well-organized. It should include timelines, milestones, and clear roles and responsibilities for all team members.
4. Training your team members: It's essential to provide them with the training they need to implement Lean Six Sigma effectively. This training should include the principles and methodologies and the tools and techniques required to make meaningful improvements.
5. Using data-driven decision-making: One of the fundamental principles of Lean Six Sigma is using data to drive decision-making. During uncertain times, relying on data to make informed decisions and measure progress toward goals is especially critical.
6. Engaging all stakeholders: Effective implementation of Lean Six Sigma requires buy-in from all stakeholders.

This work, *Lean Six Sigma: International Standards and Global Guidelines, Third Edition*, intends to clarify the best common understanding of the approaches, tools, and methodologies for successful implementation. It offers a proven framework for improving efficiency, reducing costs, enhancing quality, and fostering innovation, all of which are critical for success in uncertain times.

Terra Vanzant Stern, PhD
CEO
Simple, Smart, Decision-Making, Inc.
dba SSD Global Solutions, Inc.

Acknowledgments

American Society of Quality Project Management Institute
SSD Global Solutions Clients and Partners ASQ Lean Enterprise Division

Author

Terra Vanzant Stern, PhD, is a popular IT Pro TV host and CEO of Simple, Smart, Decision-Making, Inc. dba SSD Global Solutions (SSD). SSD specializes in Change Management, Process Improvement, and Project Management for M&A and government clients.

Dr. Stern is a PMP and Six Sigma Master Black Belt. She also holds SPHR, GPHR, Facilitation, ISD, and Quality Engineering certifications.

Other books by Dr. Stern include *Lean and Agile Project Management*, *Leaner Six Sigma®*, and *HR Concepts for Project Managers*.

Dr. Stern is currently exploring The Business Case for Forgiveness in the Workplace and The Importance of Ethics in Change Management.

NEW GLOBAL STANDARDS

I

Introduction: Building a Foundation for Lean Six Sigma with Solid Standards

In today's fast-paced business environment, organizations constantly seek ways to improve their processes and increase efficiency. This is where Lean Six Sigma comes in, a methodology that focuses on eliminating waste and reducing process variation to achieve optimal performance. However, for this approach to be successful, it is essential to have solid standards in place. Standards provide a framework for consistency and continuous improvement, making them a crucial component of any Lean Six Sigma initiative.

Lean Six Sigma is a robust methodology that combines Lean principles and Six Sigma techniques to improve efficiency and reduce waste in processes. At its core, Lean Six Sigma focuses on achieving optimal performance by eliminating non-value-added activities, reducing defects and errors, and streamlining workflows.

To understand Lean Six Sigma, it's essential first to grasp its fundamental principles. One of the main principles is the concept of continuous improvement, also known as Kaizen. This means organizations should constantly strive for incremental enhancements in their processes rather than settling for the status quo.

Another fundamental principle is the emphasis on data-driven decision-making. Lean Six Sigma practitioners rely on data and statistical analysis to identify and address the root causes of problems. This ensures that solutions are based on factual evidence rather than assumptions or opinions.

DOI: 10.4324/9781003397649-1

Additionally, Lean Six Sigma promotes a customer-centric mindset. It encourages organizations to meet and exceed customer expectations by delivering high-quality and valuable products and services. Organizations can align their processes and resources by understanding and prioritizing customer needs.

Furthermore, Lean Six Sigma emphasizes the importance of collaboration and teamwork. It encourages cross-functional collaboration, involving employees from different departments and levels of the organization. This collaborative approach allows for a holistic understanding of processes and facilitates the sharing knowledge and expertise.

By understanding the principles of Lean Six Sigma, organizations can clearly understand its purpose and potential benefits. This knowledge is a solid foundation for implementing the methodology and effectively leveraging its tools and techniques.

Lean Six Sigma is a methodology that aims to improve efficiency and eliminate waste in processes. However, without solid standards in place, organizations will struggle to achieve the full benefits of this approach. Standards provide a framework for consistency and continuous improvement, guiding organizations to follow in their Lean Six Sigma initiatives.

One critical step in implementing standards is to involve all stakeholders. This includes top management, process owners, and frontline employees. By engaging stakeholders in the process, you can gather valuable insights and ensure that the standards reflect the realities of the organization. Implementing practical standards is not a one-time task. It requires ongoing monitoring, review, and adjustment to ensure the standards remain relevant and valuable. By following these steps, organizations can implement standards that support successful Lean Six Sigma practices and drive sustainable improvements.

Chapter 1

ISO 13053 International Standard for Six Sigma

For the International Lean Six Sigma (ILSS) practitioner new to International Organization for Standardization (ISO), it is important to review the basics about ISO standards before understanding the worldwide impact of ISO 13053 for Six Sigma. Understanding ISO certification will also help the ILSS practitioner when they are working with an ISO-certified company.

ISO is a global federation of national standards bodies. ISO publishes over 22,000 standards covering all industries to include but not limited to technology, food safety, manufacturing, and healthcare.

Standards offer organizations the ability to apply for ISO certification. Certification means that, according to an ISO auditor, the organization involved has met the requirements set forth in a specific standard. ISO technical committees conduct the work of preparing the standard. These committees include subject matter experts as well as ISO representatives. Not all standards lead to certification. Standards can also be guidelines.

The ISO 9000 framework helps assess a company's ability to meet the needs of the customer. Simplified, this standard requires organizations to (1) identify their quality management system (QMS) and (2) continually improve the QMS process. The first step is registering.

The process of registration involves the following steps:

- A certified ISO registrar receives the application;
- The certified ISO registrar does a two-part assessment:
  - Readiness Survey
  - Quality Management System Review;

DOI: 10.4324/9781003397649-2

- Registration is either granted or not granted. Companies have the opportunity to correct their activities and try again.

The next step is certification. To become certified the company must demonstrate that they have documented their management system, identified their core business processes, and then implemented the quality management system. To stay certified the company must demonstrate that they are working toward continual improvement.

Generally speaking, companies hire a consultant to prepare for registration. The consultant may be independent or be an employee of a certified ISO registrar. An internal audit is one method used to prepare.

The best-known ISO standards in the United States belong to the ISO 9000 series. ISO 9001, updated regularly, is the original management standard. The most current ISO 9000 standard is ISO 9000:2015. This standard, reviewed in 2021, remains the current standard.

To understand the value of the Six Sigma ISO Standard, it is beneficial to understand ISO in general. Although previously noted that ISO publishes over 22,000 standards, the most commonly used standards are in the ISO 9000 series.

The ISO 9000 series is a collection of standards designed to help organizations improve their processes and operations. Each standard has its own specific set of requirements, and one of the most important is the ISO 16 core standards. These standards include:

- Quality Management System
- Documentation Requirements
- Control of Documents
- Control of Records
- Internal Auditing
- Corrective and Preventive Actions
- Configuration Management
- Measurement, Analysis, and Improvement
- Maintaining the Integrity of Quality Records
- Handling Customer Property

ISO 9000 as well as the standards governing Six Sigma all include foundational thought in the eight management principles also promoted in ISO 9000:2015. ISO standards all support the process approach, continual improvement, and customer focus. Leadership and the involvement of people are prime factors for success.

From the earliest days of business management, there have been certain principles that have stood the test of time. These principles are as relevant today as they were decades ago, and they will likely never go out of style. Here is a summarized version:

1. Delegation: Delegation is an essential management skill. It means entrusting tasks and responsibilities to others who are capable of carrying them out. It is not only a matter of assigning tasks to the right people, but it is also a way to empower them to take on more responsibility and be part of the team's success.
2. Being Decisive: Decisiveness is a fundamental part of good management. A leader needs to be able to make decisions quickly, confidently, and efficiently. In order to be a successful manager, it is important to know when to act and when to wait. The ability to make timely decisions will help to keep the organization on track and keep it from getting bogged down in indecision or unnecessary delays. It is important for managers to take into consideration all available information and facts before deciding.
3. Effective Communication: Effective communication is essential for any successful business. It is important to make sure that everyone in the organization is on the same page, especially when it comes to understanding key objectives and tasks. Leaders must also ensure their team members have the information they need to make decisions and complete tasks.

   In order to communicate effectively, it is important to create an environment of open communication and respect. Individuals are encouraged to speak up and contribute. This allows for the free exchange of ideas and suggestions. Clear guidelines are established. Everyone is aware of what kind of information is acceptable for sharing and what should remain confidential.
4. Be Proactive: Being proactive is one of the most important management principles that will never go out of style. It is about being ahead of the game. Anticipating what needs to happen before it becomes an issue is an example of proactivity. It means taking a proactive approach to problem-solving, planning, and decision-making.

   For managers, being proactive means looking for opportunities to improve processes or systems, rather than waiting for problems to arise. It means staying one step ahead of potential obstacles, setting goals and creating action plans in advance. It also involves actively seeking feedback and responding to it quickly and effectively.

5. Relationship Building: Good managers understand the importance of building relationships with their team. Developing strong relationships can help foster an environment of trust, respect, and collaboration. This makes it easier to motivate and engage team members, as well as helps managers to better understand the needs of their team.

   Building relationships starts with getting to know your team. Be available to chat with each member of the team and get to know them on a more personal level. Ask questions about their background, hobbies, interests, and what they are looking to achieve from their career. When team members feel valued, respected, and heard, they will be more likely to contribute ideas.
6. Clear Expectations: Expectations are an important part of any successful management plan. When expectations are clear, it allows employees to understand their roles and responsibilities more easily. It also helps to ensure that everyone is on the same page and working toward the same goals.

   When setting expectations, it is important to be as specific as possible. By outlining the expectations in a detailed manner, it can help to avoid any misunderstandings. It is also important to ensure that employees have all the information they need in order to meet those expectations. This includes providing deadlines, instructions, and other relevant details.

   Additionally, it is essential that employees understand the consequences of not meeting expectations. Clearly communicating this in the beginning can help to keep everyone motivated and focused on their tasks.
7. Leading by Example: Leading by example is an important part of any successful management team. In order to ensure a team's success, it is essential for the manager to lead by example. This means that the manager should set the standards and be the role model for their team. Showing how to get things done in an effective manner and maintaining a professional attitude can inspire others to do the same.

   Leaders who lead by example demonstrate their commitment to the team, its values, and objectives. This encourages employees to take ownership of their roles and do their best to achieve their goals.
8. Continuous Learning: One of the most important principles of successful management is the need to continuously learn. By staying up to date with industry trends, you can develop a better understanding of your team and their goals, as well as stay on top of any potential

changes in the market or business environment. Additionally, by seeking out new opportunities for growth and development, you can help ensure your team remains productive and engaged.

In all ISO documentation there are key terms. Here is a list with the summarized explanations:

- Quality Management System (QMS) – A QMS is the system that outlines the policies, processes, and procedures necessary to meet the requirements of the ISO 16 standard.
- Documented Information – This is any information that is necessary to ensure the effectiveness of the QMS and made available to any parties involved.
- Risk-based Thinking – This refers to the process of considering potential risks and opportunities during the planning and operation of processes in order to reduce their potential impact on product quality.
- Continual Improvement – This is an ongoing process that includes the identification of areas of improvement. This increases the effectiveness of the QMS.
- Customer Focus – This term refers to a commitment to understanding customer needs and striving to exceed them, as well as creating and maintaining relationships with customers.
- Leadership – Leaders are responsible for providing direction and guidance, as well as setting a good example for those around them.
- Involvement of People – The success of any QMS depends on its employees; this term recognizes their importance and promotes their involvement in all aspects of the system.
- Process Approach – This involves the application of a system of activities in order to create an effective QMS. It involves planning, controlling, and managing processes in order to meet objectives and customer requirements.
- System Approach to Management – This approach involves managing the QMS as a system, rather than managing individual processes separately.
- Mutually Beneficial Supplier Relationships – This refers to relationships between the organization and its suppliers that are mutually beneficial and support Continuous Improvement.
- Fact-based Decision-Making – This involves using data and facts to make decisions, rather than relying on opinions or assumptions.

The primary goal of ISO initiatives is to increase customer satisfaction. This standard provides better management controls and engaging in continuous process improvement. The ILSS practitioner is able to influence this initiative by eliminating errors, reducing waste, and providing sustainability models.

The second most recognized standard in the United States is ISO 14001. ISO 14001 focuses on the management of environmental issues. These include the following:

- Environmental review
- Environmental policy creation
- Documenting the Environmental Management System
- Audit and review

The ILSS practitioner interested in working with ISO 14001 should be familiar with the environmental efforts of the company as well as any compliance issues for that specific industry and governmental regulations.

The introduction of ISO 13053 for Six Sigma is an exciting development for the ILSS practitioner. This standard is for Six Sigma, but it contains components typically associated with Lean Manufacturing, Continuous Improvement (CI), and Operational Excellence (OE). For the ILSS practitioner, working in ISO 9000 or ISO 14000 environments, the Six Sigma standard adds another layer of credibility to process improvement.

Six Sigma professionals often rely on the American Society for Quality (ASQ) Six Sigma Black Belt Body of Knowledge (ASQ-SSBOK). This outlines the topics covered in the ASQ Six Sigma Black Belt certification examination.

Topics listed in the ASQ-SSBOK are the same as those covered in ISO 13053. However, differences also are evident. For example, ASQ-SSBOK supports more references to the history and value of Six Sigma, leadership, and the maturity of teams. ISO 13053 places more emphasis on tools, implementation, and the maturity of an organization.

ISO 13053 includes two subordinate standards: ISO 13053-1 and ISO 13053-2. ISO 13053-1 covers the Define–Measure–Analyze–Improve–Control (DMAIC) methodology. ISO 13053-2 covers tools used in the DMAIC process.

ISO 13053 helps to promote continual improvement in product safety and reliability. It encourages organizations to review and update their quality management systems on a regular basis in order to stay ahead of any changes or developments in the industry. This helps to ensure that any new products will be of a consistently high quality and meet the relevant safety standards.

By implementing ISO 13053, organizations can also benefit from improved cost savings. As the system requires regular reviews and updates, it enables companies to identify any issues quickly. Additionally, following this system can also help organizations reduce waste and inefficiency, as they can more effectively manage processes such as supply chain management.

Overall, ISO 13053 provides organizations with an effective framework for improving product safety and reliability, as well as providing other benefits. By following this system, businesses can improve their customer satisfaction and cost savings, while ensuring that their products meet the necessary safety and quality standards.

1.1 ISO 13053-1

This part of ISO 13053 records the best practices in each of the phases of the DMAIC model. It makes management recommendations and gives an overall understanding of the roles and responsibilities in a Six Sigma project. In the typical Lean Six Sigma (LSS) project, often the ILSS practitioner will need to wear a variety of hats. Understanding how each role should function independently offers insight as well as a solid checklist.

The standard outlines activities involved in a Six Sigma project such as gathering data, extracting information from those data, designing a solution, and ensuring the desired results. ISO 13053-1 states that a reliable fiscal management model should be in place before beginning a process improvement.

In contrast, the ASQ-SSBOK specifically notes that Six Sigma project awareness should include an understanding of market share, margin, and revenue growth. Specific emphasis is on the following:

- Net Present Value
- Return on Investment
- Cost of Quality

ISO 13053-1 promotes a basic maturity model. Maturity models are popular in other process improvement programs as well. Maturity model levels are markers and milestones. These levels may also monitor success and build evaluation metrics. These levels of maturity are:

- Level 1—the starting point
- Level 2—managed
- Level 3—defined
- Level 4—quantitatively managed
- Level 5—optimized

This particular model is familiar to students of Capability Maturity Model Integrated (CMMI). CMMI is a process improvement approach designed to improve enterprise-wide performance. Defense contracts or software-related projects use CMMI. According to the Software Engineering Institute, CMMI helps “integrate traditionally separate organizational functions, set process improvement goals and priorities, provide guidance for quality processes, and provide a point of reference for appraising current processes.”

ISO 13053-1 emphasizes the Voice of the Customer (VOC). The ASQ-SSBOK includes reference to VOC as well. VOC is the attention to customer feedback and understanding customer requirements. Customer requirements are also known as Critical-to-Quality (CTQ) factors. CTQ factors are more heavily stressed in LSS as compared to ISO 13053-1 or ASQ-SSBOK, thus exceeding the objectives of both documents. In LSS, the concept of “voices” is also captured in the following:

- Voice of the Employee (VOE)
- Voice of the Business (or rather Voice of the Industry)
- Voice of the Process (VOP)

As with all documents related to Six Sigma or LSS, ISO 13053-1 fully explains the Sigma statistic and normal distribution table by using the term Defects per Million Opportunities.

ISO 13053-1 discusses Cost of Poor Quality (COPQ) and relies on the Total Quality Management definition of this term. Producing and fixing defects resulting from an internal or external failure creates the COPQ.

LSS confirms this definition but also includes what-if scenarios in the explanation of COPQ. For example, what is the cost of doing nothing? What is the potential lost revenue? What are all the costs associated with providing inferior products or services?

There are three areas normally considered in articulating the COPQ:

- Appraisal costs
- Internal failure costs
- External failure costs

The ISO 13053-1 standard explains human resource roles within a Six Sigma project. Roles outlined in the competency model consist of the following:

- Champion
- Yellow Belt
- Green Belt
- Black Belt
- Master Black Belt
- Deployment Manager

These terms are universal and also appear in the ASQ Six Sigma Body of Knowledge. Lean Six Sigma includes the following roles as well:

- White Belt
- Process Owner
- Sponsor

The ASQ-SSBOK does not go into detail about the various roles and responsibilities but does place a premium on things not included in the ISO 13053-1 document such as team types. The team types include the following:

- Formal
- Informal
- Virtual
- Cross-functional
- Self-directed

ISO 13053-1 outlines how to prioritize projects and offers suggestions for project selection originally introduced by Edwards Deming that includes considerations such as the following:

- Are there measures?
- Will the potential project improve customer satisfaction?

- Is the potential project aligned to at least one of the business measures?

The standard speaks to project scoping, inputs/outputs, and general information before moving to the model. Project scoping and documentation of the scope are crucial activities for CI and OE initiatives as well. The ILSS practitioner can often help in the CI and OE effort by clarifying the scope.

ISO 13053-1 captures essential information for each phase of the DMAIC. A more in-depth explanation of the DMAIC phases may be located in Section II of this book, *Lean Six Sigma, Operational Excellence, and Continuous Improvement.*

1.2 ISO 13053-2

The primary purpose of 13053-2 is to introduce tools that will help execute the DMAIC process. The standard presents the following concepts and fact sheets:

- Affinity diagram
- Brainstorming
- Cause-and-effect diagram
- Control charts
- CTQ tree diagram
- Data collection plan
- Descriptive Statistics
- Design of Experiment
- Determination of sample
- FMEA (Failure Mode and Effects Analysis)
- Gantt chart
- Hypothesis testing
- Indicators of key performance
- Kano
- Measurement systems
- Monitoring/control plan
- Normality testing
- Prioritization matrix
- Process mapping and process
- Project charter

- Project review
- QFD (Quality Function Deployment—House of Quality)
- RACI (Responsible, Accountable, Consulted, and Informed) Matrix
- Regression and correlation
- Reliability
- Return on Investment (ROI), Costs, and Accountability
- Services delivery
- SIPOC (Suppliers, Inputs, Processes, Outputs, Customers)
- Value stream
- Waste

The ASQ-SSBOK and LSS toolkit recognizes the above-referenced tools. Students of OE or CI programs likewise use these tools. However, the ASQ-SSBOK does not offer specific instructions or fact sheets for these tools.

LSS philosophy will consider the scalability of the tool when making a tool decision. For example, if the project is small, tools such as DOE (Design of Experiment), Hypothesis Testing, and QFD may not be useful. Lean Six Sigma theory supports the thought that a person should only use the tool if it is necessary. There is a tendency in both the ISO and ASQ documentation to use particular toolboxes on every assignment.

The ASQ-SSBOK also covers Design for Six Sigma (DFSS). ISO 13053-2 does not address DFSS. Tools commonly used in DFSS are, however, included in the toolbox promoted by the ISO standard.

Design for Six Sigma is a process methodology used when no existing process is in place. A popular DFSS model is Define–Measure–Analyze–Design–Verify (DMADV). The first three phases of the model are the same as the DMAIC model, which is why it is a popular choice for the ILSS practitioner. The argument for DFSS is that processes created from scratch require a design component. Technically the DMAIC model does not have a design component.

ASQ-SSBOK places more emphasis on specific statistics and manual calculations. ISO 13053-2 promotes statistical thinking captured within the tools as opposed to individual statistical knowledge. LSS tends to slant toward the use of MS Excel-based statistical software with the intent of simplifying statistical concepts.

In summary, if the ILSS practitioner has not worked in an ISO environment, reviewing ISO 9001:2015[8] is essential. This standard is valuable to the ILSS practitioner even if certification is not the goal. ISO standards, in general, provide strong and defendable guidelines on what is necessary to implement, monitor, and evaluate process improvements. This particular standard provides specific instructions for a successful QMS.

The introduction of ISO 13053 for Six Sigma provides a visual road map for the ILSS practitioner. It enhances the credibility of process improvement procedures and provides a common vocabulary and guidelines. The ILSS practitioner should also review and understand the ASQ-SSBOK as well as various LSS toolkits. The theories and concepts governing Continuous Improvement and Organizational Effectiveness are equally important to consider.

ISO 13053 is essential for quality management. In summary, ISO 13053 is an international standard for quality management, providing guidelines for organizations to create, implement, maintain, and improve their quality management systems. ISO 13053 is essential for organizations that need to ensure quality in their products and services, as it provides a comprehensive set of processes and procedures to ensure the highest quality of goods and services.

It is an international standard that provides guidance and specifications for quality management systems. It is a valuable tool for ensuring that products, services, and processes are consistently meeting customer requirements and customer satisfaction.

ISO 13053 focuses on the principles and practices of quality management, with a specific emphasis on understanding and addressing customer needs, setting performance objectives, monitoring customer feedback, and improving customer service. The standard ensures continual improvement in quality management systems, while minimizing risks associated with the production of products, services, and processes. By implementing the ISO 13053 standard, organizations can be more confident that their products and services will meet customer expectations.

The key benefits of ISO 13053:

1. Improved Quality Control: By following the strict guidelines outlined in ISO 13053, businesses can ensure a higher level of quality control throughout their production processes. This helps minimize costly mistakes, as well as defective products and services.
2. Enhanced Efficiency: Quality management processes that are consistent and well-defined help businesses become more efficient. By following ISO 13053 standards, organizations can reduce their production time and costs, as well as improve their overall efficiency.

3. Greater Competitiveness: By following the ISO 13053 standard, organizations can demonstrate to potential customers and partners that they have taken steps to ensure the quality of their products and services. This can give them an edge over competitors who do not follow such rigorous quality standards.
4. Increased Customer Satisfaction: Quality assurance processes that are based on ISO 13053 help businesses provide better service to their customers. This, in turn, leads to greater customer satisfaction and loyalty.

By adhering to the ISO 13053 standard, organizations can reap multiple benefits such as improved quality control, enhanced efficiency, greater competitiveness, and increased customer satisfaction. These benefits can lead to greater long-term success for businesses.

Chapter 2

Lean Project Management

Process improvement programs depend on project management skills to execute and sustain improvement activities.

Project management is the discipline of planning, organizing, securing, and managing resources to achieve specific goals. Today, International Lean Six Sigma (ILSS) practitioners aspire to make these activities leaner and more agile. Basic project management is always necessary to successfully complete a process improvement project.

In the US, the Project Management Institute (PMI) is the most respected form of project management. PMI is the primary authority. This is true even though there are additional project management constructs available. However, in countries outside the US, other project methodologies are employed. These international methodologies include ISO 21500 Project Management the International Standardization (ISO) Guidelines and PRINCE2.

Internationally sensitive project management relies heavily on policy and leadership models supported by that organization or culture. The ILSS practitioner must also be aware of compliance issues governing the information technology (IT) activities of a specific country. Most enterprise-wide process improvements will include an IT component. This component may depend on the Information Technology Infrastructure Library (ITIL) or Agile. The point being that without project management in place, process improvement cannot occur.

The good news for the ILSS practitioner is that although there are different project management methodologies, there are more similarities than

DOI: 10.4324/9781003397649-3

differences. The templates, concepts, and collection of information are likewise similar.

Lean Six Sigma (LSS) has always considered basic project management essential to successful process improvement. Both basic project management and LSS are interested in establishing a sound plan, communicating with stakeholders, and conducting regular reviews. Likewise, project management and LSS are concerned with managing the schedule and containing costs. Using templates from traditional project management can assist ILSS practitioners. Once the solution is determined, templates will speed up the rollout of the project.

Throughout the Define–Measure–Analyze–Improve–Control (DMAIC) model, used by LSS, the use of basic project management tools is apparent. However, dedicated project management does not occur until the second half of the Improve Phase. This is the phase where the project plan is both created and executed. Alternative names for a project plan are execution plan, rollout plan, and implementation plan.

Before building a project plan for process improvement, the LSS model strongly encourages defining the problem, creating a clear picture of the current condition, and analyzing that condition. These activities happen in the Define, Measure, and Analyze Phases. Once the solutions are determined, the Improve Phase aims to make a solution selection.

The next task in Improve involves piloting the solution. Assuming the pilot is successful, the next step is creating the project plan. It is at that time that the International Lean Six Sigma (ILSS) practitioner becomes a full-fledged project manager. Project Management in this case means building a project plan and ensuring the execution of the plan.

Two important things to consider are: (1) if the company has a project management office established there may be a process in place to execute projects and (2) other methodologies put the creation of the project plan in a different step.

For example, in the Plan–Do–Check–Act (PDCA) model the project plan is in place prior to the second step, which is do or execute. Lean project management is about making the project manager leaner as well. This includes modifying traditional project management tools to make them work better, faster, and/or more cost-effectively depending on the project.

Lean thinking begins with identifying and reducing waste. Waste is anything that does not directly benefit the customer. A Lean project manager should, whenever possible, use Work Breakdown Structure (WBS) method.

A WBS is an outline of all the tasks. The outline begins with whole numbers: 1, 2, 3, and so on. Subtasks designations are 1.1, 2.1, or 3.1. A primary component of a work breakdown structure is the 100% rule. This indicates that the WBS encompasses all aspects of the project, as well as the person or team responsible for that component.

Creating a WBS requires the following steps:

1. Define the project.
2. Set project boundaries.
3. Identify project deliverables.
4. Define Level 1 elements. This would be the primary tasks needed.
5. Break down each of the Level 1 elements. This consists of breaking down a task into smaller and smaller pieces.
6. Identify the individual or team members responsible for completing the tasks.
7. Project the time baseline—how long will each task take. How long will the project take as a whole.
8. Project the cost baseline—the cost of each task—the cost of the entire project.

Lean Project Management requires being familiar with core documents related to project management best practices. These materials continue to evolve. For example, the International Organization for Standardization (ISO) has created a new international standard for project management, referred to as ISO 21500: Guide to Project Management. These standards increase global awareness of project management. The primary purpose of the ISO 21500 is to enable multinational organizations to coordinate their project management processes and systems. The ILSS practitioner should benefit from this document since it strives to create a common universal language around project management concepts.

Other respected documents that outline the project management approach, including the *Project Management Body of Knowledge* (PMBOK® Guide) supported by the PMI and PRojects IN Controlled Environments 2 (PRINCE2) endorsed by the UK government, are also internationally accepted collaterals.

Being familiar with the new ISO standard for project management as well as the PMBOK® Guide and PRINCE2 serves the ILSS practitioner well, as a solid educational platform. The following section explains these documents beginning with the PMBOK® Guide.

PMBOK® Guide management requires:

- Recognizing that projects are temporary—there is a beginning and an end.
- Using a validated decision process or risk assessment.
- Considering factors related to timing, cost, quality, and resources.
- Developing and articulating project scope.
- Knowing how to successfully close out a project and document any successes.

The American National Standards Institute (ANSI) recognizes the PMBOK® Guide as an American National Standard (ANSI/PMI99-001-2008) and it is also recognized by the Institute of Electrical and Electronics Engineers as the best guide for representing terminology and guidelines.

The PRINCE2 methodology encompasses the management, control, and organization of a project. It involves a highly integrated approach to project management, which includes specific inputs and outputs. It is a process-based, structured project management methodology that highlights how eight particular components, when understood and effectively addressed, can reduce risks in all types of projects.

The following information will provide an accelerated overview and highlights of ISO 21500 Guidance on Project Management, the PMBOK® Guide, and PRINCE2.

ISO 21500 Guidance on Project Management states that, for a project to be successful, it should:

- Select appropriate processes to meet the project objectives.
- Use a defined approach to develop or adapt the product specifications.
- Comply with requirements to satisfy the project sponsor, customer, and other stakeholders.
- Define and manage the project scope within the constraints while considering the project risks and resource needs to produce the project deliverables.
- Ensure proper support from each performing organization, including commitment from the customer and project sponsor.

It is vital to note that content in ISO 21500, the PRINCE2 components and processes, and the knowledge areas in the PMBOK® Guide are fairly consistent. The PMBOK® Guide is the most detailed account of project management terms and processes, PRINCE2 concentrates more on applied knowledge, and ISO 21500 provides a strong basic framework for a DMAIC project.

The PMBOK® Guide supports nine knowledge areas (all process improvement programs recognize that basic project management must be in place before process improvement may begin):

- Integration Management
- Scope Management
- Time Management
- Cost Management
- Quality Management
- Human Resource Management
- Communications Management
- Risk Management
- Project Procurement Management

The PMBOK® Guide also promotes that the following phases are necessary for a successful project:

- Initiating
- Planning
- Executing
- Monitoring and Controlling
- Closing

PRINCE2 processes highlight the following activities:

- Planning (continued throughout)
- Starting up a project
- Directing the project
- Initiating the project
- Managing stage boundaries
- Controlling a stage
- Managing product delivery
- Closing a project

Other business activities in PRINCE2 include the following:

- Defining the organization structure for the project management team
- Planning a product/service-based approach

Here is a simple comparison of the main topics in the PMBOK® Guide Knowledge Area and PRINCE2 Components

PMBOK® Guide Knowledge Area	*PRINCE2 Components*
Integration	Combined processes and components, change control
Scope, time, cost	Plans, business case
Quality	Quality, configuration management
Risk	Risk
Communications	Controls
Human Resources	Organization (limited)
Procurement	Not covered

ISO 21500 goal is to establish worldwide standards. PRINCE2 is a general framework while PMI focuses more on techniques. The major advantages of PRINCE2 are the following:

PRINCE2 has had two major revisions since its launch in 1996. The first is the PRINCE2:2009 Refresh in 2009, and the PRINCE2 2017 Update in 2017. The exam content, to become certified, has not changed drastically and relies on the original theories. However, the terminology is easier to understand and uses more mainstream project management terminology. PRINCE2 is a recognized core standard for project managers. There is recognition of the term: PRINCE2 Agile but it refers to software development approaches used by development teams. PRINCE2 updates in 2017.

Other recognized forms of project management accepted methodologies include:

- Traditional Project Management Method
- Process-based Project Management Methodology
- Agile for Project Management

Traditional Project Management is an approach that recognizes the same five developmental components as the PMBOK® Guide. It does not place emphasis on the knowledge area and is less flexible.

Process-based Project Management Methodology is an approach that uses maturity models. Capability Maturity Model Integrated (CMMI) is an example of a process improvement program developed by the Software Engineering Institute, a part of Carnegie Mellon University. Another example would be Software Process Improvement and Capability Estimation (also known as ISO/IEC15504).

Agile for Project Management has gained popularity and the content is now a part of PMI and known as Disciplined Agile. Agile, in general, promotes being adaptive instead of being preplanned. It also emphasizes human development initiatives. Agile methodology considers people factors similar to a Lean mindset. This includes items such as Leadership and Team Building. Although there are differing versions of Agile for Project Management, they all embrace the four core values:

- individuals and interactions over processes and tools;
- working software over comprehensive documentation;
- customer collaboration over contract negotiation; and
- responding to change over following a plan.

Theory of Constraints (TOC), developed by the late Eliyahu M. Goldratt, is also known as Constraint Management. The Theory of Constraints has three principles. These three principles are convergence, consistency, and respect. TOC is a stand-alone methodology. TOC also appears in different methodologies as an enhancement feature.

Also worth mentioning is the Theory of Inventive Problems Solving (TRIZ). TRIZ, although not technically considered a project management methodology, does provide analytical tools that can be especially useful to problem-solving in project management.

Most project management methodologies/approaches agree that understanding the following areas is a key factor in successful project management:

- Integration Management
- Scope Management
- Time Management
- Cost Management
- Quality Management
- Human Resource Management
- Communications Management
- Risk Management
- Procurement Management

Projects have a defined beginning and end point. This can cause confusion in the process improvement or continual improvement methodologies. Technically, process or continual improvement do not have an end. The goal is to keep improving. However, once an opportunity for process improvement occurs, project management is necessary to achieve the improvement goal. A unique feature of the Define–Measure–Improve–Analyze–Control (DMAIC) model is the opportunity to sustain the process improvement and continue the improvement. This is the purpose of Control. Still, the Control Phase of the model performs project management activities such as documenting or updating standard operating procedures, notifying stakeholders of the status, and celebrating success. An in-depth understanding of this phase is available throughout Section II of this book.

ILSS practitioners can use MS Project to manage their process improvement projects, or another process improvement software package. This includes graphic software such as Visio.

Often the process of improvement is not complex. In these cases, MS Excel will be sufficient. The advantage of using MS Excel to track or explain the project is that most employees have access to that package. The Plan–Do–Check–Act (PDCA) is a popular alternative to the DMAIC. Here are the basic steps in this methodology:

- Plan: Identify an opportunity and plan for change.
- Do: Implement the change on a small scale.
- Check: Use data to analyze the results of the change and determine whether it made a difference.
- Act: If the change was successful, implement it on a wider scale and continuously assess the results. If the change did not work, begin the cycle again.

LSS, Total Quality Management, and the PMBOK® Guide all endorse the PDCA model as a process improvement strategy. If the team has a varied background, the process improvement needs to happen immediately or if the process improvement is not complex, the PDCA is the best choice.

Most basic project management concepts do not interfere with LSS concepts. However, one theory supported by the PMBOK® Guide is that only two of the three process improvement conditions may exist at any one time. These three conditions are (1) quality, (2) speed, and (3) expense.

This theory supports that, if quality and speed (items 1 and 2) are critical to the customer, it will be expensive. If the most crucial factor to the customer is low expense and a fast turnaround, quality will suffer.

This is a deviation from LSS thinking since LSS theory is that the right methodology can improve all three conditions. Therefore, the customer does not need to make this painful decision.

Another philosophy where LSS and the PMBOK® Guide differ is the topic of scope creep. Scope represents the specific services documented in the project plan.

Scope creep may be serious if a customer wants more services than negotiated.

Scope creep has the potential of distorting timelines and increasing cost. The PMBOK® Guide strongly cautions project managers about adding post-creation services to the plan. This could push out the time and cost baselines. Whereas LSS recognizes that scope creep could be a problem, it promotes always doing a little extra. The purpose is to delight the customers.

When building a project plan, the ILSS practitioner should stay cognizant and record any possible constraints. Constraints are conditions that may hinder project completion. For example, resource allocation might be a concern and also a constraint. Documenting constraints is the first step in building a risk-management strategy.

2.1 PMI Certifications

PMI offers certifications in project management-related areas. Each certification has different eligibility requirements:

- PfMP—Portfolio Management Professional is an advanced certification that addresses portfolio management.
- PMP—Project Management Professional is the most recognized PMI certification and is highly respected.
- PMI-ACP—is an Agile Certified Practitioner.
- The Certified Associate in Project Management (CAPM)—this credential is for project team members and entry-level project managers, as well as qualified undergraduate and graduate students. The growing need

for project management knowledge and proficiency bodes well for optimistic forecasts for IT practitioners.

- Project Management Practitioner (PMP)—One of the most widely recognized PM credentials requires the demonstration of a solid foundation of project management knowledge and practice.
- Program Management Practitioner (PgMP)—This certification is for individuals who manage multiple projects or departments.
- PMI Risk Management Practitioner (PMI-RMP)—This certification is primarily for individuals who advise and make project decisions based on risk factors.
- PMI Scheduling Practitioner (PMI-SP)—Certification in project management scheduling.

2.2 PRINCE2 Certifications

There are two PRINCE2 qualification levels: PRINCE2 Foundation and PRINCE2 Practitioner.

- PRINCE2 Foundation certification involves understanding the principles and terminology used in PRINCE2 and basic project management.
- PRINCE2 Practitioner is the highest level of PRINCE2 qualification. This certification verifies that a practitioner understands how to apply PRINCE2 principles when running or managing a project.

2.3 The American Academy of Project Managers

The American Academy of Project Managers has different degrees, each requiring an elevated level of experience. These are:

- Project Manager E-Business (PME)
- Certified International Project Manager (CIPM)
- Master Project Manager (MPM)

There are other international organizations that offer project management certification. The Australian Institute of Project Management and the Project Management Association in Switzerland are two examples.

2.4 Self-Study

For those interested in a self-study program related to international project management, topics to research would include the following:

- Project Management Tools and Techniques
- Microsoft Project Management Software
- Applied Project Management
- Cultural Awareness Training

Additional factors play a role in ILSS and Project Management. The primary factors include the following:

- Change Management
- Leadership Development
- Measurement Systems Analysis
- Business Finance

Change Management has a variety of meanings depending on the area. The most popular and recognized certification is the Change Management Certificate (CCMP) offered by different vendors. Another recognized certification is Prosci. The Prosci model promotes the Awareness–Desire–Knowledge–Ability–Reinforcement (ADKAR®) change model.

Leadership Development traditionally has focused on developing leadership ability. In an ILSS organization, these methods are imperative to success but also include understanding diverse cultures, generations, and work ethics. Successful leadership development is linked to

- An individual's ability to learn
- Quality and nature of the leadership development program
- Genuine support for the leader's supervisor
- Choosing the right projects
- Choosing the right people
- Following the right methodology
- Clearly defining roles and responsibility

Measurement Systems Analysis (MSA) is a science that considers selecting the right measurement. It is necessary to study the measurement as well as the measurement device. Are measures reliable and valid? What is the measurement uncertainty? Calibration of equipment is an MSA issue.

Statistics is the science of making effective use of numerical data relating to groups of individuals or experiments. Six Sigma and Lean have always included the field of statistics when measuring and analyzing data.

Business Finance plays a stronger role for the new LSS practitioner. The buy-in and continued support of a project cannot be based solely on statistical data. Choosing the appropriate return-on-investment formula and being able to measure project success, in financial terms, have become essential.

Moving forward as LSS practitioners, it is imperative to remember that LSS is not just a matter of blending two phenomenally successful process methodologies but rather encompassing a collection of bodies of knowledge.

Lean Project Management is a way to incorporate basic project management into DMAIC projects. When considering the DMAIC model, practitioners become dedicated project managers at the bottom of IMPROVE. The first few phases (Define–Measure–Analyze) of the DMAIC model are committed to ultimately finding the solution. Tools typically used in project management can make this process smoother.

The role of Lean Project Management is to provide leadership and direction to projects. In the absence of project management, a team may move without direction, control, or purpose. It is leadership that allows and enables team members to perform at their best.

Lean Project Management is an integral part of Lean Six Sigma, a business process improvement methodology used by organizations worldwide. Project management in Lean Six Sigma involves planning, executing, and controlling a project in order to achieve the desired results. It helps to ensure on-time project completion is within the budget, while also providing direction and focus to the project team.

Project management, in general, also helps to keep costs down. With a comprehensive plan in place, teams can identify cost areas for minimization or elimination. This allows businesses to focus their resources on activities that will yield the greatest return on investment. Lean Project Management studies the cost from everyone's point of view. This would include the vendors/suppliers, employees, and the process.

Finally, project management encourages collaboration between all parties involved in the Lean Six Sigma process. This can help to foster a culture of innovation and create a keen sense of unity within the team.

By providing a structured approach for identifying and addressing risks, managing resources and timelines, and keeping costs down, project management can help ensure successful projects and maximize the potential of Lean Six Sigma.

Lean Project Management is really an evolved approach to traditional project management.

The world of project management is constantly evolving, and in the years ahead, the concept of Lean Project Management will be more important than ever. As technology advances, organizations of all sizes and industries are looking for ways to optimize efficiency, reduce costs, and improve customer satisfaction.

A Lean Project Management approach is highly effective for organizing and managing projects. As a result, organizations become more efficient, cost-effective, and productive while reducing time to market and risk. Lean Project Management has benefits to include:

- Increased Efficiency—Lean Project Management helps to streamline processes. This reduces costs and makes projects more productive.
- Improved Visibility—Lean Project Management provides an enhanced view of the project. This allows for better decision-making, improved resource utilization, and a higher level of project control.
- Faster Completion—By streamlining processes and removing waste from the production cycle, Lean Project Management helps teams complete projects faster than traditional methods. This also allows them to launch products quicker and capture market share earlier.
- Reduced Risk—Lean Project Management helps to eliminate unnecessary steps and tasks that can lead to errors or costly delays. By understanding potential risks in advance, it is possible to take proactive measures that reduce the chances of failure or wasted resources.
- Improved Quality—Lean Project Management ensures that every step maximizes quality, as well as customer satisfaction. It also helps teams to identify and address any quality issues quickly, which leads to better outcomes overall.

These are the benefits of implementing Lean Project Management in your organization. With the right tools and training, you can leverage these benefits to improve your overall project performance and profitability.

Lean Project Management is all about optimizing processes and finding ways to reduce waste. In order to achieve this, there are five key principles used as a basis for all Lean projects. These principles, known as the "Five Ps," are as follows:

1. Process—Lean Project Management involves simplifying processes and minimizing waste. This means that there should be a focus on eliminating or reducing unnecessary steps or tasks. It also means taking a look at how resources are allocated and using only what is necessary.
2. People—Lean projects require a team of people who are committed to achieving the project's goals. This team needs to be composed of individuals with diverse backgrounds, skills, and knowledge. Additionally, everyone involved should understand their roles and responsibilities.
3. Performance—Lean projects are frequently evaluated, and stakeholder feedback collected.
4. Planning—Proper planning is essential for Lean project success. Projects should have clear objectives and an action plan that includes detailed timelines and budget estimates.
5. Positioning—It is important to ensure the correct positioning of the project. This means that the product or service attracts potential customers, and the organization can benefit from the sales or services it offers.

By following these five principles, organizations can improve their efficiency, reduce waste, and create successful Lean projects. Each principle is key to the success of a Lean project.

Blending Lean Project Management with Lean Six Sigma initiatives is crucial to success. In summary, stable project management plays a vital role in LSS. Process improvement requires using project management theory as well as project management tools. The ILSS practitioner should be up to date on the project management methodology and tools already used by their company. The ILSS practitioner should also understand any special project or process improvement software utilized.

Chapter 3

Lean Government in the United States

It is worth mentioning that terms such as Lean Government and Lean Health often encompass both Lean and Six Sigma. Lean Six Sigma is the fusion of two popular business principles—Lean and Six Sigma—into one methodology. These methodologies work the best when combined but it is easier to say Lean Government, for example, than Lean Six Sigma Government. However, the evidence of Six Sigma in Lean Government is overwhelming.

The Lean Six Sigma method of process improvement is an essential tool for the government, both domestically and internationally. This process has proven to be invaluable for reducing costs, streamlining operations, and improving overall performance. Presented in this chapter are two crucial factors:

- The benefits that government agencies can reap from implementing Lean Six Sigma;
- An understanding of why Lean Six Sigma should be a top priority for government.

As a reminder, Lean Six Sigma (LSS) is a data-driven management methodology that combines the two existing methodologies of Lean and Six Sigma. Developed to optimize processes, reduce waste, and create more efficient workflows, LSS focuses on identifying problems, improving processes, and streamlining operations to increase quality and efficiency.

DOI: 10.4324/9781003397649-4

Lean Six Sigma in government focuses mostly on eliminating waste. The intention is to emphasize continuous improvement. This can help reduce costs, increase productivity, and ultimately lead to higher constituents' satisfaction.

Using Lean Six Sigma in government improves service delivery, implements better governance practices, and saves money by increasing efficiency.

For example, it can help with the process of creating new laws or regulations, which can save both time and money. Additionally, LSS monitors government departments and services to ensure they are running effectively and efficiently. This can lead to increased transparency and accountability in government operations.

Lean Six Sigma plays a role in successful government operations around the world. It is a powerful tool that allows government agencies to streamline operations, reduce costs, and improve overall efficiency. Its success in the US has caught the attention of governments around the world, leading to its adoption in countries such as Japan, India, China, and others. As more countries look to implement Lean Six Sigma, there are key lessons they can learn from the US experience.

Primarily, any government that is looking to implement Lean Six Sigma should take the time to professionally train their staff. The successful implementation of Lean Six Sigma requires all staff to understand the process and its objectives. Training should cover all aspects of the process, including defining goals, process mapping, and project management. Without proper training, the process can quickly become ineffective and costly.

Second, it is imperative to recognize that Lean Six Sigma is not a one-size-fits-all solution. Different departments and even different countries have unique needs and processes. It is essential that each government customizes Lean Six Sigma to fit its own specific requirements.

Finally, it is important to measure the success of the implementation and adjust where needed. Accomplished by regular reviews and audits of the process, LSS tracks both tangible and intangible results. Establishing basic and current metrics creates a baseline.

Overall, governments that want to implement Lean Six Sigma must recognize that it is an ongoing process. With proper training, customization, and evaluation, governments can ensure that their Lean Six Sigma implementation is successful and leads to long-term benefits.

Since its introduction to the public sector in the early 2000s, Lean Six Sigma has become a valuable tool for the US government to improve operations and reduce costs. The implementation of LSS methodology results in streamlined processes and the elimination of waste. Lean Six Sigma increases efficiency. It ultimately delivers better value to taxpayers. Popular success in the US government using Lean Six Sigma include:

- The Department of Veterans Affairs
- The Department of Defense
- The Department of Homeland Security
- The Department of Health and Human Services

3.1 Department of Veterans Affairs

The Department of Veterans Affairs (VA) is one of the largest government departments in the United States and is tasked with providing essential services to those who have served in the military. To better serve veterans and their families, the VA has implemented Lean Six Sigma principles in a variety of areas.

For example, the VA deployed Lean Six Sigma techniques to improve patient wait times and reduce operational costs. Lean Six Sigma also helps the VA streamline processes, which leads to increased efficiency and reduced bureaucracy. The VA's Office of Transformation Leadership, established in 2010, provides oversight for the implementation of Lean Six Sigma initiatives.

In 2011, the VA achieved a 47% reduction in claims processing time by using Lean Six Sigma to identify areas for improvement and redesign processes. This resulted in shorter wait times for veterans and their families and improved customer satisfaction. The VA also launched a national project to standardize its medical records system and make data available across multiple departments and locations. This initiative used Lean Six Sigma to identify inefficient processes and eliminate them, resulting in a significant reduction in the amount of time it takes to process paperwork and get information to the right people.

Overall, the VA has experienced success with Lean Six Sigma initiatives that have allowed it to serve veterans more efficiently and effectively. By reducing waste, increasing efficiency, and improving customer satisfaction, the VA is showing that Lean Six Sigma can help departments within the US government better serve citizens.

3.2 Department of Defense

The Department of Defense (DoD) is one of the most important agencies in the United States government, and it has adopted Lean Six Sigma to help streamline processes and save money. Lean Six Sigma, implemented in 2005 across the DoD network, has documented significant improvements in efficiency.

At the heart of Lean Six Sigma at the DoD is a focus on eliminating waste and reducing costs. The DoD has seen significant savings from Lean Six Sigma initiatives, such as reducing the cost of supply chain management by nearly 20%. Additionally, the DoD has saved over $3 billion in travel costs due to process improvements resulting from Lean Six Sigma.

Beyond simply reducing costs, Lean Six Sigma has also had a positive effect on morale within the DoD. After implementing Lean Six Sigma, employee satisfaction improved by 15% and morale increased by 25%. This indicates that not only is Lean Six Sigma saving money, but it is also having a positive effect on those who work within the DoD.

The DoD's success with Lean Six Sigma proves that it can be an invaluable tool for improving efficiency and saving money. It is a testament to the power of Lean Six Sigma and its ability to have a positive impact on government organizations.

3.3 The Department of Homeland Security

The Department of Homeland Security (DHS) has been using LSS to help improve its operations since 2004. With LSS, the DHS has been able to achieve greater efficiency and effectiveness in areas such as customer service, logistics management, and incident response.

The DHS deployed a Lean Six Sigma program with the goal of improving the overall effectiveness and efficiency of the department's operations. The implementation included training for the personnel in the basics of LSS, as well as providing an online resource center for employees to access materials and resources related to LSS.

The deployment of Lean Six Sigma at the DHS resulted in improved performance in areas such as process redesign, customer service, technology optimization, and problem-solving. For example, the department used LSS to design and implement a more efficient process for handling customer complaints. This resulted in a 37% improvement in customer satisfaction, with the average time needed to resolve a complaint reduced by 60%.

Another success story came from the department's use of LSS to optimize its supply chain operations. By using Lean Six Sigma methods such as streamlining processes, cutting costs, and improving accuracy, the department was able to reduce the amount of time needed for inventory replenishment by 25%, resulting in cost savings of $1 million.

Overall, the deployment of Lean Six Sigma at the Department of Homeland Security has been a resounding success. The program has enabled the department to improve the efficiency of its operations and better serve its customers.

3.4 The Department of Health and Human Services

The Department of Health and Human Services (HHS) is the United States government's principal agency for protecting the health of all Americans. Since the implementation of Lean Six Sigma, the department has made successful improvements in a wide range of areas, including healthcare access, public health, and economic stability.

For example, the department was able to streamline their service delivery system using Lean Six Sigma. This allowed them to reduce wait times for patients by 50% and improve customer satisfaction overall. In addition, they have been able to cut down on waste and streamline operations throughout the organization.

The department has used Lean Six Sigma to enhance its fiscal management systems. This resulted in a 25% decrease in audit errors. Resources are more efficient.

Overall, the HHS has seen remarkable success with Lean Six Sigma. They have been able to reduce wait times, streamline processes, increase efficiency, and save money overall.

During the 81st General Assembly in the state of Iowa, legislation passed that authorized the Department of Management to create the Office of Lean Enterprise. In the January 2012 Colorado State Address, Governor John Hickenlooper remarked that almost every department had initiated a Lean program in order to identify waste/inefficiencies and create savings. Colorado House Bill 11-1212 passed to integrate Lean Government principles. This bill promotes incorporating Lean practices, as well as training state employees, to be Lean experts within the State of Colorado.

In all of these cases, Lean Six Sigma proves to be an effective tool for improving the efficiency and effectiveness of government operations. By reducing waste, improving productivity, and increasing customer satisfaction, Lean Six Sigma is proving its value in helping non-US-based governmental entities provide better services to their citizens.

A basic premise of Lean Thinking is to study the value of the work people do and directly connect it to the quality of service provided for the citizen. These activities may cause stress among employees who do not understand the merits of Lean. Employees may fear job loss or loss of control of their daily activities. If Lean Six Sigma is not a normal practice, Chapter 17 addressing Change Management as well as Chapter 18 on Training methods will help employees feel more comfortable and motivated to embrace LSS.

In the initial process, value stream mapping (VSM) can be extremely useful for governmental agencies. VSM refers to the activity of developing a visual representation of how a particular process, product, or service flows through the system.

VSM also identifies time frames, handoffs, and resources involved throughout the process. VSM, similar to flowcharting, has a set of symbols that represent various processes, materials, and information.

The purpose of a Value Stream Map is to identify areas of overt, as well as hidden, waste. Bottlenecks, redundancy, and rework are also more apparent. The map tracks the time, from the moment of the request through the delivery of that request.

VSM has extra advantages for employees who may not be eager to incorporate the methodology. By presenting the core process visually, it is easier to show the faults in the current system. This may instill a sense of urgency as well as the feeling that learning a new method is constructive.

In the beginning, another useful tool is Kaizen Events, also known as Rapid Improvement Events. Kaizen Events, designed to yield quick results, often provide the ancillary benefit of increased employee buy-in. Being able to see benefits in real time encourages workers to commit to new processes. They also typically bring together a cross-functional team for 3–5 days to study a specific process. It is important that the members of this team have the ability to make decisions.

The events, conducted by a facilitator, use a model for process improvement. The Plan–Do–Check–Act (PDCA) model is popular. If the problem is complex the Define–Measure–Analyze–Improve–Control (DMAIC) model is a better choice. However, proprietary models, such as

Select–Clarify–Organize–Run–Evaluate, or SCORE, are another option. The Kaizen approach endorsed these activities:

- Assessment
- Planning
- Implementation
- Evaluation

In the Assessment Phase, the major goal is to determine the Critical-to-Quality (CTQ) factors. A common definition of CTQ is the quality of a product or service in the eyes of the Voice of the Customer (VOC).

It is always a promising idea to identify the critical quality parameters as they relate to what is important to the customer at large. Once the CTQs achieve consensus with the team the next step is the development of metrics.

The Planning Phase considers ideas for implementation and the corresponding impacts. Process improvement and tracking results happen in the Implementation Phase. Finally, the Evaluation Phase measures the results on the basis of the metrics developed during the Assessment Phase.

The success of any rapid improvement event depends on

- Teamwork
- Personal discipline
- Employee morale

In addition to rapid improvement events, another way to kick off a Lean Government program is by initiating a workplace organizational model such as the 5S. Similar to a VSM, the 5S model offers visual validation.

3.5 International Government Communities

Now, it is gaining traction in the public sector, particularly in non-US-based governmental entities. With its success in the corporate sector, non-US-based governmental entities are now turning to Lean Six Sigma as a way to improve efficiency and performance. This subsection will discuss the successes of Lean Six Sigma in non-US-based governmental entities proving its effectiveness in the public sector.

Lean Six Sigma offers noteworthy benefits to government organizations looking to streamline operations and improve efficiency. By utilizing the methodology, government organizations can reduce waste and save money while improving performance. With Lean Six Sigma, organizations are able to reduce overhead costs and increase productivity by better understanding their processes. This enables them to identify opportunities for improvement and then take steps to address those issues. Additionally, Lean Six Sigma helps to reduce bureaucracy and promote collaboration between departments, leading to greater efficiency across the organization. Finally, Lean Six Sigma provides a system of measurement and analytics. This allows government entities the ability to track progress/measure results. This procedure ensures on-time goals are met with efficiency.

Lean Six Sigma is becoming increasingly popular in non-US-based governmental entities, as leaders look for ways to become more efficient and improve services. Governments around the world are using Lean Six Sigma to improve public services, reduce costs, and streamline processes. Counties and governmental agencies are actively training staff in Lean Six Sigma principles and practices.

One of the most notable applications of Lean Six Sigma in government is in the United Kingdom. This includes the Department of Health, which uses Lean Six Sigma to reduce waiting times in hospitals, and the Department for Work and Pensions, which uses it to help people find employment. The UK has also adopted Lean Six Sigma to improve public safety, with the National Police Chiefs Council introducing it to reduce crime and make roads safer.

In Canada, the government has adopted Lean Six Sigma to improve both customer service and productivity. This has included an effort to reduce processing times for passport applications, as well as streamlining government procurement processes. In addition, the Canadian government has adopted Lean Six Sigma to improve the delivery of healthcare services, such as reducing wait times for surgeries and increasing access to specialists.

In Australia, Lean Six Sigma helped to reduce the government's paperwork burden by half, enabling staff to spend more time on other activities. In India, it enabled a reduction in the processing time for pension applications by about 50%.

In one case study from Hungary, the implementation of Lean Six Sigma resulted in a decrease in processing time for applications from five days to two days. This enabled more people to access the service in a timely manner and helped to reduce the costs associated with providing it.

Governments around the world are using Lean Six Sigma to improve their services and save money. With its focus on continuous improvement,

Lean Six Sigma can help governments deliver better services more efficiently. By adopting Lean Six Sigma principles, governments can ensure that their citizens receive better services at a lower cost.

The implementation of Lean Six Sigma in non-US-based governmental entities has seen positive results. In particular, it has been able to significantly reduce the cost of government services, increase the efficiency of processes, and improve the quality of services delivered. In addition, it has helped to create an improved working environment for staff and improved the overall satisfaction of citizens with their government.

In summary, Lean Six Sigma has helped government organizations to become more transparent and accountable by creating systems for monitoring performance and providing feedback on results. This has enabled them to better meet the needs of their constituents.

Overall, Lean Six Sigma has the potential to transform the way governments operate by providing a structure for process improvement that leads to increased efficiency, improved service delivery, and cost savings.

LEAN SIX SIGMA, OPERATIONAL EXCELLENCE, AND CONTINUOUS IMPROVEMENT

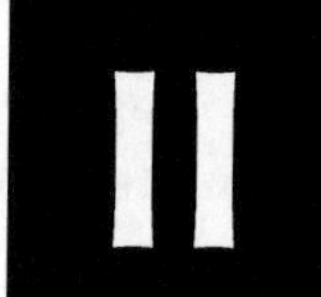

Introduction

The following chapters are multipurpose. For those new to Lean Six Sigma, the chapters are intended to provide a fundamental self-study guide. For those considering developing an in-house Lean Six Sigma program, the chapters provide a basic curriculum. This section includes questions at the end of each chapter as well as suggestions for additional reading.

For the International Lean Six Sigma (ILSS) practitioner, additional consideration should be given to how different cultures respond to training. Chapter 18, Training Modules: Using Instructional Systems Design for Lean Six Sigma Training, provides a blueprint on how to develop and format training programs that need to consider diversity. As an ILSS practitioner, it may be necessary to do shorter, mini training sessions related to specific process improvement topics.

The goal of every organization is to continuously improve and increase efficiency. To achieve this, many organizations have turned to Lean Six Sigma, Operational Excellence, and Continuous Improvement. These three concepts, while related, have distinct differences that can be difficult to navigate.

DOI: 10.4324/9781003397649-5

Lean Six Sigma, Operational Excellence, and Continuous Improvement are three distinct strategies that organizations often use to optimize their performance. While they all have the goal of improving the quality and efficiency of processes, they each have their approaches and benefits. Lean Six Sigma focuses on removing waste from processes and streamlining them for maximum efficiency. Operational Excellence is about setting ambitious goals for an organization and then identifying opportunities for improvement. Finally, Continuous Improvement is an ongoing effort to find new ways to improve processes. All three methods can benefit by using standard Lean Six Sigma tools and all three approaches have similar tools in their toolkit.

An example of a mini-session is when the ILSS practitioner focuses training on one phase of the Define–Measure–Analyze–Improve–Control (DMAIC) model. For example, if the Define and Measure Phases are complete, training may need to focus only on analytical problem-solving to satisfy the next phase, Analyze. Another example of a mini-session might be training a group on a specific tool, such as a fishbone diagram.

It is also essential to consider how different cultures understand and synthesize the concept of Operational Excellence (OE) as well as the basic theories involved in Continuous Process Improvement (CPI). Globally, the term Operational Excellence is described as the systematic management of the process, personal safety, environment, reliability, and efficiency to achieve world-class performance. Lean and Six Sigma practices may be applied to all of these major processes. Operational excellence is often seen as the direct result of applying Lean Six Sigma. However, this train of thought may need to be explained or explored in other cultures.

The most respected award in OE is the Shingo Prize. The mission of the Shingo Prize is to create excellence in organizations through the application of universally accepted principles. These include the alignment of management systems and the intelligent application of improvement techniques across the entire organizational enterprise. The term Continuous Process Improvement is generally considered a subset of OE. In Lean Six Sigma, CPI is an important part of the Control Phase of the DMAIC model. CPI tools are often needed simply to sustain the current process control.

However, some organizations perceive CPI more as a stand-alone program. In these businesses, much emphasis is placed on the Plan–Do–Check–Act (PDCA) model. Most of the concepts in the stand-alone CPI model adopt the Total Quality Management (TQM) philosophy. The initiatives are very similar to Lean Six Sigma with the exception that the PDCA model is used as a core model rather than DMAIC.

How a culture responds to the terms Operation Excellence or Continuous Process Improvement should be considered when initiating a process improvement. Some other terms or words may not be fully understood. For example, there is a lot of confusion over the term waste. In Lean Six Sigma something may be labeled as waste simply because it does not directly contribute to the process improvement. It is important that the employee or student realizes when something is labeled as waste; it does not always mean that an activity is not significant or will not be completed. It simply means that, for that particular process improvement, it is unnecessary.

As a reminder, most process improvement professionals would categorize waste as something related to one of these areas:

- Defects
- Overproduction
- Waiting
- Overprocessing
- Transportation
- Inventory Motion
- Unused Employee Ability

OE and CPI terminology often use unfamiliar words intended to provide a more individualized touch. For example, unused employee ability in some OE models is rephrased as unexploited employee creativity. In some Continuous Improvement Models, the term Non–Value Added is used to explain overproduction/processing. Even in English, these expressions need explanation and definition so it is important to be aware of the types of words being used in other countries.

The leadership models must also be considered when delivering training in other countries. For example, in Egypt, employees tend to revolve around a strong leader who usually allocates tasks rather than specific roles or functions. This makes recognizing concepts, such as non-value production or non-value processing, difficult for the team to grasp. In Taiwan, as in other countries, a safe, harmonious work environment that is functioning as a team is respected. Therefore, discussing topics such as unused employee ability or creativity is nearly impossible.

In the United States, a great deal of emphasis is placed on brainstorming activities. Lean Six Sigma, OE, and CPI include several structured brainstorming tools. The purpose of these tools varies. Sometimes, the purpose of brainstorming is to decide on solutions. In other cases, brainstorming is used to determine the contributing factors to a problem. In cultures where this concept is not as readily embraced, the ILSS practitioner may need to use structured brainstorming as a map to create the right questions to be asked individually.

Lean Six Sigma, Operational Excellence, and Continuous Improvement are all terms used in business process improvement. These three approaches have distinct features, but they also intersect in numerous ways.

When it comes to Lean Six Sigma, the focus is on efficiency, improving processes, and reducing waste. This approach seeks to streamline processes and remove any steps that are not adding value. Lean Six Sigma uses a system of rigorous analysis and data-driven decision-making to identify issues and potential solutions. The ultimate goal is to achieve maximum efficiency with minimal resources.

Continuous Improvement is about taking a never-ending approach to process improvement. It is an attitude of continuous learning and experimentation that encourages teams to continuously assess their current practices and look for better ways of doing things. It focuses on slight changes over time and looks for incremental improvements to make processes faster and more efficient.

Operational Excellence is a set of principles and practices aimed at achieving high performance in operations. It focuses on the customer experience, employee engagement, process design, and results. Operational Excellence relies on data and analytics to ensure that processes are running optimally and that any changes will have positive outcomes.

The intersection between these three areas lies in their mutual focus on efficiency, customer experience, employee engagement, process design, and results. Lean Six Sigma helps to identify issues quickly, while Continuous Improvement takes a never-ending approach to improvement and Operational Excellence focuses on optimizing existing processes. All three approaches can work together to create a comprehensive system of business process improvement that delivers the desired outcomes. All process improvement programs benefit from understanding the tools and methodologies promoted in Lean Six Sigma.

Chapter 4

Core Knowledge

Lean Six Sigma (LSS) uses a variety of process improvement models. Whereas the Define–Measure–Analyze–Improve–Control (DMAIC) model is the most prevalent, LSS also relies on additional problem-solving methodologies. This includes the Plan–Do–Check–Act (PDCA) model, well-liked in Lean Manufacturing and basic project management as well as alternative improvement models such as Select, Clarify, Organize, Run, and Evaluate (SCORE). Lean Six Sigma may also borrow from the Systems Development Life Cycle (SDLC) and/or facets of Agile.

In the most popular DMAIC model, the five phases, sometimes called steps, are the basis of most LSS training.

Each phase (or step) of this model supports tools, ideas, and templates. After each phase, there is a tollgate review. A tollgate is a check sheet to ensure activities have been completed. In a formal Six Sigma project, it is rare to start activities on the next phase until the previous phase is completed.

Lean Six Sigma is a little more flexible. In other words, if there is an opportunity in Define to satisfy parts of the Measure requirements, this is acceptable. It is not the goal to move to one phase before the previous phase is complete, but it is allowed in Lean Six Sigma. Generally, this is because a Lean Six Sigma project has the same manager from cradle to grave, whereas the Six Sigma project has several owners and there may be a different resource for each phase due to the size of the project. This could mean a different department is responsible for each phase, making it necessary to fully complete the phase before moving on to the next.

DOI: 10.4324/9781003397649-6

4.1 Define, Measure, Analyze, Improve, and Control

The Define–Measure–Analyze–Improve–Control (DMAIC) model is composed of a five-phase problem-solving system:

- Phase 1: Define
- Phase 2: Measure
- Phase 3: Analyze
- Phase 4: Improve
- Phase 5: Control

In typical problem-solving, there is a tendency to state the problem and then rush to the solution. The problem statement might not be fully ready. This would allow for two phases before execution:

- Phase 1: State the problem or opportunity for improvement.
- Phase 2: List the solutions and choose one.

In the DMAIC model, the brainstorming of solutions does not take place until after all the data have been captured and analyzed, in Phase 2 and Phase 3, Measure and Analyze. Both the list of solutions and the subsequent project plan do not happen until Phase 4, Improve. The theory is that a good list of solutions cannot be created without clearly defining the problem, creating a measurement system, and then doing intense analysis. The advantage is that when a list is created after defining, measuring, and analyzing, the response will not be "We tried that before and it didn't work," because the project manager would already have that information. Comments such as "we cannot afford that solution" would not be voiced because the project manager would know how to proactively address this concern if they worked through the first three phases of the DMAIC.

Although the DMAIC is the most popular model, another set of models referred to as Design for Six Sigma (DFSS) or Design for Lean Six Sigma (DFLSS) are also available. DFSS and DFLSS models are the same. In other words, any model with the reference DFSS could also be a DFLSS model. These models also have various phases along with activities and tools. However, all of the tools used in DFSS could apply to the DMAIC.

4.2 Plan–Do–Check–Act

Although the DMAIC model is the flagship of Lean Six Sigma, using the Plan–Do–Check–Act (PDCA) model is acceptable.

The PDCA cycle is a well-known project model. It can be used independently or within any phase of the DMAIC or as a stand-alone problem-solving tool. There are times when the DMAIC may be the preferred model but because of time or the significance of the problem, a PDCA may be a better choice. The plan–do–check–act cycle can be used for carrying out a change. In this case, just as a circle has no end, the PDCA cycle should be repeated again and again.

The PDCA cycle is made up of four steps for improvement or change:

- **Plan**: Recognize an opportunity, and plan the change.
- **Do**: Test the change.
- **Check**: Review the test, analyze the results, and identify key learning points.
- **Act**: Act based on what is appropriate.

4.3 DMAIC and PDCA

Sometimes, when the DMAIC is the preferred model but there is a time constraint, PDCA is used as a substitute. Sometimes, PDCA is used to prove that the DMAIC may be necessary. Sometimes, the PDCA model is referred to as the PDSA model. This is the same model but "S" is substituted for "C" for Check to indicate Study. The choice of PDSA over PDCA would depend primarily on whether the project manager planned to "Study" the results or "Check" the results.

Since the DMAIC is considered a process improvement methodology, some International Lean Six Sigma practitioners believe that another model would be useful if a product or service was being designed from the ground up. Usually, DFSS/DFLSS models still resemble DMAIC. The most popular DFSS model, Define–Measure–Analyze–Design–Verify (DMADV), has the same first three phases.

The downside of DFSS/DFLSS models is the consistency. Whereas popular models such as DMADV are properly documented, many other DFSS/

DFLSS models do not have consistent documentation, or because they are proprietary models there is no general documentation available.

Originally, the purpose of DFSS models was to include specific design steps in the process. Typically, design steps would be items such as

- Needs Analysis
- Finding the Right Designer
- Establishment of Priorities
- Mockup
- Implementation of Feedback
- Testing
- Final Design
- Launch
- Marketing and Promotions
- Plans for Updates/Changes/Additions

A strong understanding of the DMAIC is still necessary to properly utilize or modify any DFSS/DFLSS model; however, DFSS/DFLSS models are gaining popularity. The adage was to only use DFSS if the processes were so broken that no one could apply the DMAIC. Now, many process improvement professionals see a benefit in including a specific Design Phase. Most International Lean Six Sigma practitioners support the idea that design occurs in the Improve Phase of the DMAIC model.

It is somewhat confusing that some models are considered DFSS/DFLSS simply because they were developed in-house with a different set of terminology. Others add or subtract a step from the DMAIC model. In these cases, the DFSS model may not have a design component at all. Over the years, DFSS has evolved to encompass models that are simply variations of the DMAIC.

Some projects are simply projects that must be completed via a prescribed project plan. Process Improvement projects, in Lean Six Sigma, take advantage of one of three methodologies: DMAIC, PDCA, or DFSS, with DMAIC being the preferred model.

4.4 Rapid Improvement or Kaizen Event Models

A rapid improvement, also known as Kaizen Event, is necessary for several reasons. They include but are not limited to safety, financial and first-to-market scenarios. It is not uncommon to use the DMAIC or PDCA models when facilitating these events; however, several models use Lean Six Sigma tools.

One popular model is SCORE®, developed by BMGI, a vendor of Lean Six Sigma training and consulting. It involves the following phases:

- **S**elect—1 day to 1 week
- **C**larify—1 day to 1 week
- **O**rganize—1 day to 1 week
- **R**un—3 to 5 days
- **E**valuate—up to 3 weeks

Many rapid improvement/Kaizen Events are conducted by using a proprietary model designed at a specific company but most subscribe to the following steps:

1. Define the problem.
2. Document the current situation.
3. Visualize the ideal situation.
4. Define measurement targets.
5. Brainstorm solutions to the problem.
6. Develop a Kaizen plan.
7. Implement a plan.
8. Measure, record, and compare results to targets.
9. Prepare summary documents.
10. Create a short-term action plan, ongoing standards, and sustaining plan.

Determining the methodology for a Lean Six Sigma project is necessary as each model has specific nuances and tools that benefit the success of a project. Whereas Lean Six Sigma favors the DMAIC model as does ISO 13053, there are times when other models are more appropriate. All models, however, can benefit by using Lean Six Sigma tools.

4.5 Discussion

1. What are the primary differences between the DMAIC model and typical problem-solving techniques?
2. What is the significance of PDCA for International Lean Six Sigma practitioners?
3. What is DFSS and how is it different from DMAIC?
4. What are the best circumstances to use DMAIC, PDCA, or DFSS?
5. What is the significance of the DMADV model?

Chapter 5

Lean Six Sigma Basics

This chapter is an accelerated overview of the Lean Six Sigma (LSS) basics. However, the material in this chapter is also covered in more depth throughout this book. It is also a good test prep for standardized exams.

Lean Six Sigma supports the Project Management Body of Knowledge (PMBOK® Guide) and assumes that most International Lean Six Sigma practitioners already have essential project management knowledge. There are, however, deviations in Lean Six Sigma that are not supported by the *PMBOK® Guide.*

The most significant deviation from the *PMBOK® Guide* is that the International Lean Six Sigma practitioner must begin with the fundamental belief that most processes need improvement. Essential project management supports that, on any project, we must decide which two of the three conditions are the most important to the project:

- Quality
- Speed
- Expense

In other words, it will be costly if quality and speed are essential to the customer. But, on the other hand, if the most important thing is the low expense and a quick turnaround, quality will suffer, and so forth.

One core thought of Lean Six Sigma is that the customer does not have to make that choice by following the correct methodology and implementing problem-solving tools. All three are possible.

The second apparent deviation from the *PMBOK® Guide* has to do with scope. Scope represents the services provided. The *PMBOK® Guide* is

DOI: 10.4324/9781003397649-7

genuinely concerned about scope creep. Scope creep is a consideration when the client asks for more benefits than initially negotiated. The *PMBOK® Guide* recommends closely monitoring any additional duties for costing purposes. Lean Six Sigma is also concerned about scope creep but promotes always doing things in addition to the project requirements that will truly "delight" the customers. Lean Six Sigma is so committed to this philosophy that there are often chapters dedicated to "delighters" in some Lean Six Sigma material.

Aside from these two theories, most of the *PMBOK® Guide* is incorporated and actively encouraged in Lean Six Sigma.

One of the reasons Lean Thinking and Six Sigma Methodology blend so well is that they both use the same analytical problem-solving tools, sometimes referred to as the Seven Quality Tools, demonstrated in the next chapter.

Six Sigma uses statistically driven data. This is also true of Lean; however, Lean allows the practitioner to consider things such as "gut" feeling, company culture, and economies of scale in decision-making. In addition, Lean Thinking and philosophy soften the Lean Six Sigma agenda, making it more people-focused. However, even when good data is captured and analyzed, strong people skills are still needed to pull a team together to solve problems. Therefore, items prevalent in almost all Lean Six Sigma material that are somewhat minimized in a book covering only Six Sigma are attention to leadership, team building, and basic communication skills.

How the message is presented and articulated is also a concern in Lean Six Sigma. Lean Six Sigma promotes using the most straightforward graph and explanation when offering research and problem solutions.

Six Sigma strives for defect reduction, process improvement, and customer satisfaction and is based on "statistical thinking." There is an assumption that everything is a process and that all procedures have inherent variability. The Six Sigma theory relies heavily on data to understand the variability and drive process improvement decisions. As mentioned earlier, it is all about reducing errors, mistakes, or defects.

Lean is concerned about waste which includes "hidden" waste. For example, two employees may be doing the same job. Waste may be necessary, called, aptly, "necessary" waste, which may involve things such as compliance issues. However, Lean has many suggestions for reducing daily identifiable waste. These areas include the following:

- Waiting time
- Overproduction

- Transportation time
- Repeated transactions

A popular concept in Lean Six Sigma is value stream mapping (VSM). The VSM intends to help identify all forms of waste. VSM was originally a simple pencil-and-paper tool where only those processes and items contributed directly to the product, service, or recording project completion. In project management, this is similar to a critical path. VSM can also now have sophisticated graphics and symbols—identical to a process map. The easiest way to construct a VSM is to create a process map first. Think of a process map as simply everything that needs to be accomplished for the project to succeed. It is the main to-do list.

After these items are listed, cross off anything that does not directly contribute to the completed project. It might be necessary to "walk the process" to make sure. For example, let us say extensive paperwork needs to be completed, but the project could be finished even without completing the paperwork. These items don't get erased but are put into a different bucket. The idea behind a VSM is that the viewer can easily see where most of the resources should be dedicated.

Lean Six Sigma is a systematic approach to eliminating defects and reducing waste. It typically uses the DMAIC (Define–Measure–Analyze–Improve–Control) model discussed in this section of this book. Each step in the DMAIC model has statistical and analytical problem-solving tools.

In the beginning, Lean Six Sigma students are often obsessed with the actual meaning of Sigma. In the context of Lean Six Sigma, however, it simply means reducing errors to 3.4 per million opportunities. This is close to zero defects.

Here are the various Sigma levels:

Sigma Level	*Defective Items (PPM)*	*Faulty Items (%)*
1	697,700	69.77
2	308,700	30.87
3	66,810	6.681
4	6210	0.621
5	233	0.0233
6	3.4	0.00034

Sigma levels examples are often related to pizza delivery. For example, when the above scale indicates one million on-time pizza deliveries may not seem too alarming. However, if a pilot is flying in an airplane or a patient is about to enter surgery, these levels have a different meaning.

Another way to think of Six Sigma levels is a popular explanation promoted by the American Society for Quality that explains why 99% accuracy is essential. This chart suggests that functioning at 4, Sigma could cause the following events to occur:

- Two short or long landings at major airports each day;
- 5,000 incorrect surgical procedures every week;
- No electricity for almost 7 hours each month;
- At least 200,000 wrong drug prescriptions each year.

Lean Six Sigma principles also embody Critical to Quality (CTQ). However, statistically, this is sometimes difficult to measure due to the subjectiveness.

Lean Six Sigma is concerned with process capability. What can the process deliver? It is equally concerned with Measure Systems. Lean Six Sigma is so worried about measurement systems that there are analyses to measure the measurement system. This may seem like overkill, but the entire process is flawed if the system is not accurately measuring.

Lean Six Sigma strives to stabilize processes. Stabilized and predictable processes are easier to improve. As mentioned earlier in this book, one of the big pluses of Lean Six Sigma methodology is that it incorporates popular management tools. For example, brainstorming, flowcharts, and checklists are frequently utilized.

Since Six Sigma is the dominant methodology, Lean Six Sigma uses the following belts to denote the area of expertise. Here is a quick summary of the roles:

- Yellow Belt—this person understands the basic theory and has participated in formal training. They can assist Green Belts in administrative duties.
- Green Belt—this person can apply the theory and use various tools. They participate in longer training sessions and must complete hands-on activities.

- Black Belt—this person can lead a Lean Six Sigma project and manage Green and Yellow Belts.
- Master Black Belt—this person is a trainer, mentor, and supervisor of Black Belts. Master Black Belts are often a part of the project selection.

Most recruiters use these designations to determine levels of expertise when filling a job posting. Companies that have committed enterprise-wide to Lean Six Sigma may offer internal training programs and encourage everyone to use the designations. Other companies may hire a Black Belt as a Quality Engineer.

Typically, in a company that has adopted Lean Six Sigma, a Green Belt will have a regular position and use Lean Six Sigma methodology for projects within their department. Black Belts often are assigned to a specific department, and Lean Six Sigma implementation is their principal duty. Many companies that do not have an internal training program do not have a Master Black Belt on staff. Black Belts mentor and support Green Belts. Master Black Belts usually mentor Black Belts and often are in charge of training for the company.

Companies hire Green, Black, or Master Black Belts for specific projects. Green Belts are sometimes preferred for contract work when the company knows what project they want to implement. Black and Master Black Belts are often chosen as contractors and consultants when the company does not have a clear idea of where the mistakes and waste occur.

One recent trend, with the variety of training available, is that recruiters look for candidates with external certifications achieved by attending vendor or university training. As a result, internal company programs must be more specialized or customized to cover all the Lean Six Sigma basics.

The statistical aspects covered later in this book are the most resistant to Lean Six Sigma. The good news is that the statistics for Green Belt projects may be limited to basic statistics such as mean, median, mode, range, and variance, also covered later in this book. In addition, statistics studied by Black Belts are often performed via statistical packages or templates. Whereas it is helpful that the statistical concept is understood, the computer or the template does all the heavy lifting.

The DMAIC model can be implemented using little math or statistical tools; hence, a lack of statistical or mathematical knowledge should not prevent the International Lean Six Sigma practitioner from getting started.

5.1 Discussion

1. How is Six Sigma Methodology different from Lean Thinking?
2. What are the advantages of blending Six Sigma and Lean?
3. What are two deviations that Lean Six Sigma promotes that are not included in the *PMBOK® Guide*?
4. What are the advantages of understanding essential project management when implementing Lean Six Sigma?
5. Explain the various martial arts designations for Lean Six Sigma.
6. What is the advantage of being externally certified by a vendor instead of attending an internal program?
7. What are examples of waste?
8. What are examples of "hidden" or "necessary" waste?
9. What is the purpose of a value stream map?
10. What are CTQs, and why are they important? How would you get a CTQ?

Chapter 6

Analytical Problem-Solving Tools

The Seven Tools of Quality are essential principles used in the business world for years. These tools are necessary for any company to improve its processes and increase efficiency and profits. In addition, these tools are frequently used by businesses and other disciplines, such as science.

Different names know the following tools. The generic term is *analytical problem-solving tools*; however, the most popular name is still the Seven Tools of Quality. Because the term *Quality* also encompasses cost and time considerations, they have also gained a reputation as the most popular process improvement tools.

Each tool serves its purpose, but they all work together to help organizations achieve higher levels of quality and efficiency.

These include:

- Flowchart
- Check Sheet
- Cause-and-Effect Diagram (Fishbone Diagram)
- Histogram
- Pareto Chart
- Scatter Diagram
- Control Chart

These tools make statistical analysis less complicated and are vital visual aids. For those interested in trying out these tools, the American Society for

DOI: 10.4324/9781003397649-8

Quality offers free templates online for these tools and others. Go to www.ASQ.org and query Quality Tools and Templates.

Interestingly, although people have received credit for creating these tools, Walter Shewhart, Edwards Deming, and Joseph Juran heavily promoted their use, and Kaoru Ishikawa popularized the toolset.

These seven tools, when used together, form an immensely powerful toolkit.

6.1 Flowcharting

A flowchart is a diagram that illustrates the sequence of steps in a process. It helps troubleshoot and analyze strategies. No one claims responsibility for being the founder of the flowchart. Start and end symbols are represented as ovals or rounded rectangles. These symbols usually contain the word Start or End or something that represents the beginning and end.

- Processing steps, represented as rectangles.
- Arrows coming from one symbol and ending at another symbol representing that control passes to that symbol.
- Parallelogram representing Input/Output.
- Diamonds representing conditions or decisions.

A flowchart is a means of visually presenting data flow through an information processing system. It reflects the sequence of events. A flowchart is a blueprint. There are advantages to flowcharting, including the following:

- Communication
- Analysis
- Documentation
- Coding
- Debugging Capability
- Program Maintenance

Flowcharts in the Define Phase of the DMAIC (Define–Measure–Analyze–Improve–Control) model map the current process. In the Measure Phase, flowcharts are often used to study or identify variations that can be learned and measured. In the Analyze Phase, flowcharting is a way to reason through the steps in a process—what would happen if an action were removed?

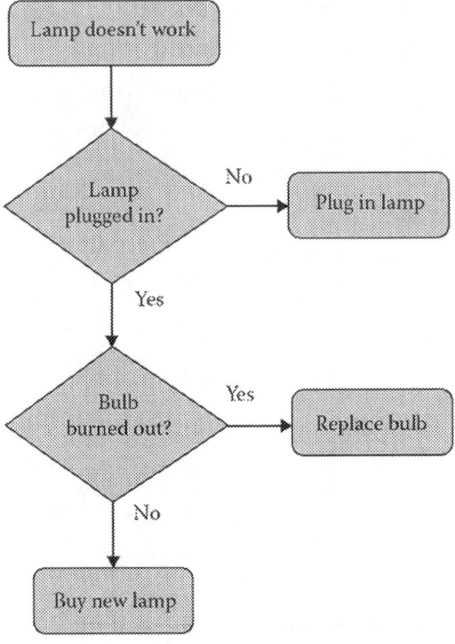

Figure 6.1 Flowchart.

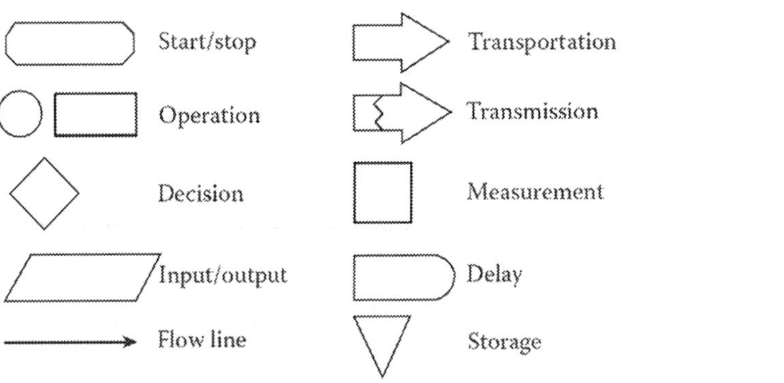

Figure 6.2 Basic flowcharting symbols.

To be practical and valuable, flowcharts should not be complicated. Figure 6.1 is an example of a simple flowchart, and Figure 6.2 shows basic flowcharting symbols.

6.2 Check Sheets

The simple check sheet is one of the most commonly used and powerful Lean Six Sigma tools. A check sheet is a list of things to do. A tollgate is an example of a check sheet. This check records the activity status of each phase.

Check sheets allow the collection of data in an easy, systematic, and organized manner. In addition, opportunities for process improvements are based on information obtained from the data collected in the process.

Check sheets are easy to understand; however, the collected data must be accurate and relevant to analyzing the quality problem. Information has to be accurate. To collect reliable data, a data collection plan is beneficial.

There are four steps needed in data collection:

- Establish a purpose for collecting these data.
- Define the type of data collected.
- Assign the collector of the data.
- Decide when the data collection time limit is.

The check sheet is used for collecting data in real time and at the location where the data is generated. A document is typically a blank form designed for the quick, easy, and efficient recording of the desired information. For example, a standard check sheet in Lean Six Sigma includes the defective item, defective location, defective cause, and checkup confirmation. The check sheet is sometimes called a tally sheet.

There are five types of check sheets:

- Classification
- Location
- Frequency
- Measure
- Checklist

Classification check sheets reflect a trait such as a mistake or failure. These mistakes and failures have two categories. Location is a check sheet concerned with a trait's physical location. For example, a picture can indicate the item evaluated. Frequency is a check sheet showing the absence or presence of quality or number of occurrences. Measurement check sheets are scales divided into intervals, and measures are indicated by checking an appropriate interval. Finally, checklists are check sheets that list items to be performed, a to-do list. A significant use of check sheets is as "toll gates." Toll gates, in the DMAIC model, are often presented between the phases to ensure all requirements for that particular phase are met. This is more or less a double-check and is used as a mistake-proofing tool.

Figure 6.3 is an example of a simple check sheet typically used by the Automotive Industry Action Group.

AIAG CHECKLIST

Customer or internal part no. Revision level

	Question	Yes	No	N/A	Comment/action required	Person responsible	Due date
1							
2							
3							

Revision date: __________

Prepared by: __________

Figure 6.3 Check sheet.

6.3 Cause-and-Effect Diagram

This particular tool, the fishbone diagram, is also known as the Ishikawa diagram.

A cause-and-effect diagram consists primarily of two sides. The right side (the effect side) lists the problem or the quality concern under question, while the left side (the cause side) lists the primary causes of the pain. Best done by brainstorming, there are different techniques available that are specific to the topic.

This tool allows a team to identify, explore, and graphically display, in increasing detail, all the probable causes related to a particular effect needed to be said. The major categories of reasons contributing to the impact are assigned to the major branches of the diagram.

The tool defines the problem, identifies possible and probable causes, and organizes these causes to highlight the major ones. It also helps groups systematically generate ideas and check that it has correctly stated the direction of causation. Finally, the format is valid when the findings need to be presented to others.

The possible leading causes of the problem (the effect) are drawn as bones off of the main backbone. Different names can be chosen to suit the situation, or these general categories can be revised. The key is to have three to six main categories listing all possible issues or influences. Then, brainstorming is typically done to add possible causes to the prominent "bones" and more specific reasons for the bones on the major bones.

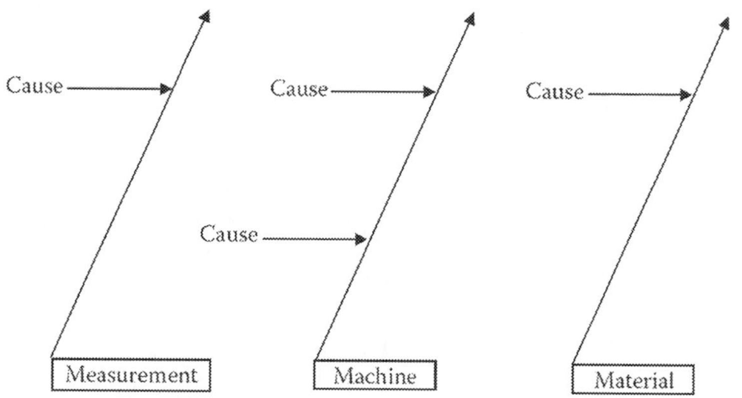

Figure 6.4 Cause and effect (fishbone).

One option is to use the 4 Ms. The 4 M categories from the major bones to help improve the structured brainstorming approach include:

- Materials
- Machines
- Manpower (now called workforce)
- Method

The most common method is to draw the diagram on a whiteboard or flip chart. The facilitator first presents the main problem and then asks for assistance from the group to determine the leading causes; these are drawn in later, splintering off from the prominent bones of the diagram. The team assists by making suggestions, and, eventually, the entire cause-and-effect chart is filled out.

Figure 6.4 shows the format for a basic cause-and-effect (or fishbone) diagram.

6.4 Histogram

A histogram is a bar chart used to represent groups of data graphically. A histogram is used to graphically summarize and display the distribution of a process data set. A histogram is a specialized type of bar chart. Individual data points are grouped in classes so that the viewer can get an idea of how frequently data in each class occurs. A histogram illustrates the shape, centering, and spread of data distribution and indicates whether there are any outliers.

A histogram is the easiest way to determine the center, spread, and shape of the data's distribution points.

A simple way to explain how a histogram is formed is to say that the form is obtained by splitting the range of the data into equal-sized bins (called classes). Then, the number of points from the data set that fall into each bin is counted for each container.

The questions a histogram answers include the following:

- What is the most common system response?
- What distribution (center, variation, and shape) does the data have?
- Does the data look symmetric or skewed to the left or right?
- Does the data contain outliers?

The steps involved include the following:

1. Count the number of data points—there must be at least 30.
2. Determine the highest and lowest number. Calculate range.
3. Divide the range into equal classes—the number of bars that will appear.
4. Count the number of each occurrence within each class.

Figure 6.5 is a simple histogram showing the frequency of calls to a help desk.

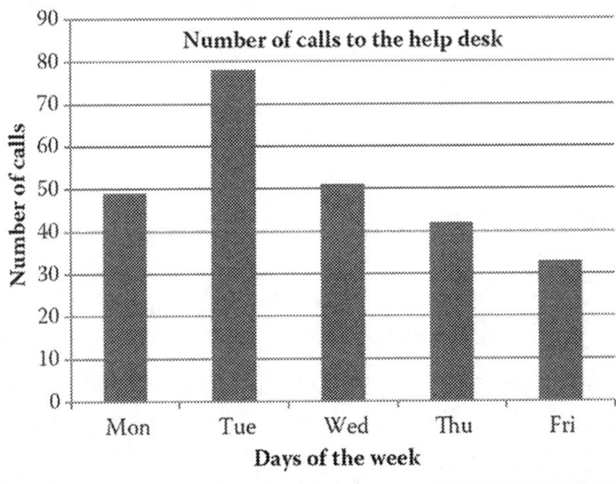

Figure 6.5 Histogram.

6.5 Pareto Chart

Developed by the Italian economist Vilfredo Pareto, this tool describes the frequency distribution (the 20–80 rule). Pareto determined that a small percentage of any given group (20%) accounts for a high amount of a particular characteristic (80%).

The purpose of the Pareto chart is to prioritize problems. Companies need more resources to tackle every problem; thus, they must prioritize.

Typically, on the left vertical axis is the frequency of occurrence. The right vertical axis is the cumulative percentage of the total number of events, total cost, or a total of the particular unit of measure.

In the previous example, the histogram showed the frequency of calls to the help desk. A Pareto chart would list the "Types of Calls" to the help desk. Both frequency charts (histograms) and Pareto charts are helpful when trying to determine root cause issues.

Figure 6.6 shows the annual cost for each cost center for the company. First, the data would have been gathered on a chart and arranged from highest to lowest amount. Then, from this charted data, a Pareto chart would be used to show the relationship visually.

In Figure 6.7, an accumulation line has been drawn to show the relative significance of each item. This Pareto chart shows that Parts and Materials, along with Manufacturing Equipment, account for roughly 20% of the overall cost.

Cost center	Annual cost	
Parts and materials	$	1,325,000.00
Manufacturing equipment	$	900,500.00
Salaries	$	575,000.00
Maintenance	$	395,000.00
Office lease	$	295,000.00
Warehouse lease	$	250,000.00
Insurance	$	180,000.00
Benefits and pensions	$	130,000.00
Vehicles	$	125,000.00
Research	$	75,000.00

Figure 6.6 Pareto chart information.

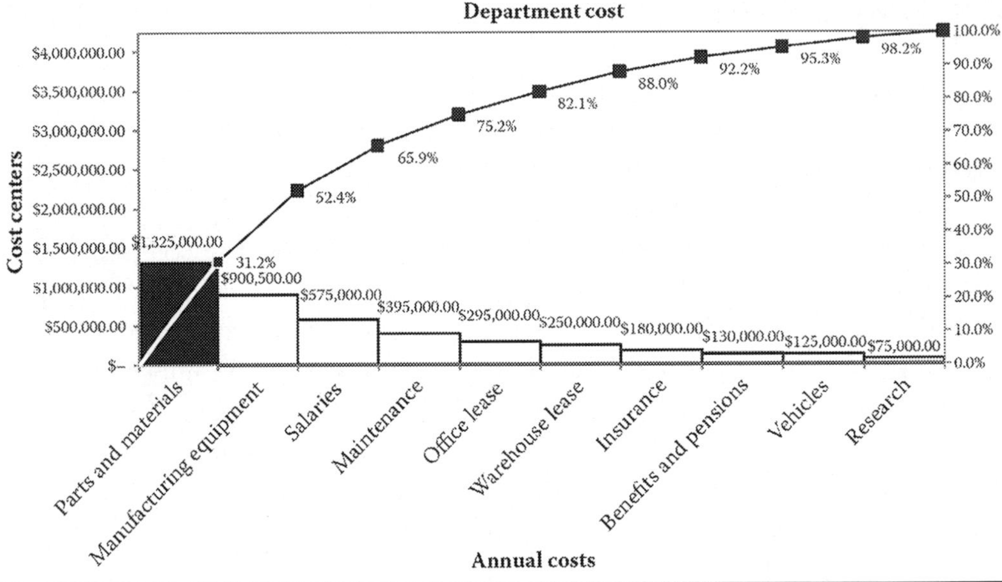

Figure 6.7 Pareto chart.

6.6 Scatter Diagram

Scatter diagrams compare two variables to see if there is a relationship. The relationship can be positive or robust, negative or none. The scatterplot shows this correlation graphically.

- Strong positive correlation—data points are tightly clustered along a trend line with an upward slope (as one variable increases, so does the other).
- Strong negative correlation—data points are tightly clustered along a trend line with a downward slope (as one variable increases, the other decreases).
- No correlation—data points look like a shotgun blast.

For example, Variable A could be the number of employees trained on a new software package. Variable B could be the number of calls to the help desk about the latest software. The assumption is that employee training reduces the number of calls to the help desk.

In this case, the numbers plotted would be the number of people trained on the software versus the number of calls to the help desk about that particular package. Other examples might include comparing height to weight, water consumption to daily temperatures, or the amount of education compared to income levels.

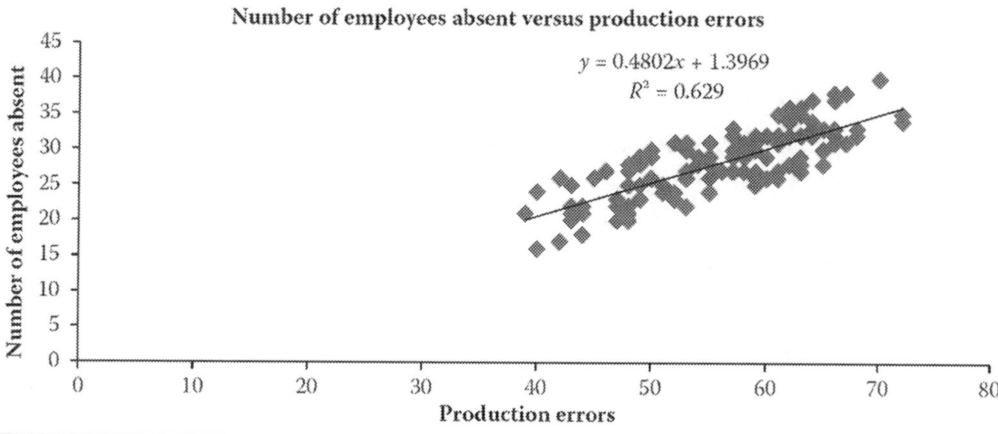

Figure 6.8 Scatter diagram.

Scatterplots are a useful diagnostic tool for determining association, but if such an association exists, the plot may or may not suggest an underlying cause and effect. It is common to hear the expression that correlation does not mean causation.

The information plotted on this scatter diagram (Figure 6.8) indicates a strong correlation between employee absences and production errors.

6.7 Control Charts

Initially, control charts were only used in manufacturing; however, they are now used in all industries. For example, the Joint Commission (formerly JCAHO) frequently used control charts in health care to understand, monitor, improve, and verify process improvement.

Control charts show a picture of whatever is being measured over a period. It is essential to understand variation. For example, building two storage sheds and making them look identical without a standardized plan is almost impossible. Without specific instructions, the same applies to widely diverse services, such as dry cleaning or training. Even with all the instructions and standards available, there is still room for variation. Reducing the deviation is necessary before overall process improvement. This is also known as stabilizing.

For example, Common Cause Variation and Special Cause Variation are often discussed in Lean Six Sigma. A common cause is sometimes called the system cause, and a special cause is sometimes called the local cause.

Common causes are problems inherent in the system itself. They are always present and affect the output of the process. Special causes are problems that arise periodically. They are somewhat unpredictable.

Examples of the common cause may include:

- Poor training
- Inappropriate production methods
- Poor workstation design

Examples of the particular cause may include:

- Operator error
- Broken tools

There are distinct types of control charts. Figure 6.9 is an example of a basic control chart. All control charts would have these components.

When considering the dynamics of a control chart, it is helpful to think of a bell curve showing normal distribution. The line from the top of the bell straight down represents the mean. When the bell chart is perfectly shaped, not leaning to one side or the other, the process is said to be in control or stable (Figure 6.10).

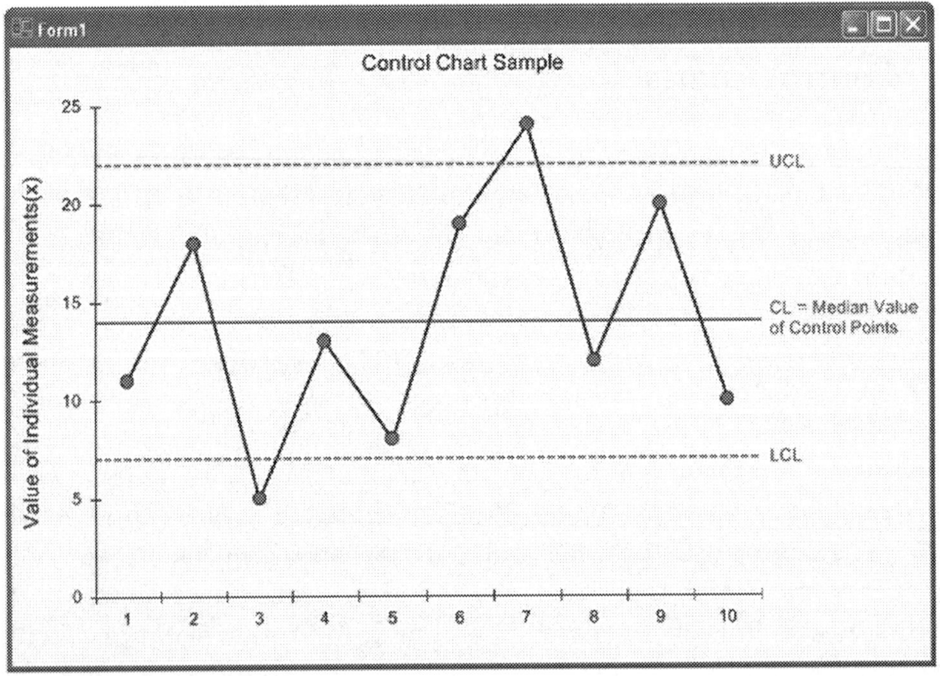

Figure 6.9 Basic control chart.

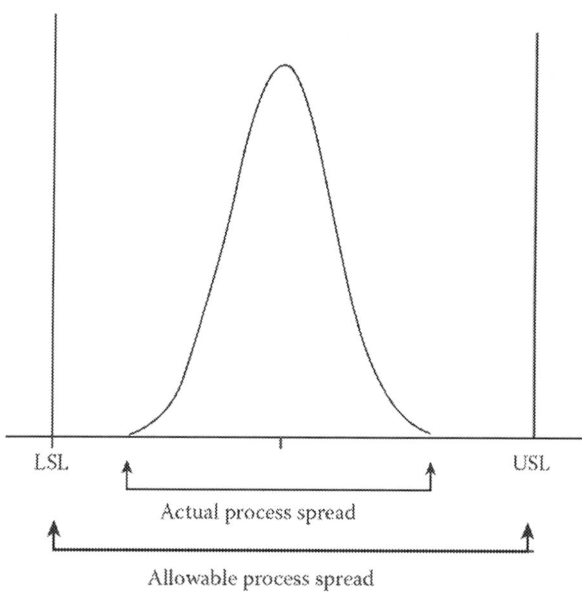

Figure 6.10 Bell chart showing normal distribution.

It is essential to use each tool correctly to maximize their benefit. Furthermore, these tools can also be used in combination with each other to create an integrated approach to quality improvement. By employing these tools correctly, organizations can drastically improve the quality of their products and services and save time and money in the process.

Using the Seven Tools of Quality can immensely benefit businesses of all sizes. Implementing these tools into your operations can help you maximize efficiency, increase accuracy, and decrease waste. In addition, by utilizing the tools, you will better understand your process and make improvements that result in a higher-quality end product.

One of the primary benefits of using the tools is improved customer satisfaction. By understanding the flaws in your process and making corrections, customers are more likely to have a positive experience with your product or service. This increased customer satisfaction can lead to more loyal customers and more referrals.

The Seven Tools of Quality can also help you improve efficiency within your business. You can identify improvement areas by accurately measuring how your processes work. Making these adjustments can allow you to increase production and reduce waste. This results in greater efficiency, lower costs, and higher profits for your business.

Finally, the Seven Tools of Quality can help you stay competitive in today's marketplace. Delivering high-quality products or services quickly can give you an edge over your competition and make you more attractive to potential customers.

In summary, using the Seven Tools of Quality can benefit businesses of any size. By understanding and improving processes, companies can increase customer satisfaction, improve efficiency, save money, and remain competitive. Implementing the tools is a fantastic way to maximize quality and ensure success overall.

6.8 Discussion

Note: These templates are available online for free through the American Society for Quality.

1. How would a cause-and-effect diagram be developed with heavy traffic as the root problem?
2. How would you prepare a histogram and Pareto chart that could be used for an IT help desk?
3. How would a scatter diagram be created on two related topics: cost and housing or weight and height?
4. How would a control chart be designed using the following data: 5, 10, 15, 12, 23, 67, 4, and 6?
5. What are the above chart's lower control limit (LCL) and upper control limit (UCL)?
6. What are some other tools you think would be good critical thinking or analytical problem-solving tools?
7. What is the typical design of a flowchart?
8. What components included on a check sheet ensure project completion?
9. Explain the differences and similarities between a value stream map and a process flowchart.

Chapter 7

DMAIC Basics

Define → Measure → Analyze → Improve → Control

The DMAIC methodology is an incredibly powerful problem-solving and process improvement tool. It is a five-step process that stands for Define–Measure–Analyze–Improve–Control and can be used to improve any business process. It helps organizations identify potential sources of waste and inefficiency to create more efficient processes and operations.

The DMAIC framework offers benefits for improving customer satisfaction. Businesses can reduce customer complaints and provide better service using the DMAIC framework to identify and solve problems. Additionally, by improving processes with the DMAIC framework, companies can reduce customer wait times and respond faster to customer inquiries.

Overall, the DMAIC framework provides a systematic approach to improving customer satisfaction. By taking the time to implement the steps of the DMAIC framework, businesses can gain valuable insight into their customers' needs and expectations and make the necessary changes to improve customer satisfaction.

After each phase of the model, a toll gate exercise may occur.

A toll gate is a list of questions to answer before moving to the next phase. Think of the toll gate as a checklist to ensure everything has been completed. In straight Six Sigma, starting activities on a phase is rare until the previous phase is complete. Lean Six Sigma is a little more flexible. In other words, if there is an opportunity in Define to satisfy the Measure requirements. Remember that Lean Six Sigma is about speed, efficiency, and getting good, solid data.

DOI: 10.4324/9781003397649-9

Sometimes, a DMAIC work breakdown structure (WBS) is created at the beginning of the project. This WBS lists the tasks in each phase of the model. Then, the WBS shows up again in the Improve Phase. The structure is the same at that time, but the WBS is used to form a project plan.

Unlike a typical WBS, which is intended to be a project road map, the WBS will constantly be revisited and updated as participants work through the various phases of the model. This is because each phase of the model is intended to enlighten and expand the project, and the project manager will only know some of the components that must be completed. For this reason, project managers don't want to think of the WBS in typical terms where a baseline might be created to measure progress but rather as an overview of the basic plan.

7.1 Overview of DMAIC

Each phase of the model has various tools that may be used and activities that should be performed. The following briefly examines each phase and the critical components for success.

DEFINE → Measure → Analyze → Improve → Control

Examples of activities in this phase include:

- Defining the improvement process
- Identifying, prioritizing, and selecting the opportunities
- Developing project team charters
- Building effective teams
- Identifying the customer segments and requirements

The primary duty of Define is to finish with a strong project charter that clearly explains the process that should be improved, along with a strong business case.

Define → **MEASURE** → Analyze → Improve → Control

Examples of activities in this phase include:

- Determining the parameters measured
- Managing the measurement process

- Understanding variation
- Evaluating the measurement system and selecting the measuring devices
- Determining the process performance

In the Measure Phase, consideration of the CTQ is significant. Critical to Quality is the accepted term used to define customer requirements. However, we now use that term interchangeably with Critical to Satisfaction or Critical to Success. Although CTQs are relevant throughout the entire model, this is the phase in which the CTQ is determined.

Define → Measure → **ANALYZE** → Improve → Control

Examples of activities in this phase include:

- Identifying potential root causes
- Implementing alternative methods
- Conducting sources of variation studies
- Conducting correlation analysis

The Analyze Phase is crucial to the outcome.

Define → Measure → Analyze → **IMPROVE** → Control

Examples of this phase include:

- Generating solutions
- Identifying alternatives
- Ranking the alternatives
- Selecting the best solution
- Discussing the implementation aspects
- Implementing the final solution as per the plan

In the Improve Phase, implementing the best solution usually involves more than one department. Therefore, discussing the implementation aspects of the best solution with everyone affected is necessary before finalizing and implementing the plan.

Define → Measure → Analyze → Improve → **CONTROL**

Examples of this phase include:

- Developing a control plan (specify the checkpoints and control points)
- Implementing a suitable monitoring system for control
- Reviewing and evaluating the impact of changes
- Updating the documents, incorporating process changes
- Closing the project, rewarding the team members, and disbanding the team

In the Control Phase, there is a check regarding data integrity. The Control Phase also includes the control and transition plan. The idea behind the control plan, a deliverable, is that the control plan is written in a way that even those not exposed to Lean Six Sigma can review and understand it.

Success in Lean Six Sigma is not based on complicated or high-tech procedures. It relies wholly on tried-and-tested systems. It simplifies things by reducing complexities. One way to reduce complexity is to have everyone on the project team follow a basic road map.

Teams need to do what is expected of them. This is another area where having a standard improvement model is functional. It provides couples with a road map. DMAIC is a structured, disciplined, rigorous approach to process improvement consisting of the five phases mentioned, where each phase is linked logically to the previous and subsequent phases. DMAIC, although not the only road map in Lean Six Sigma, remains the most popular.

Process mapping and value stream mapping (VSM) are concepts used in all facets of the model. A process map, or flowchart, is used to display processes visually. It illustrates how a product or transaction is processed. VSM demonstrates the flow of material and information as a product or service passes through the value stream. VSM and process mapping are similar.

Value stream mapping is a Lean Manufacturing technique used to analyze the flow of materials and information required to bring a product or service to a consumer.

The significant difference between a VSM and a process map is that a VSM gathers and displays a broader range of information; it is higher level (does not map every single item) and identifies the critical path. Also, the items on the map are all considered essential to the process. In other words, if a step in the current process is eliminated, would the procedure still be able to flow? If the answer is yes that step is not included in VSM.

All process steps are recorded on a process map to get an accurate as-is picture.

Because of the emphasis on basic project management skills, all International Lean Six Sigma practitioners should have a copy of *A Guide to the Project Management Body of Knowledge*, Third or the newer Fourth Edition (*PMBOK® Guide*) Guides by Project Management Institute. This guide is available in hard copy, soft copy, or as a CD. Information about the *PMBOK® Guide* may be obtained at http://www.PMI.org.

Material from PRINCE2, many of which are public domain, can also help you learn basic project management skills. The United States website is http://www.prince2.com.

Using the DMAIC framework allows organizations to systematically analyze their processes, measure the effectiveness of improvements, and develop appropriate controls. The process begins with defining the problem and collecting data to measure it. Once the problem is defined, it is analyzed to determine root causes and potential solutions. Next, improvement activities are implemented, and the effects of these changes are monitored. Finally, control activities are implemented to ensure the changes are sustained over time.

This framework helps organizations ensure that their quality improvements are systematic and practical. The DMAIC approach provides a structured way of identifying and solving problems, reducing variation, and improving customer satisfaction. By following the steps outlined in the DMAIC process, organizations can ensure that their quality efforts are efficient and successful.

The DMAIC methodology has five distinct phases that each play a role in improving the process:

1. Define: The first phase of DMAIC focuses on understanding the problem. This is where you identify the process, the objective, and the customer requirements that need to be met. This step also includes defining a baseline performance measurement.
2. Measure: This phase measures current process performance against the baseline. Collecting and analyzing data is essential to accurately assess the current process and how it can be improved.
3. Analyze: Root causes are identified and evaluated. This will help determine whether the processes will be modified or eliminated.

4. Improve: This phase focuses on finding solutions that will improve the process and help it meet the customer's needs. Solutions can include changes in processes, procedures, technology, or other areas.
5. Control: The Control Phase ensures practical and sustained improvements. This includes setting up controls to measure performance, monitor trends, and respond to issues.

By following the five steps of DMAIC, businesses can ensure that their processes meet customer needs and work efficiently and effectively. It is important to remember that each step in the process should be documented and tracked so that progress can be monitored and improvement goals achieved.

7.2 Practice Exercises

1. Take a project and list the high-level activities that should happen in each of the following phases:
   Define
   Measure
   Analyze
   Improve
   Control
2. You have been asked to implement a Lean Six Sigma Training Program at the company. What high-level activities should occur in each of the following phases?
   Define
   Measure
   Analyze
   Improve
   Control
3. Create a process map entitled Mail Delivery and map the steps it takes for you to receive mail from the mailroom.
4. Create a VSM of the process map in Exercise 3.

Chapter 8

Define

Define → Measure → Analyze → Improve → Control

The Define Phase of the DMAIC model is often overlooked, yet it is one of the most critical steps in the process. A clear understanding of the problem is crucial to any improvement project's success. In addition, the Define Phase is the foundation for the entire DMAIC project, as it helps to identify and understand the process, root cause, customer needs, and gaps in the current system. In short, it helps define the scope of the problem and identify potential solutions.

The Define Phase of the DMAIC model is the first step in problem-solving and process improvement. The objective of this phase is to define the problem clearly. To complete this phase, one must understand the problem and identify the main drivers or causes influencing the issue. This helps to determine the objectives and goals that need to be achieved and develop an effective plan for process improvement. Additionally, by properly defining the problem, organizations are confident that their solution is effective and meets all requirements.

The Define Phase is also essential for identifying stakeholders, setting expectations, and gathering resources. By accurately defining the problem and identifying key stakeholders, organizations can better assign tasks and responsibilities to team members interested in the project's success. This phase also helps organizations anticipate potential problems during the process and respond appropriately to mitigate them.

DOI: 10.4324/9781003397649-10

The primary objective in the Define Phase is to clarify and document the process improvement goal. What is the problem? What process improvement needs to be made? Is it reasonable to take this specific existing process and invest time in making the process better, faster, or more cost-effective? The DMAIC model determines the next steps that will lead the project manager to "how the problem will be solved." The Define Phase is responsible for problem definition and establishing buy-in that exploring the process improvement is worth the time and effort.

Since one of the primary jobs of the DMAIC model is to provide reasonable solutions, in the Define Phase, the project manager is working with "projected" ROI. Projected ROI is determined by what overall benefit might occur.

This first phase is also about securing an agreement on the current process. This is usually established by designing a current process map. Although process solution discussions begin at the end of the Analyze Phase in the DMAIC model, often crucial insight is gained by simply mapping the current process.

Define intends to clarify the process improvement objectives and to determine what would constitute a successful outcome.

Critical tools for the Define Phase include:

- Process Map
- Project Charter
- SWOT (Strength–Weakness–Opportunity–Threat)
- Critical-to-Quality (CTQ) Definitions
- Stakeholder's Analysis
- SIPOC (Supplier–Input–Process–Output–Customer) Diagram
- QFD (Quality Function Deployment/Design)
- DMAIC WBS—Project Tracking Tool
- Affinity Diagram
- Kano model

The Define, Measure, and Analyze Phases of the DMAIC model are creative. In the Define Phase, for example, there are only two rules. First, to qualify as a DMAIC project, before leaving the Define Phase, the project manager must have a map of the current process and a project charter. Indeed, all the other activities suggested in the Define Phase will lead to tremendous project success; however, these two documents are the only hard and fast requirements in the Define Phase.

8.1 Process Mapping

Process mapping can be simple or complex. The only rule is that it must reflect the current state: How are things working now? When a process map is provided, the project manager should still "walk the process," as things may not be recorded or may have been eliminated or added since the last map was established. It is surprising how many project managers try to improve a process without fully understanding the current state. A process map is often done with visuals using flowcharting symbols but may also be depicted by using a bulleted list or a list that reflects Step 1 in the process, Step 2 in the process, and so forth.

Process mapping is simply taking the steps in the process and applying graphic symbols. A flowchart may reflect the ideal or perception rather than the actual steps. Therefore, physically walking through the process is valuable. Posting the process flowcharts in a conference room for functions that are not confidential or labeled security issues will allow everyone involved to review the information. Even if a conference room is not available, posting these on the wall of an office or cubicle provides visual motivation.

One type of process mapping is a value stream map (VSM), discussed in the Analyze Phase. Value stream mapping is a paper-and-pencil tool that helps the viewer understand the flow of material and information as a product or service passes through the value stream. For example, if a process is already in place, identify any "hidden processes." The VSM combines several charts, such as Swim Lane and PERT, also discussed in the Analyze Phase, to visually show the process flow.

8.2 Project Charter

The primary purpose of a project charter is documentation. A project charter is a document that records the project's goal and additional information, including why the project is initiated and who will be working on the project. In a typical project management scenario, often a project plan is prepared. This would include a list of the tasks to complete and an estimated time, costs, and resources necessary to complete the project.

A process improvement project charter is more like a proposal. It lists the process, as well as why the process needs improvement. The objective is to be permitted to work on the project and to ensure that all parties involved understand the specific process improvement that has been targeted.

Sometimes, a basic project charter has already been established before entering the DMAIC process. If this is not the case, the project charter must be fully developed in the Define Phase. Leaving the Define Phase and entering the Measure Phase with a clearly defined project charter is possible.

Most project charters begin with recording the problem statement. The problem statement may be a real problem that needs to be solved, or an activity that needs to be accomplished. A vague project definition leads to unsuccessful proposals and unmanageable documents. Naming a topic is not the same as defining a problem, but it is an excellent place to start.

A problem statement in a project charter is similar to writing a thesis statement. However, a problem statement is specific.

When brainstorming possible problem statements, here is a methodology that may be useful:

- Make a list of everyone involved.
- Find out what users consider to be the problem.
- Group the problems into categories.
- Condense the main categories into a problem statement.

A solid project charter aids in overall mistake-proofing efforts. Mistake-proofing is a constant theme throughout the DMAIC model. *Poka Yoke* is the Japanese phrase for "do it right the first time" and is labeled mistake-proofing methodology.

Before a project is selected, the project manager needs to determine the criteria. In some companies, a transparent methodology will explain the project selection process. For example, the selection may be based on ROI, process capability, or "green" (environmental) factors. When a selection methodology is not clearly understood, a tool called SWOT analysis may be helpful.

There are reasons why a project charter is necessary to facilitate the DMAIC model. A solid alliance will:

- Provide a clear statement of work.
- Outline critical success factors.
- Define expected benefits.
- List key stakeholders.
- Clarify what team expectations are.
- Keep the team focused.

- Keep the project and team aligned with organizational priorities.
- Name constraints and assumptions.

Project charter templates are readily available; however, if the company has an existing template, it is best to use that as a foundation.

8.3 SWOT Analysis

A SWOT analysis looks at quadrants to determine, via brainstorming, the Strengths, Weaknesses, Opportunities, and Threats of a project. The SWOT diagram takes on additional factors such as threats (risks) to the project and opportunities or possibilities. The SWOT analysis is helpful in overall decision-making. A Force Field Analysis only lists the pros and cons, so a SWOT analysis is more thorough.

One of the advantages of SWOT is that the project manager can determine immediately if there is a solid reason to move forward with the process improvement. It forces the project manager and the team to state what needs improvement. For example here are some existing processes you may want to consider improving:

- the student enrollment system
- the car rental process
- the method of designing online applications

What would be the pros and cons of improving each of the above examples? What would be the possible opportunities? What would be the risks?

Projects generally begin with a sponsor. A sponsor is a person funding the project. However, having a person function as a champion is also helpful. Champions help with issues such as change management and publicity about the project. A SWOT analysis is often practical when recruiting a champion. It gives the champion a quick overall picture of the issue.

8.4 Critical to Quality

In the Define Phase of the DMAIC model, once the problem statement has been determined, the next step is to consider CTQ factors. An effortless way to think of CTQs is "anything important to the project's success." This makes customer requirements and expectations, by default, CTQs. However,

CTQs should not be limited to only the customer and should include anything that needs to be considered to complete the process improvement successfully.

CTQs are the key measurable characteristics of a product or process. A CTQ usually is interpreted from a qualitative customer statement to an actionable, quantitative business specification. CTQs are what the customer expects of a product. Discussing the process boundaries and the customer's goals is essential to success.

One tool to develop CTQs is looking at the stakeholders and what they want to see happen. Stakeholders are people impacted by the project. A stakeholder analysis is a matrix (chart) that describes each stakeholder's commitment level. These become CTQs along with the customer requirements.

The "Voice of the Customer" (VOC) is the term used to describe the stated and unstated needs or requirements of the customer. This may be accomplished by direct discussion, interviews, surveys, focus groups, and even complaint logs. Other methods include warranty data, field reports, and customer specifications. The VOC is critical to the project and to determine the validity of the CTQs.

As discussed, one of the Define Phase's significant outcomes is clarifying the process improvement. CTQs can be especially useful in this quest. In addition, CTQ knowledge can provide valuable information on the link to the business or department initiatives.

8.5 SIPOC Diagram

SIPOC is a diagram that helps determine CTQs. SIPOC stands for:

- Supply
- Input
- Process
- Output
- Customer

A SIPOC can be formal or informal but is a crucial risk management tool. It helps identify the people and things impacted before embarking on a project. It replaces the quality circles Total Quality Management (TQM) promoted.

SIPOC									
Who are the suppliers for our product or service?		What do the suppliers provide to my process?		What are the start and end point of the process associated with the problem and the major steps in the process?		What product or service does the process deliver to the customer?		Who are the customers for our product or service? What are their requirements for performance?	
Suppliers		Input		Process (high level)		Output		Customers	
1		1		Start point:		1		1	
		2						2	
		3				2		1	
2		1						2	
		2		Operation or activity		3		1	
		3		1				2	
3		1		2		4		1	
		2		3				2	
		3		4		5		1	
4		1		5				2	
		2		6		6		1	
		3		7				2	
				8					
				9					
				10					
				11					
				End point:					

Figure 8.1 SIPOC.

TQM suggested that everyone who touched the process should be involved. Although a stellar idea at the time, this proved to be very costly. Instead, a SIPOC may be used as a problem-solving tool to identify all the stakeholders in a project or as a tool in the Measure or Analyze Phase of the DMAIC to determine critical factors to measure or analyze. In addition, SIPOC can assist in process mapping.

Figure 8.1 is an example of a robust SIPOC format.

8.6 Quality Function Deployment

Quality Function Deployment/Design (QFD) is more complicated. The QFD portion is gathering the customer requirements and mapping these requirements to the technical capabilities required to facilitate the needs. The output of QFD is the House of Quality. The house used to be a fairly standard template but now may take diverse forms. The common thing in all places, however, is listing the CTQs and seeing the correlation between the CTQs and the technical capabilities of the person performing the project.

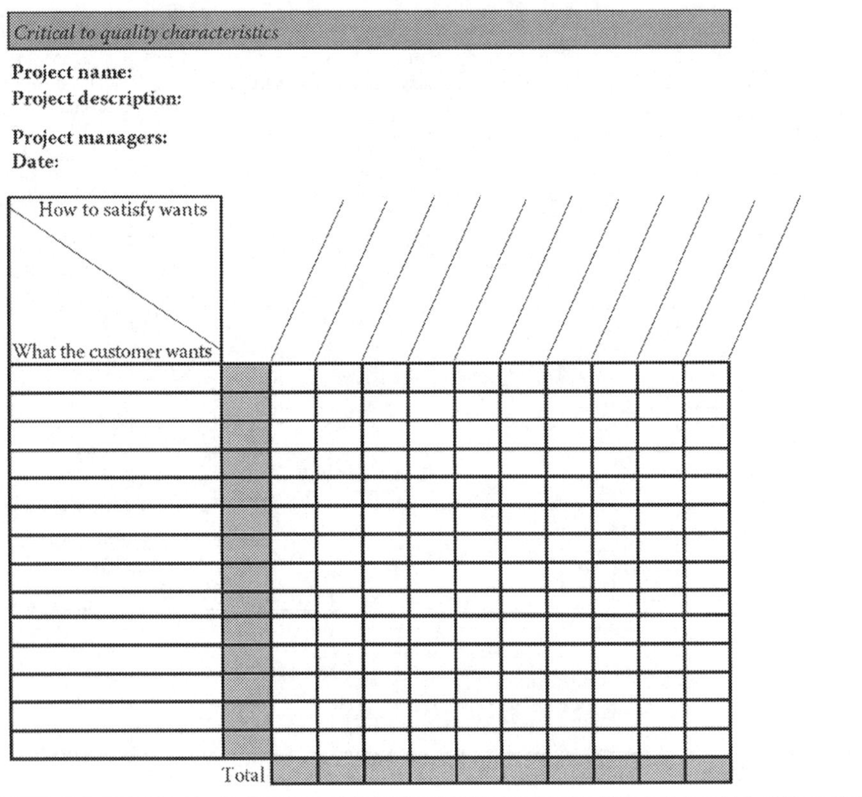

Figure 8.2 CTQ Tree.

Today's House of Quality format varies from complex engineering examples to simplistic graphics. However, in the center of the House of Quality is the CTQ Tree (Figure 8.2).

8.7 DMAIC WBS

A DMAIC WBS (work breakdown structure) may be applicable because it provides a map of what will happen. This is closely related to a project plan. Unlike a project plan, however, the DMAIC model is a discovery model.

The DMAIC WBS takes each category of the DMAIC and presents it in outline form. The outline shows the anticipated steps in each phase. The DMAIC WBS looks very much like a project plan. However, in this case, there is no baseline. It is simply a to-do list using the standard outline, for example:

1. Define
    a. Project Charter
    b. Design Process Map
    c. Perform QFD
2. Measure
    a. Data Collection Plan
    b. Benchmarking Study

The DMAIC WBS is a projection of what will happen in each phase. The detail will not be available, but there will be a high-level view of the planned accomplishments.

Two popular visual tools used in the Define Phase are affinity diagrams and a Kano model or analysis. These tools allow participants to identify critical elements of project success quickly. In addition, both tools are helpful when a large group of people is working on the same project or when there is chaos or conflict.

8.8 Affinity Diagram

The affinity diagram organizes ideas into their natural relationships. The first step is simple brainstorming and listing the ideas in categories.

8.9 Kano Model

A Kano model is a product development theory, now also applied to the service industry, suggesting that customer preferences be divided into categories, including delighters, satisfiers, and dissatisfiers.

In a Kano model, topics are grouped according to how they will delight, satisfy, or dissatisfy the customer. Professor Noriaki Kano classified them into these five themes:

- Attractive
- One-Dimensional
- Must-Be
- Indifferent
- Reverse

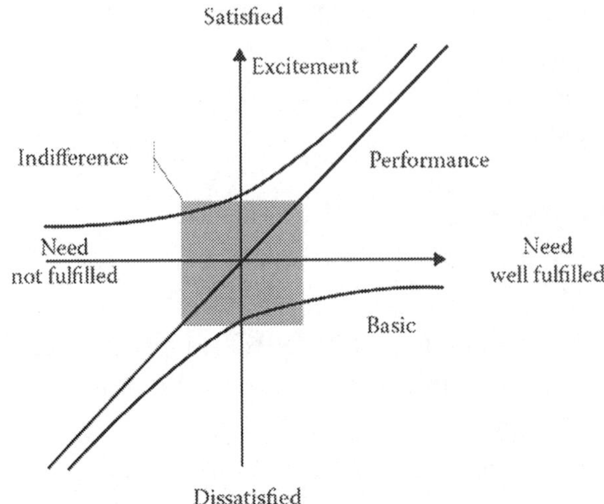

Figure 8.3 Kano model.

Later, the categories changed to delighters, satisfiers, and dissatisfiers.

The Kano is an essential paper-and-pencil tool and typically follows the format in Figure 8.3.

A toll gate is reviewed at the end of each phase in the DMAIC cycle. Think of a toll gate as a checklist of everything that needs completion before the next step begins. Toll gates will always carry specific components related to the project; however, some general items listed in the Define Phase would include:

- CTQs identified and explained
- Project charter
- Processes mapped
- Team readiness

Throughout the DMAIC cycle, basic project management skills are needed, especially in the Improve Phase. However, the most apparent use of project planning tools is in the Define Phase.

It's critical to spend sufficient time on this phase to accurately identify and quantify the desired outcome and areas of improvement. Without the proper definition, it's almost impossible to identify the causes of problems and prioritize solutions that can bring about positive change.

Defining the problem correctly also helps keep the project on track by clearly understanding what needs to be done and how much time and effort will be required to complete the project. It also sets expectations for all stakeholders to work from the same assumptions and facts.

In conclusion, the Define Phase of DMAIC is essential for developing an effective plan for solving a problem. It allows organizations to identify key stakeholders, set objectives, and gather necessary resources to ensure the project's success. Additionally, by properly defining the problem, teams can better ensure that the implemented solution is effective and meets all requirements. Finally, by specifying the situation correctly, companies can be sure to invest in solutions that will solve their problems and bring about positive change.

8.10 Discussion

1. What is the purpose of a project charter?
2. When would it be appropriate to use a Kano model?
3. What is the purpose of an affinity diagram?
4. How is SIPOC used?
5. How are CTQs determined?
6. What items should be included in a stakeholder's analysis?
7. How is a DMAIC WBS built?
8. Construct a stakeholder's analysis for a project.
9. Design a SIPOC for a specific industry.
10. From the SIPOC, determine one CTQ for each group S–I–P–O–C.
11. What elements could be reasonably added to a project charter?
12. What elements in Define contribute to the overall concept of mistake-proofing?

Chapter 9

Measure

Define → **MEASURE** → Analyze → Improve → Control.

In any project, it is essential to be able to measure the results you are achieving. This is especially true for projects that use the DMAIC process. Data is the cornerstone of any successful business. From the minor details of a product's cost to the broadest understanding of a customer's behavior, data helps organizations understand and improve their operations.

The DMAIC process uses data as a foundation for improvement. The "Measure" stage, in particular, requires companies to measure key performance indicators (KPIs) and other relevant metrics.

When it comes to the DMAIC process, measuring is one of the most critical steps. This is because measuring allows you to gain insight into what's happening in your organization. It will enable you to determine whether or not the changes have an effect and, if so, how significant that effect is. In addition, by measuring, you can accurately identify areas of improvement.

Measuring also allows you to create a baseline to compare the results of your efforts. For example, if you measure before and after implementing a new process, you can quickly tell if it has the desired effect. This data can be used to inform future decision-making and help guide the direction of your organization.

Measuring helps provide clarity when looking at complex systems. By understanding what is happening in a plan, you can more easily pinpoint

DOI: 10.4324/9781003397649-11

areas of opportunity and focus resources on them. This can lead to better optimization of processes and higher levels of efficiency throughout the organization.

Moreover, measuring also helps provide clarity when looking at complex systems. By understanding what is happening in a plan, you can more easily pinpoint areas of opportunity and focus resources on them. This can lead to better optimization of processes and higher levels of efficiency throughout your organization.

Auditing and measuring are both essential parts of the DMAIC model. While these two processes may have different goals, they also have similarities.

Measurement and auditing are two critical components of the DMAIC model. The DMAIC model stands for Define, Measure, Analyze, Improve, and Control and is used to improve organizational processes. To properly use the DMAIC model, it is necessary to understand the relationship between measurement and auditing.

The purpose of measurement in the DMAIC model is to collect data that can be used to identify process problems and quantify the extent of those problems. This data is analyzed and used to improve the process. Auditing is evaluating a function and documenting any issues or non-compliance with established standards. Auditing often identifies potential problems and risks before they impact the organization.

The relationship between measurement and auditing is simple: size provides the data necessary to inform an audit, while the audit provides insight into areas of concern that may need further analysis. Measurement can identify problems or inefficiencies in a process, while auditing can provide the context to understand why those problems exist. Measurement and auditing work together to ensure that functions operate at their highest efficiency and compliance level.

Edwards Deming, the father of modern quality control, said that anything that is measured gets better. The primary purpose of the Measure Phase is to establish a clear as-is picture of where the existing process is today and ensure that the tools used to measure the activity are reliable and valid. In this phase, a conscious effort is made to eliminate critical or biased information.

Two documents are brought to the Measure Phase when leaving the Define Phase: a process map and a project charter. The project charter document is used as a reference document throughout the DMAIC phases.

The process map is used to decide what functions in the process should be measured.

If the process map developed in the Define Phase is at a high level, the map is often set in a more detailed diagram. A clear process map is a quick way to determine what activities should be measured.

The reliability of the tool used to measure is also considered in this phase. This may mean the calibration of specific instruments used in the measurement process in manufacturing environments. In service industries, where simple observation is often used to determine how well things are going, it may mean documenting to whom and how the words are being made. For example, is the method used to measure fairness?

Establishing how long each activity takes and how much each cost is imperative. This information is necessary to demonstrate that a process improvement has occurred once the solution is implemented.

In the Measure Phase, tasks are related to recording defects, mistakes, or variations and identifying process improvement opportunities. These measurements need to be reliable and valid. There are diverse definitions for reliability and accurate; however, Lean Six Sigma considers reliability as relating to the measurement tool. For example, is a measuring tape a reliable instrument to measure inches? Normally yes. The validity, in this case, means if it has meaning related to the project. In other words, is the measurement chosen related to the problem?

One of the significant activities of Lean Six Sigma is gathering data. Other improvement methodologies often attempt to process improvement without the appropriate data to understand the underlying causes of the problem. Unfortunately, having the correct data can result in short-lived or disappointing results.

The purpose of the Measure Phase in the DMAIC model is to understand the as-is or current state clearly.

Critical tools for the Measure Phase include:

- Process Mapping (Detailed Look)
- Input and Output Definition (*X*s and *Y*s)
- Benchmarking
- Scorecards
- CTQs—Measurement
- Cp and Pp Index
- Failure Mode and Effects Analysis (FMEA)
- Sigma Calculations

- Measurement Systems Analysis (MSA)
- Data Collection Plan

9.1 Detailed Process Map

In the Measure Phase, a process map should contain all the details. In the Define Phase, the process map is a high-level map recording the significant steps in the process. A more detailed process map will help identify relationships and bottlenecks. The process map designed in the Define Phase now takes on more facts. One of the goals of the Measure Phase is to pinpoint the location or source of a problem as precisely as can be determined. Then, measure whatever makes sense to measure. The detailed process map provides a way to view relationship graphics.

$$Y = f(x)$$

Y: the outcome or outcomes, result or results, that you want. *X*: the inputs, factors, or whatever is necessary to get the outcome (there can be more than one possible *x*). F: the function or process that will take the inputs and make them into the desired outcome.

9.2 Benchmarking

Benchmarking is an effective and popular technique to define the as-is state. There are distinct types of benchmarking:

- Internal
- Competitive
- Functional
- Collaborative
- Generic

Internal benchmarking compares activities and processes within the organization to another operation in the same company. Competitive benchmarking is the most challenging as it compares against competitors, and this information is sometimes difficult to secure. Functional benchmarking analyzes and compares a function—think of tasks as activities. Collaborative benchmarking is the most futuristic, aiming to improve industries such as health care or world initiatives. It sets the standard for a specific field or industry. Finally, generic benchmarking looks at any activity, operation, or process.

9.3 Scorecards

Scorecards are another way to measure. For example, the Balanced Scorecard, developed by Kaplan and Norton at Harvard University in the early 1990s, focused on these quadrants: Finance, Customer Service, Business Process, and Learning. These are good designations; however, a scorecard may pick any four areas related to the project and compile measurements around those categories.

Using scorecards is an excellent way to gather measurements because each quadrant may already have developed metrics. For example, one standard financial measure would return on investment (ROI).

Yet another place to start measuring would be the Critical-to-Quality (CTQ) factors developed in the Define Phase. Since the objective is to get a clear "as-is" picture of where the project is today, determining how well the CTQs perform.

A prioritization or decision matrix is a valuable technique used with team members or users to achieve consensus about an issue. The matrix helps rank problems or issues. The purpose is to prioritize tasks, issues, and alternatives to aid in selecting what tasks, issues, or alternatives to pursue. The goal is to evaluate and prioritize a list of options. The team first establishes an index of weighted criteria and then estimates each chance against those criteria.

This tool may be a Pugh matrix, decision grid, selection matrix or grid, problem matrix, problem selection matrix, opportunity analysis, solution matrix, criteria rating form, or criteria-based matrix.

A simplified way of thinking of a decision matrix is to make a list of things that are important when choosing a job. Then, give each factor a rating from 1 to 10. Next, make a column for each position considered. If it meets the rating factor, a plus goes in that column. If not, place a minus symbol. The column with the most pluses wins.

Process Cycle Efficiency is a calculation that relates the amount of value-added time to the total cycle time in a process. For example, a Lean approach is one in which the value-added time in the process is more than 25% of the total lead time of that process.

Process			
Description	Metric used	Actual	Target
People			
Description	Metric used	Actual	Target

Figure 9.1 Balanced Scorecard worksheet.

There are presentation templates to show the Balanced Scorecard results, and, often, companies have developed their format. However, this worksheet may quickly gather the necessary information (Figure 9.1).

9.4 Failure Mode and Effects Analysis

FMEA is a tool used throughout the DMAIC model. For example, an FMEA would measure the current process controls in the Measure Phase. Process control is what is currently in place to manage the risk of something going wrong. FMEAs can also be forms used to identify every possible failure mode of a process or product. These forms can also rank and prioritize the possible causes of failure.

Safely used, the FMEA provides benefits that include:

- Improving product/process reliability and quality
- Increasing customer satisfaction
- Early identification and elimination of potential product/process failure modes
- Documenting risk
- Developing actions to reduce risk(s)

FMEA forms may contain various information. Additional information may include formulas that calculate risk, occurrence, or detection. Companies can create their FMEA forms.

Risk, Occurrence, and Detection may have industry-associated formulas that determine, on a scale from 1 to 10, the severity of the problem (Risk), how often the pain may occur (Occurrence), or how likely the company may catch the problem before it becomes a problem (Detection).

Function	Potential failure	Possible effect	Possible causes	Current control/s

Figure 9.2 FMEA worksheet.

In its simplest form, however, FMEA is designed to identify a project's key activities, functions, or processes. Then, the FMEA determines the ramifications of that activity's failure. Other essential factors are determining why the action could fail and what things (controls) are currently in place to avoid that.

A worksheet to gather critical information that may be used on any FMEA form or analysis is shown in Figure 9.2.

Although the basic FMEA information and process are the same, the variations of FMEA forms include:

- System
- Service
- Software
- Design
- Process

System FMEAs, for example, may include product specification, design considerations, and company or industry constraints.

A Service FMEA may consider additional information specifically related to one of these areas:

- Purchasing
- Supplier selection
- Payroll

- Supplier payment
- Customer service
- Recruitment
- Sales
- Project planning
- Scheduling of services

Software FMEAs may include various system analytics or industry benchmarks, whereas Design and Process FMEAs may include customer requirements and standards.

9.5 Sigma Calculations

Sigma calculations are handy in the Measure Phase to determine the current sigma level of an activity or transaction. To calculate the Defects per Million Opportunities (DPMO), three distinct pieces of information:

- The number of units produced
- The number of defect opportunities per unit
- The number of defects

The actual formula is:

$$\text{DPMO} = \left(\text{Number of Defects} \times 1{,}000{,}000\right)$$

$$\left(\text{Number of Defect Opportunities / Unit}\right) \times \left(\text{Number of Units}\right)$$

Two conditions must exist to use the sigma level effectively as a measurement form. The first condition is that you are dealing with countable items. Second, everyone must agree on what constitutes a mistake or defect.

9.6 Cp and Pp Indexes

Statistics measure process capability. A capable process is one where almost all the measurements fall inside the specification limits. Capability Metrics (Cp) is a measurement similar to sigma, measuring process capability.

A process Capability Analysis is a technique used to determine how well a process meets specification limits. A Capability Analysis is based on a sample of data taken from a process and usually produces:

- An estimate of the DPMO
- One or more capability indices
- An estimate of the sigma quality level at which the process operates

A process is capable if it falls within the specification limits. If the histogram data fall within the specification limits, then the process is capable. Often manufacturing environments prefer to use Cp. Traditionally, a one or higher index indicates that the process is capable in Cp. In manufacturing, usually, the number needs to be 1.33, which is the same as 4 Sigma. The number 2 in the index represents Six Sigma. The process capability index, or Cpk, measures a process's ability to create a product within specification limits.

Process capability refers to the ability of a process to produce a defect-free product or service in a controlled manner. An index often measures this. For example, the process capability index determines how well the process is "centered" within the specification limits.

A more sophisticated Capability Analysis is a graphical or statistical tool that visually or mathematically compares actual process performance to the performance standards established by the customer. In summary, the capability of processes may use indices called Cp and Cpk. These two indices, used together, can tell us how capable our process is and whether or not we have a centering issue. Cp is the potential capability of the process; Cpk is the actual capability of the process.

Histograms track the frequency of events. A quick way to study process capability is to review the size and shape of the histogram. For example, if the histogram's bar shape looks like a normal distribution (bell-shaped). The process would appear capable of managing most issues. If, on the other hand, the bell is leaning to the right or left, this may indicate an opportunity for process improvement.

A nonmathematical way to determine capability is to examine the CTQ objectives thoroughly. During production, the performance of the process is monitored. This helps detect and prevent possible variations. A method is considered capable if the process is centered on the specified target and the range of the specified limits is more comprehensive than the actual process variations.

As mentioned in the Define Phase, each phase is completed by reviewing a toll gate. Once again, there will always be items specific to the project that will be included in the toll gate. At this toll gate, a prominent item would be the data collection plan, ensuring that it has been established and documented and that data has been collected on critical measurements. Again, remember that the objective is to develop a clear picture of the current process.

A basic understanding of fiscal management is helpful in the Measure Phase. Just as Lean Six Sigma assumes a specific basic project management knowledge, there is also an assumption that practitioners have been exposed to information such as Finance and Accounting for the Non-Financial Manager. This is necessary because many measurements may be based on finance or basic accounting.

Although no one expects an International Lean Six Sigma practitioner to have the same financial knowledge as a CPA (certified public accountant) or CFO (chief financial officer) of a company, the following concepts are essential and not covered in this material:

- Accounting Terminology and Underlying Concepts
- The Role of Various Financial Statements
- Distinguishing Income from Cash Flow
- The Accounting Process
- The Quality of Earnings
- Financial Decision Making
- Analysis of Financial Reports
- Approaches to Valuation
- Calculating Return on Investment

A critical factor in the Measure Phase is the question of reliability and validity.

Reliability is the consistency or stability of indicators. A reliable instrument yields the same results on repeated measures. However, a device may be reliable but not valid.

There are distinct types of validity:

- Face Validity (Assumptions of a logical tie between the items of an instrument and its purpose)
- Content Validity (The extent to which a measure represents all facets of a given construct)
- Criterion-Related Validity (The relationship between the subject's performance on the measurement tool and the subject's actual behavior)

9.7 Measurement Systems Analysis

MSA is a mathematical method of determining the variation within the measurement process that contributes to overall process variability. It considers the following: bias, linearity, stability, repeatability, and reproducibility.

MSA builds a foundation in the Measure Phase. Therefore, it is a component of the analysis.

An MSA is a specially designed experiment that seeks to identify the components of variation in the measurement. Just as processes that produce a product may vary, obtaining measurements and data may have variations and product defects.

MSA is knowledge first developed by the Automotive Industry Action Group (AIAG).

AIAG concentrates on the following measurement analysis conditions:

- Bias
- Stability
- Linearity
- Repeatability and
- Reproducibility

Bias is a measure of the distance between the average value of the measurements and the "True" and "Actual" deal of the sample or part. Stability refers to the capacity of a measurement system to produce the same values over time when measuring the same sample. Linearity measures Bias's consistency over the measurement device's range. Reproducibility assesses whether different appraisers can measure the same part/sample with the same measurement device and get the same value. Repeatability assesses whether the appraiser can measure the same part/sample multiple times with the same measurement device and get the same value.

9.8 Data Collection Plan

A valuable tool in the Measure Phase is a data collection plan. The purpose of a data collection plan is twofold. First, it is a communication tool. Second, the data collection plan is a strategy. A data collection plan should document the phases, including pre-data and post-data collection.

The five steps involved should include the following:

- Clearly defining goals
- Reaching an understanding (authority)
- Ensuring that the data is reliable
- Collecting the data
- Following through with results

Data collection takes various forms, but capturing data using a Histogram or Pareto chart is common. Histograms track the frequency of events, whereas Pareto charts track the types of events.

Remember, when leaving the Measure Phase of the DMAIC model, the goal is to present a clear as-is picture of the various activities in the process. For example, what are these activities costing now? How long do these activities take now? Who or what department is responsible now? What, if any, bottlenecks are occurring in the process now?

The consequences of not measuring the results of a process can be significant. Measurable data lets you know if your changes have successfully improved the process. However, this can lead to costly and time-consuming rework, wasted resources, and delays in delivery. Furthermore, it can lead to missed opportunities for improvement as issues.

When it comes to the DMAIC process, measuring is essential to ensure the process functions correctly and identifies improvement areas. With accurate measurements, it is possible to determine whether or not the process is achieving its desired outcomes. In addition, metrics are necessary to track progress and optimize the process.

With proper measurement and data tracking, the process may be more effective. However, by not measuring, you cannot properly analyze the results of your improvements and make informed decisions about how to proceed. Additionally, with measurements, you can quantify your successes and failures and compare them with similar processes.

Overall, proper measurement is essential for the success of the DMAIC process.

Data is an invaluable asset for making improvements and reaching goals. When used correctly, data can help you make decisions quickly and accurately. In the Measure Phase, follow these steps:

1. Collect relevant data: This data should come from reliable sources and accurately represent the current state of your process or product.
2. Analyze the data: Once you have collected your data, it is time to analyze it and draw conclusions about what the data shows.

Data analysis tools like Excel, SQL, and Power BI constantly improve. As a result, you can compare data sets and discover patterns, trends, and correlations.

3. Make decisions based on the data: Once you have analyzed your data and concluded, you can use this information to make decisions and formulate strategies to reach your desired outcome. Data-driven decisions are typically more accurate than intuition.

Using data throughout the DMAIC process ensures that all decisions are based on accurate and up-to-date information. This will help you optimize your process or product more efficiently and with greater confidence in the results.

In conclusion, measuring is essential to the success of the DMAIC process. It allows you to track progress, create baselines for comparison, and gain insight into the workings of complex systems. In addition, this data can inform future decision-making and help guide the organization's direction.

9.9 Discussion

1. How would a Pareto chart be used differently in the Measure Phase than the Define Phase?
2. List the different types of FMEAs.
3. List the different types of benchmarking.
4. Design a priority matrix for choosing a new job.
5. List the major components of a good MSA.
6. List the major components of a data collection plan.
7. What is the primary goal in the Measure Phase?
8. What is the purpose of a Capability Analysis?
9. What is the importance of the $Y = f(x)$ relationship?
10. What toll gates would you include in the Measure Phase?
11. What accounts for long-term versus short-term variation?
12. What is the difference between common cause and particular cause variation?

Chapter 10

Analyze

Define → Measure → **ANALYZE** → Improve → Control

Process improvement projects are essential for the success of any organization. Schemes are used to increase efficiency and reduce costs by streamlining processes and identifying improvement areas. However, one of the essential components of any process improvement project is the Analysis Phase. By performing a thorough analysis, organizations can gain valuable insights into their operations and determine which changes are necessary to make their process more effective.

When entering the Analyze Phase of the DMAIC model, the project manager knows what process improvement needs to be explored (Define) and the current picture (Measure). These two crucial pieces often lead to immediate ideas for improving the process. However, often the data and information need to be analyzed first. Sometimes, analyzing the info involves putting the data in a chart or graph to make it digestible. Sometimes, depending on the complexity of the process improvement, it requires more thought or more complex data analysis.

The objective of the Analyze Phase is to leave the phase with three to five solid process improvement solutions. Each solution needs to be evaluated for a variety of conditions. These conditions include but are not limited to concerns such as affordability, sustainability, time concerns, and capability issues.

The Analyze Phase is the process of breaking down a problem or cycle into its parts to understand better how it works. It involves examining a situation or system, looking at all the components that make up the whole,

DOI: 10.4324/9781003397649-12

and understanding how they interact. By doing this, we can identify underlying issues and uncover the root causes of any existing problems. Analysis can be used to identify areas for improvement, develop solutions and strategies, and ultimately create an effective plan of action for implementing change. The study is essential to any process improvement project and can help us better understand the situation and identify potential solutions.

The Analyze Phase requires listing all the possible solutions to the problem based on the information received from the Define and Measure Phases. It includes running "what-if" calculations on the keys. Only those solutions that meet the conditions of the what-if calculations would make the final list. The list is then passed on to the Improve Phase.

The Analyze Phase is often the most labor intensive. Formal training classes spend most of the classroom instruction time working with tools used in this phase. Many of the tools used in the Analyze Phase have already been covered in Define or Measure but may take on a different nuance. One of the objectives in this phase is to identify and analyze the gaps between current performance and desired performance.

Additional activities in the Analyze Phase focus on

- Identifying Variation
- Determining Vital Few *X*s, $Y = f(x)$ Relationship
- Determining Root Cause(s)
- Evaluating Impact

Since Lean Six Sigma is concerned with reducing waste and eliminating defects, identifying the sources of variation is critical. Variation is the fluctuation in process output—an instance or magnitude of change. Identifying the variation happens in the Measure Phase. In the Analyze Phase, the variation is analyzed. Although additional variation may become apparent, the main question is what it means and how it affects the project.

Whereas in the Measure Phase, the *Y*s and *X*s may have been identified, the Analyze Phase concentrates on which are the most critical *Y*s and *X*s. Sometimes, this will be called the Vital Few *X*s and *Y*s. They are also called KPIV and KPOV—Key Process Input or Output Variables.

Determining the root cause can be as simple as using the 5 Whys or a more sophisticated Failure Mode and Effects Analysis, discussed in the Measure Phase.

In large projects, it becomes necessary to determine the vital inputs and outcomes instead of all the information and outputs so that the project manager can focus on which problem is causing the most issues.

In Analyze, the objective is to determine the causes of the problems and decide which specific issues need improvement. Designing strategies to eliminate the gap between existing performance and the desired level of performance is often part of this phase. This involves discovering the cause of the defects. This is done by identifying the key variables most likely to create variation.

Critical tools for the Analyze Phase include:

- General
  - Correlation Analysis
  - The 5 Whys
  - 7 Quality/Process Improvement Tools
    - Process Map
    - Fishbone Analysis
    - Pareto Chart
    - Histogram
    - Checklist
    - Scatter Diagram
    - Control Charts
- Sophisticated—Statistical Package Based
  - Hypothesis Testing
    - Analysis of Variance (ANOVA)
    - Probability Models/Distributions
  - Linear Regression
  - Statistical Process Control (SPC)

Once it is determined that the data received from the Measure Phase are reliable and valid, it is time for the Analyze Phase to begin. To find these solutions, the following factors were analyzed:

- Correlation—Is there a common bond (positive or negative)?
- Root Cause—Why are things the way they are?
- What are areas that can be stabilized (variations)?
- What impact do the variations have on the solution?

Creativity is not encouraged when analyzing data. However, remember that the voice of the customer, business, employee, and process is valuable when making decisions. This is done by asking the right questions and using the right tools to identify, clarify, and reveal ideas.

Dozens of tools are available to analyze data. Unfortunately, Lean Six Sigma classes often focus on the devices alone. The trick with Lean Six Sigma is remembering to start with the most accessible tool first. Then, if that tool does not yield the results, try something more sophisticated. It is only sometimes necessary to select a complicated device. By using this approach, all the required data will have been collected by the time a more sophisticated tool is needed.

10.1 Correlation Analysis

Correlation analysis determines if two variables have a positive relationship, a negative relationship, or no relationship at all. This analysis can be done using a simple scatter diagram. It is often helpful to think of a correlation in terms of one thing versus another; for example, eating soup versus snowy days, rainy days versus employees who are late to work.

10.2 The 5 Whys

The 5 Whys is a simple but effective tool for determining root cause analysis. A question is asked five times based on the information received in the previous answer until a conclusion is reached. Sometimes, this simple tool can solve the problem. A famous example of this tool is as follows:

You are on the way home from work, and the car stops:

- Why did the car stop? Because it ran out of gas.
- Why did it run out of gas? Because I did not buy any gas on my way to work.
- Why didn't you buy any gas this morning? Because I did not have any money.
- Why didn't you have any money? Because I lost it all last night in a poker game.

Please note in this particular example there are only 4 Whys. This is to demonstrate that you don't necessarily have to ask 5 times to get to the root cause. Sometimes the answer will come sooner. The idea is, that after 5 whys, if you don't have a root cause, you may want to select another tool.

10.3 The Seven Tools for Process Improvement

Generally, these tools include the following charts and graphs:

- Process Map
- Fishbone Analysis
- Histogram
- Pareto Chart
- Checklist
- Scatter Diagram
- Control Charts

The Analyze Phase of the DMAIC model uniquely uses these charts. For example, a Process Map visually shows the steps in a process. This map is used in Define as an information tool and in Measure to decide what measurements should be taken.

The Process Map would determine bottlenecks and process flow in the Analyze Phase. Instead, it is often used as a pencil-and-paper tool where steps are moved around or eliminated to see the total impact on the process improvement.

A fishbone analysis in Define may be used to determine if the right problem is being explored, or in the Measure Phase; a fishbone may be used to determine variations that should be measured. In Analyze, the fishbone is almost always used to discover the root cause.

Both histograms and Pareto charts in Analyze place information in bins or buckets to determine the root cause. When used in Define, these charts determine if a problem exists; and in Measure, the tools are used to gather information on the current as-is state.

A checklist is used to collect information in all phases of the DMAIC model. Scatter diagrams are generally specific to the Analyze Phase because they show correlation and control charts are used to analyze patterns within the process. Control charts are often used in Measure to collect current as-is data, and in the Control Phase, they are used as a sustainability tool.

10.4 Statistical Thinking

The Analyze Phase in a Lean Six Sigma project may be accomplished using less complicated tools such as Pareto charts or histograms. All International

Lean Six Sigma practitioners should be exposed to the following topics. These topics usually require hands-on experience in a project to grasp the concept. Various software packages are available to make the process easier. These concepts include:

- Statistical Hypothesis Testing
- Statistical Analysis

A hypothesis is a tentative statement that proposes a possible explanation for a phenomenon or event. A valid inference is a testable statement.

Usually, a hypothesis is based on previous observations, such as noticing that many trees lose leaves in the winter and the weather is colder. Are these two events connected? How are they related? The null hypothesis would be that many trees lose leaves in winter because of the freezing weather. The alternative view would be that many trees lose leaves in winter, which is not attributed to the cold weather.

Sophisticated tools used for hypothesis testing are performed via statistical software. They are only necessary if there is much data to digest. To conduct a hypothesis test, the premise must first be determined. Then, the belief becomes the alternative hypothesis, and the opposite statement becomes the null hypothesis. The null hypothesis is mutually exclusive, which means if the alternative view is accurate, then the null hypothesis is untrue. In theory, hypothesis testing is a great way to analyze data if there is a large amount of data.

Although several are available, a popular tool for hypothesis testing is ANOVA. An ANOVA is an analysis of the variation present in an experiment. Another tool in hypothesis testing is probability models. Using basic probability theory, specific tests are applied. This will help to determine the likelihood of an event.

A statistical hypothesis test is a method of making statistical decisions from and about experimental data. Null hypothesis testing answers how well the findings fit the possibility that chance factors alone might be responsible. Fortunately, this analysis is done by using statistical software. Generally speaking, it is only necessary when working with huge pieces of data.

Hypothesis testing is used to formulate a test regarding a theory that is believed to be accurate. A typical example would be claiming that a new drug is better than the current drug for treating the same symptoms. The null hypothesis, H0, represents a theory considered accurate. The alternative view, H1, is a statement of what a statistical hypothesis test is set up to establish. In a hypothesis test, a Type I error occurs when the null hypothesis is rejected when it is, in fact, true; that is, H0 is wrongly rejected. Type II error occurs when the null hypothesis, H0, is not rejected when it is, in fact, false. When working with hypothesis testing, terms that are likely to be used are:

- *p*-value
- *t-Test*
- ANOVA

A *p-value*, a hypothesis testing component, is the probability value (*p-value*) of a statistical hypothesis test of getting a matter of the test statistic better than observation alone.

The *t-test* assesses whether the means of the two groups are statistically different from each other.

An ANOVA is a mathematical process for separating the variability of a group of observations into assignable causes and setting up various significance tests. This statistical technique is performed in a package designed to analyze experimental data. Minitab Statistical Software is the leading statistical package used to analyze data for Six Sigma, but several other packages exist. For example, most statistical analysis for Lean Six Sigma may be performed using MS Excel; however, statistical software better serves some more sophisticated exercises, such as ANOVA.

An ANOVA may be used even when hypothesis testing is not being considered just as a general information tool. For example, a *t-test* only looks for the difference in mean (average) between two data sets, and an *F-test* looks at more than two data sets to determine the standard; an ANOVA also calculates items such as median, mode, maximum, and minimum, and confidence level.

10.5 Statistical Process Control

Statistical Process Control (SPC) is a powerful tool that has revolutionized how businesses operate and measure their processes. It involves using statistical methods to monitor and control production processes to improve quality, reduce costs, and increase efficiency. The benefits of SPC are impressive and can make a real difference in a company's success. Statistical process control (SPC) is building and interpreting control charts.

Statistical Process Control is an invaluable tool for detecting potential problems in manufacturing processes. Quality engineers can monitor critical process variables through SPC and notice any variations before they become serious issues. This early detection helps to reduce waste and eliminate potential losses due to rework or scrap.

Operators and quality engineers need more visibility into the underlying process parameters in a traditional manufacturing process. This can result in costly issues that could have been prevented if detected early. SPC helps provide real-time insight into the process and quickly and efficiently catch potential problems.

Detecting potential problems early also reduces downtime and improves overall efficiency. Manufacturers can minimize the risk of unexpected downtime or catastrophic failure by implementing SPC and closely monitoring key process variables.

Overall, using SPC for early detection of problems gives manufacturers the confidence to focus on improving their process rather than chasing down unknown issues. In addition, with greater visibility into the production process, manufacturers can take proactive measures to prevent downtime and eliminate future problems.

There are varying types of control charts. The most popular are:

- X-bar/R chart
- p chart
- np chart
- c chart
- u chart

The X-bar/R chart is used for numerical data that are captured in subgroups in some logical manner. For example, three production parts are measured every hour. A particular cause, such as a broken tool, will then appear as an abnormal pattern of points on the chart. So it is two charts—X-bar and range chart. The X-bar chart monitors the process location over time based on the average of a series of observations called a subgroup. The range chart monitors the variation between observations in the subgroup over time.

A p chart is an attribute control chart used with data collected in subgroups of varying sizes. Because the subgroup size can vary, it shows a proportion of nonconforming items rather than the actual count. p charts show how the process changes over time. The process attribute is described in a yes/no, pass/fail, and go/no-go form.

An np chart also shows how the process, measured by the number of nonconforming items it produces, changes over time. The process attribute (or characteristic) is always described as yes/no, pass/fail, or go/no-go. For example, the number of incomplete accident reports in a constant daily sample of five would be plotted on an np chart. Np charts determine if the process is stable and predictable and monitor process improvement theories' effects.

The c chart evaluates process stability when there can be more than one defect per unit. The c chart is helpful when counting the number of defects is easy, and the sample size is always the same. It is often referred to as simply the count.

A u chart is an attribute control chart with data collected in varying-sized subgroups. The u charts show how the process changes over time, measured by the number of nonconformities per item or group. Nonconformities are defects or occurrences found in the sampled subgroup. They can be described as any characteristic that is present but should not be or any characteristic that is not present but should be. For example, a scratch, dent, bubble, blemish, missing button, and tear are all nonconformities. U charts are used to determine if the process is stable and predictable and to monitor the effects of process improvement theories. The u chart is used to count things by units. Sample sizes may be constant or variable.

Statistics and Business/Financial Math is useful in any phase of the DMAIC model. However, this phase is an appropriate place to do a primer, as analyzing data often depends on these two sciences.

First, consider the order of operators when looking at any formula. This is a topic that constantly comes up in all mathematical works. For whatever reason, there is a tendency for many students to do the multiplication first. However, the rule is Parenthesis, Exponents, Multiplication, Division, Addition, and finally, Subtraction (PEMDAS).

Mean, median, and mode are three ways to measure the middle. In Lean Six Sigma, since the goal is to standardize, which means bringing things to the middle value, having three different measures of central tendency can be helpful. If the mean, mode, and median are drastically different, it may indicate that we need to reassess where we think the middle falls.

- The mean, or average, of a set of numbers is found by dividing the sum of the numbers by the number of numbers added.

- The median is the number in the middle. The two middle numbers are divided if there is an even set of numbers.
- The mode is the number that appears most frequently.

The only tricky thing with these measures of central tendency is that, with medians, the numbers must first be placed in sequential order. In all three steps, remember that if a specific number appears multiple times, it has to be recorded each time.

The range is the highest number in a data set minus the lowest number in the data set. Therefore, how many numbers are in the data collection often determines how confident we are that we gathered the correct data.

10.6 Stem-and-Leaf Diagram

Viewing data can take various forms. Two simple ways to view the data that have been collected are by using a Stem-and-Leaf Diagram and by using a frequency table. Either way, once data is collected, it must be organized logically so the viewer can draw appropriate conclusions.

In a Stem-and-Leaf Diagram, the first number becomes the stem, and any numbers after that become the leaves. Thus, for example, if the number set were 12, 13, 23, 24, 26, 31, 32, and 33, the diagram would look like this:

1: 2, 3
2: 3, 4, 6
3: 1, 2, 3

A Frequency Diagram is a way of tabulating data with the independent variable listed. The frequency, the number of times the independent variable occurs, goes on the right-hand column. Taking this information and making a bar chart can also be known as a histogram.

With both a Stem-and-Leaf Diagram and a Frequency Diagram, we are trying to determine how often things occur. Therefore, sometimes a Frequency Diagram will be expanded to show relevant frequency. In other words, a third column may be added to explain how much of the sample percentage is representative of the overall population.

If, for example, the data were represented as 8, 9, 8, 7, 10, 9, 6, 4, 9, 8, 7, 8, 10, 9, 8, 6, 9, 7, 8, 8, the initial table would look like this:

X	*f (Frequency)*
10	2
9	5
8	7
7	3
6	2
5	0
4	1

10.7 Type I and Type II Errors

How a sample is taken from a population is critical to analyzing data. A population is a collection of data whose properties are investigated. The population is the complete collection to be studied; it contains all subjects of interest. A sample is a part of the population of interest, a sub-collection selected from a population. There are factors to consider when choosing an example; however, Lean Six Sigma is generally concerned with size. The larger the sample, the less likely a mistake will be made.

A larger sample contributes to avoiding a Type I or Type II error, which is simply a false positive or a false negative. A sample is being studied because it would only be practical to study some of the population before making a claim. If the whole population was explored and an assertion was made, it would have close to a 100% confidence level that a Type I or Type II error has not happened. Anything less than 100% lowers the confidence level in the data.

The decision to study only a sample is often based on time, resources, and data availability. Ten percent of the population for a sample is a good rule if the population isn't huge or too small. For example, if ten surveys were sent out and only 10% were returned (1 survey), there would be insufficient data to infer or draw a conclusion. Likewise, if one million products were produced by a relatively small company, choosing 10% or 100,000 to study may not be realistic regarding time, money, and resources.

10.8 Design of Experiment

Statistical data and statistical data packages are often used to help in decision-making if there is a large amount of data. Data handled on a simple spreadsheet do not typically need sophisticated tools. Since most spreadsheet packages handle pivot tables, which filter data well, sometimes tools such as ANOVAs and Design of Experiments (DOEs) are unnecessary.

MS Excel pivot tables are the easiest for filtering data. A pivot table may summarize information without writing a formula or copying a single cell. Still, the most notable feature of pivot tables is that data are arranged logically. Creating neat, informative summaries out of vast lists of raw data is valuable in digesting the data.

When there are variables, and those variables have characteristics, it might be necessary to use a DOE to analyze data. A DOE is a tool available in most statistical packages. The term *experiment* is a systematic procedure carried out under controlled conditions. DOE, or experimental design, is the design of all information-gathering exercises where variation is present, whether under the complete control of the experimenter or not.

> DOE has definitive characteristics. For example, the data analysis approach is determined before the test. The testing is always planned using a scientific approach.

DOEs are also powerful tools to achieve manufacturing cost savings by minimizing process variation and reducing rework, scrap, and the need for inspection. Because these designs have become very sophisticated, the typical role of the International Lean Six Sigma practitioner is not to create the design but rather to make sure that the appropriate, most reliable, and valid data is entered into the spreadsheet before the DOE is initiated.

The DOE information can be gathered via a histogram. Other components that may be used as stand-alone tools include SPC and regression analysis.

In SPC, the project manager makes interpretations primarily from control charts. SPC is a decision-making tool. Control charts can help the project manager determine the appropriate change when a process exceeds the agreed-upon limits.

A control chart would have these components:

- A clear title
- Labels on the *Y* and *X* axis

- Appropriate scale
- A middle line, typically indicating a mean (but could have other meanings)
- A UCL and LCL

Statistical quality control ensures those goods and services satisfy the customer's needs.

A regression analysis is similar to a correlation analysis. However, while correlation analysis assumes no causal relationship between variables, regression analysis assumes that one variable is dependent upon the other.

10.9 Analysis of Variance

The essential ANOVA compares the mean average of two groups, also known as a *t-test*. ANOVAs have more sophisticated functions and can-do as identifying the possibility of Type I or Type II error. There are several types of ANOVAs depending on the number of treatments and how they are applied to the subjects in the experiment.

- One-way ANOVA tests for differences among two or more independent groups.
- Two-way ANOVA is used when the data are subjected to repeated measures, in which the same subjects are used for each treatment.
- Factorial ANOVA is used when the experimenter wants to study the effects of two or more treatment variables.

The analysis is essential to any process improvement project, as it helps identify problems and find solutions. By thoroughly analyzing a process or system, organizations can identify areas where improvements can be made and determine the best action. In addition, analysis allows organizations to understand better the strengths and weaknesses of their processes and any potential threats or opportunities for growth.

Analysis helps organizations make informed decisions based on data rather than opinion or guesswork. By analyzing data and performance metrics, organizations can identify areas of concern and take proactive steps to improve their processes. The analysis also allows organizations to gain insight into customer needs and preferences to tailor their products and services better to meet those needs.

In addition to identifying problems, the analysis allows organizations to develop solutions. By analyzing the current process, organizations can identify areas where improvements could be made and develop plans to implement these changes. They can also use analysis to develop new processes that are more efficient and cost-effective.

Finally, analysis helps organizations keep track of their progress over time. By regularly analyzing the performance of their processes and systems, organizations can determine if they are meeting their goals and objectives. This can help them identify areas where additional resources may be needed and where costs could be cut, or efficiency improved.

Overall, analysis is an essential part of any process improvement project. It helps organizations identify problems and develop solutions, gain insight into customer needs, and keep track of their progress over time. As a result, analysis can help organizations optimize their processes, increase efficiency, reduce costs, and ultimately increase profits.

10.10 Discussion

1. What is the difference between a Capability and a Measurement Systems Analysis?
2. What is the primary tool used in SPC?
3. How would a Pareto chart or histogram be used differently in this phase than in the Measure Phase?
4. What are the conditions in measurement systems analysis (MSA)?
5. What is the purpose of hypothesis testing?
6. Design a simple hypothesis and then give examples of Type I and Type II errors.
7. When would a project manager use the 5 Whys rather than a Cause-and-Effect Diagram?
8. What is the difference between attribute and variable data?

Chapter 11

Improve

Define → Measure → Analyze → **IMPROVE** → Control

In the Define, Measure, and Analyze Phases of the DMAIC model, much creativity is involved, and many different choices and directions may be taken. As long as the primary objectives are met, the project manager works within the DMAIC confines. There are limited rules and mostly suggestions and ideas about mistake-proofing the project.

The Improve Phase in the DMAIC model aims to take the solutions identified in the Analyze Phase and use them to improve a process, product, or service. This phase is about creating, testing, and implementing solutions to improve the quality of the product or service. During this phase, teams work to develop and test potential solutions that are expected to result in significant performance improvements. Teams also use benchmarking techniques to compare their current performance with industry standards or "best practices" and evaluate the effectiveness of potential solutions before they are implemented. The Improve Phase also focuses on designing and testing experiments to determine the best solutions and select those that will be implemented. In addition, teams use data collection and analysis techniques to measure and track improvements over time and create plans for sustaining them. In the Improve Phase, there is a specific step-by-step journey map. For ultimate success, this map needs to be followed precisely. The steps are:

1. List three to five solutions.
2. Be prepared to provide all crucial documentation.

DOI: 10.4324/9781003397649-13

3. Achieve consensus on which solution will be tried.
4. Perform a pilot.
5. Design a project plan.
6. Roll out the solution.

The project manager only leaves the Improve Phase once an improvement is made. The progress is shown by comparing the before picture (Measure) to the after picture (Improve) after implementation.

Essential tools and activities for the Improve Phase include:

- Brainstorming
- Decision Matrix
- Pilot
- Project Plan
- Failure Mode Effects Analysis (FMEA)

The Improve Phase includes five basic steps. The first step is to list the solutions discovered in the Analyze Phase, along with the research and logic. The next step is to gain consensus on which solution to try, followed by a pilot. Next, the DMAIC suggests activities that can be done to accomplish the significant objectives in each phase. However, in the interest of mistake-proofing, the DMAIC only promotes implementing a solution after trying it out first (piloting). Although the pilot may need a creative approach, it must be done. The final steps in the Improve Phase include rolling out the project plan and determining the benefit of the project.

The target process of the Improve Phase is designing creative solutions to fix and prevent problems in the future. In addition, the phase involves developing and deploying an implementation plan.

This phase involves developing potential solutions, defining operating tolerances, assessing the possibility of failures, and designing a deployment plan upon completing a successful pilot.

In the Improve Phase, the solution is rolled out. Therefore, of all the phases, this is the most vital phase to engage in mistake-proofing. FMEA is a type of mistake-proofing tool.

A prevalent mistake-proofing tool used in the Improve Phase is Poka Yoke. Poka Yoke is used in processing, setup, missing parts, operations, and measuring errors. The steps involved include:

- Identifying the operation or process problem—based on a Pareto chart. Analyzing the 5 Whys and understanding how a process can fail deciding on an approach.
- Thinking about what might trigger this result.
- The solution is tried out first.
- Training everyone.

All mistake-proofing tools are concerned with what could go wrong, anticipating this possibility, and fixing it beforehand. Another popular tool in this phase is the Pugh matrix, which is a decision matrix. This involves compiling a chart listing the problems on the left side and deciding on a rating system on the right side.

Factors to consider in the Improve Phase include:

- Change Management
- Solution Selection Techniques
- Criteria Selection and Solution Ranking
- Pilot Planning
- Pilot Implementation Schemes
- Time Management
- Giving Feedback
- Communication Skills
- Managing Stress

Change management involves understanding that different people react differently to change. However, it can also mean the process and procedure to suggest a change, monitor the difference, and evaluate it.

Having a handy matrix that shows criteria selection and solution rankings is an excellent quick way to answer this question. In addition, distributing this type of document in a meeting will keep questions relevant to the discussion.

The solution must always be subject to a pilot. How the pilot is implemented is of great importance. Were the right people included? How were the results measured? What was the actual cost of the pilot?

Essential time management plays a crucial role in this phase. An implementation plan, the ultimate time management plan, is an expected deliverable. For practitioners who have problems managing their time, a quick primer in time management techniques is suggested.

Giving feedback, general communication skills, and managing stress are part of the puzzle. Although not typically addressed in a regular Six Sigma class, Lean Six Sigma believes these issues are crucial to successfully implementing any project.

On the more technical side, the objective is to:

- Perform a Design of Experiment (DOE)
- Define Operating Tolerances of Potential System
- Assess the Failure Mode of Potential Solutions

DOE includes the design of all information-gathering exercises where variation is present, whether under the complete control of the experimenter or not. It is another area mainly addressed in manufacturing, but having components that can relate to any industry.

DOE is a systematic approach to the investigation of a system or process. A series of structured tests are designed in which planned changes are made to the input variables of a process or system.

In the experiment, deliberate changes to one or more process variables (or factors) are made to observe the effect the changes have on one or more response variables.

The order of tasks to use this tool starts with identifying the input variables and the output response to be measured. Then, for each input variable, several levels are defined that represent the ranges for which the effect of that variable is desired to be known. Several methods are available. The Taguchi method is a popular choice. It refers to techniques of quality engineering that consider both statistical process control and new quality-related management techniques. This approach favors Lean Six Sigma since it believes management techniques and statistics are in its path.

Another area that has to be examined and refined in the Improve Phase is defining the operating tolerance of the potential system. Is the system robust enough? Will it work well enough to meet any criteria previously set?

Naturally, assessing failure modes is crucial. This can be done by using a simple FMEA, as discussed earlier.

In this phase, creating and rolling out the project plan is necessary. Some industries will refer to this as the execution plan or deployment. Some companies have methodologies, including releasing the risk management plan or other documents in the same package. The project plan uses a Work Breakdown Structure (WBS).

Before the rollout, a pilot must be performed. Simulation software is more prevalent in some industries than others but is a valuable tool when a live pilot is not possible or too expensive. Sometimes, a small focus group may be used to perform a pilot. Only move forward once the idea is evaluated.

Even after the idea has been evaluated, mistake-proofing exercises need to continue. Once an outline of the project has been created, including all necessary steps to improve the process, each item on the WBS should be investigated. It is required to calculate the time and expense of each entry. At this point, applying FMEA thinking might be appropriate. Checking on each essential activity and ensuring that a risk management plan is in place and that proper process controls are being recognized as necessary. When the project plan is completed, it should be presented to all involved in draft form for possible revisions before creating the baseline.

Toll gates in this phase primarily focus on the successful completion of the project.

Once an improvement has been recognized and documented, moving on to the final phase is safe. However, the project plan will not be complete at this time because the project plan will still have close-out functions that cannot be completed until the Control Phase.

11.1 Project Plan

A good project plan balances time, cost, scope, quality, and expectations effectively. Most experts agree these factors should be considered when designing a project plan. Taking all of these factors into account will help mistake-proof the project.

- Definition/Scope: The primary purpose of the project, including significant functions, deliverables, and the project's goal relative to the organizational whole.
- Resources: The financial, technical, material, and human resources needed.
- Time: Elapsed time and actual work time required to complete the project.
- Procedures: The various organizational requirements, policies, procedures, methodologies, and existing quality program.

- Change: New or different future conditions, requirements, events, or constraints discovered within or imposed on the project.
- Communications: Meetings, status reports, presentations, and complexities that will affect communication.
- Commitment: The degree of the sponsor, user, and other stakeholder support.
- Risk: The potential constraints to project success.

Designing a project plan requires listing all the steps necessary for success. Each step is then assigned a resource, a timeline for completion, and an essential cost. Once the project plan has been reviewed, a time and cost baseline are made. This baseline is used from the beginning to the end of a project to determine if the project is within the acceptable parameters. Although there are various project plan methodologies, Lean Six Sigma supports using WBS discussed earlier in this text. Project plans may be developed quickly in MS Excel, although most International Lean Six Sigma practitioners prefer using MS Project because MS Project offers other applications useful in project management.

Project plans need to be concerned with constraints (things that could get in the way of project completion) as well as assumptions (items that are assumed will be in place) to mistake-proof the project plan. Resource allocation is always a significant concern. A process improvement project plan follows all the same rules as a typical project plan as supported by material produced by the Project Management Institute. A good project plan should include the overall expectations, definition, schedule, and risks of the project to the organization and the blueprint (list of activities). The project plan shows the project activities and how these activities will be controlled throughout the project.

This is a quick way to develop a draft of a project plan:

1. Create a task list and WBS.
2. Indent or outdent tasks to finalize the WBS.
3. Enter task durations or work estimates.
4. Create dependencies between tasks.
5. Assign resources.
6. Pass the draft around for feedback.

Although risk management should be one of the considerations in the Analyze Phase when compiling a list of possible solutions, risk management is critical in the project plan phase. Risk management manages threats and often alerts the project manager to additional process improvement opportunities.

The Improve Phase, for an instructor, is often the most accessible phase to teach. This is because it is the strictest phase of the DMAIC model and offers less flexibility. Solutions are chosen, a project plan is developed, and the answer is rolled out. Each of the steps requires mistake-proofing. How much to mistake-proof the project plan depends entirely on the complexity of the project itself.

The Improve Phase of the DMAIC model is designed to solve problems and implement solutions identified in the Analyze Phase. It involves using data-driven techniques to develop, evaluate, and improve processes.

To conduct the Improve Phase, you need to identify the best solution to the problem, develop a detailed plan to implement it, and track results to determine if the answer is practical.

First, you need to identify and analyze possible solutions. Brainstorm with your team to produce ideas for possible solutions. Then evaluate each solution to determine which is most likely successful. Consider cost, time, complexity, and whether the answer can be applied across the organization or just in specific departments.

Once you have identified the best solution, develop a detailed implementation plan. This plan should include steps such as selecting resources, scheduling tasks, and defining criteria for success.

Finally, track results to determine if the solution is effective. Develop a system to measure results, such as customer feedback surveys or sales data. Monitor progress regularly and adjust the plan as necessary.

By following this approach and the specific roadmap outlined at the beginning of this chapter, you can ensure that your team is taking the proper steps to solve problems and improve processes within your organization.

11.2 Discussion

1. What is the purpose behind conducting a DOE?
2. How is an FMEA different from mistake-proofing?
3. Why would simulation software most likely be used in this phase rather than other phases of the DMAIC model?
4. What are the key deliverables in this phase?

5. What are the key activities and tools used in this phase?
6. Why are change and time management meaningful in this phase?
7. What is the Taguchi method?
8. Why should pilots always be performed in this phase?
9. Why would some practitioners consider this the most "stressful" phase?
10. Why are books on change, such as *Who Moved My Cheese?*, still relevant today?
11. Change agents are necessary throughout the process. What is their particular relevance in the Improve Phase?

Chapter 12

Control

Define → Measure → Analyze → Improve → **CONTROL**

An improvement must be shown and documented to enter the Control Phase. However, the project still needs to be completed. Close-out activities are performed in the Control Phase. Also, the Control Phase shows a plan to sustain the process improvement. Despite its importance, it is sometimes given less attention than the other steps.

Although Control is often overlooked, it is an essential step in the DMAIC process. It is the last step, but it is the key to ensuring that the improvements made in the previous steps are sustainable. The purpose of the Control step is to monitor and maintain the gains made during the Define, Measure, Analyze, and Improve Phases.

Control involves setting up measurements and criteria to determine whether the improvements have succeeded. It also establishes processes to maintain, monitor, and improve the new approach over time. Finally, Control helps to ensure that the new method consistently delivers the desired results.

Control is also an essential part of risk management as it can help to identify areas where changes could lead to unwanted consequences. In addition, by regularly monitoring and assessing the performance of the new process, organizations can quickly spot any problems and take corrective actions before they become serious.

The first activity in the Control Phase is to articulate the dollar improvement. This is easy if, in the Measure Phase, the tool used to show the current

DOI: 10.4324/9781003397649-14

process state was financial. This was the return on investment (ROI) in Measure (where we started). This is the ROI after the improvement was made.

However, a financial impact statement must be compiled if the tool used to show the current state is only sometimes shown in dollars.

For example, in Measure, if the sigma level was 3.0 and the process improvement yielded a 4.0, what does that mean in dollars? If a scorecard was used in the Measure Phase and the score was represented as a letter grade of "C," and via the process improvement, the process is now rated as an "A," what does that mean financially?

The second activity in the Control Phase is to develop a sustainability plan. For example, how can the company keep the process improvement in place—what are the red flags that should be watched? This may also include a transition plan.

Finally, all the activities usually associated with project closure should be considered.

Critical tools for the Control Phase include items such as:

- Sigma calculations if applicable
- Standard work if some tasks are repeatable
- Control charts, if needed to study the process moving forward
- Transition plan template

Tasks in this phase may also include:

- Developing a transfer plan
- Handing off the responsibility to the process owner
- Verifying things such as benefits, cost savings, the potential for growth
- Closing out the project
- Finalizing the documentation
- Celebrating!

Many activities in the Control Phase include normal activities done whenever a project is closed, such as recording the best practices or notifying team members and the company that the project has been completed. Everything usually done to close out a project happens in the Control Phase. However, the ultimate purpose of the Control Phase has three essential characteristics.

The third is to do a normal close-out.

12.1 ROI Calculations

ROI is an approximate measure of an investment's profitability. ROI is calculated by subtracting the initial cost of the investment from its final value, then dividing this new number by the cost of the investment, and finally, multiplying it by 100.

Showing and documenting process improvement is imperative. This needs to be demonstrated in a way that the new owner understands. Using sigma levels to show how the sigma has increased is also suggested. Control charts, discussed in the Analyze Phase, are a quick way to help the new process owner watch the process's stability.

12.2 Sustainability

The Control Phase communicates the plan for keeping the process in control and stable. A control plan methodology or a control form may be in place in some companies. When creating the control plan from scratch, remember that the objective is simply the steps needed to keep the process improving in business. The guide should be written in basic terms to include dates and times when certain activities should occur. A control plan has two major components:

- How processes are standardized
- How procedures are documented

This may include a transition plan for the new owner. Even if the project manager plans to continue to monitor the process, this documentation is required. A transition plan gives the new process owner all the information needed to move forward. The transition plan is the document that explains how to contact resources and use any tools presented in the control plan.

A decisive transition plan should include the following:

- An introduction
- Scope
- Transition activities
- Roles and responsibilities
- References and attachments

The transition plan provides the framework for identifying, planning, and conducting activities. Transition planning aims to ensure a seamless and continuous service when changing hands to new providers.

The deliverables in this phase focus on documentation. Processes are standardized. Procedures must be consistent. Transfer of ownership is established, and project closure is completed.

Transfer of ownership examines several areas. The purpose of the transfer of ownership document is to establish day-to-day responsibilities. It contains checks and balances to make sure the process continues to improve. A good plan would also include components such as knowledge and learning. It may include job descriptions, staffing information, and where to locate future benchmarking data.

Success in this phase depends upon how well the previous four steps were implemented. Therefore, a strong emphasis is placed on change management. In addition, the team develops a project handoff process and training materials to guarantee long-term performance.

Many factors could affect the adjusted input and output. Therefore, the process needs to stay "in control," which is the most critical factor of this phase.

Showing and documenting standardization is an essential part of the Control Phase. Standardization enables the high-quality production of goods and services on a reliable, predictable, and sustainable basis. Standardization is making sure that all elements of a process are performed consistently. Standardization allows the reduction of variation and makes the process output more predictable. It provides a way to trace problems and provides a foundation for training. It also gives direction in the case of unusual conditions. Standardization can even be the main objective, especially if the project was designed to meet ISO (International Organization for Standardization) requirements.

The following might be the questions in the toll gate for Control:

- What process controls are being implemented?
- Who is the process owner?
- How often will the transition plan be revisited?
- What is the expected improvement in terms of cost reduction?

Finally, the Control Phase is about developing and capturing best practices. The term is frequently used in health care, government administration, education, and project management.

An area that is addressed in the Control Phase is a response plan. What are the critical parameters to watch? Is there a closed-loop system meaning that nothing can fall through the cracks? Does a troubleshooting guide or Frequently Asked Questions document need to be prepared?

Activity within the Control Phase is creating a transition plan. A transition plan explains how the day-to-day operations should be overseen. It includes information about any of the forms necessary and where to locate information and resources required to ensure success.

In this phase, the document retention practices of the company should be considered. A document retention program involves the systematic review, retention, and destruction of documents received or created during the business. How the document retention program is implemented involves balancing potentially competing interests, such as legal obligations, efficiency considerations, and prelitigation concerns.

Some companies have an automated process. These systems partner well with the Lean Six Sigma theory since Lean Six Sigma is designed to eliminate waste and speed up processes. If these principles are applied to document retention, it will yield immediate results. Electronic records management is a critical component of success.

Several compliance issues govern how long documents should be retained for particular industries. As a result, many companies need help with document retention. This is an excellent opportunity for process improvement. How a company manages its documents can determine the future success of other process improvement programs.

The sheer volume of business information has increased over the past decade. Even e-mail messages are now considered to be corporate records. As a result, companies that can implement a successful document retention strategy realize significant savings.

There are several opportunities for process improvement:

- Is there a reliable and valid indexing system in place?
- Can documents (including e-mail messages) be reproduced upon request?
- Is there a data repository as well as a backup system?

12.3 5S Plans

Although 5S may very well be implemented before the DMAIC process begins, it might also be used to sustain the overall improvement or as a suggestion at the end of a project. 5S, as mentioned early in this book, is a physical, organizational system.

5S is a popular Lean Six Sigma tool designed to instill a sense of responsibility in employees and promote a disciplined approach. Unfortunately, the original Japanese terms *Seri*, *Seiton*, *Seiso*, *Seiketu*, and *Shitsuke*, used to describe the 5S model, are frequently replaced by many English words. The attempt to develop English equivalents, starting with the first letter "S," has sometimes caused translation confusion for those trying to implement the model.

For example, almost all English translations of the 5S model will use the word *Sort* as the first S rather than the Japanese word *Seri*. Seri is translated as "the identification of the best physical organization of the workplace." Seri (or Sort) is often accomplished by discarding all unnecessary items. In English, however, the word *Sort* usually means "to place in different piles," but placing things in different groups happens in the second S, Seiso.

Seiso is technically intended to arrange things in various piles or bins. In some models, Seiso, again in keeping with the S theme, is called "Systemic Arrangements." In other models, it is called "Set in Order." The terms used here are Sort, Set in Order, Shine, Standardize, and Sustain to represent the 5S model. However, remember that several S-word variations are intended to describe the original Japanese terms. For instance, Shine, the third S, is referred to as Spic and Span in other models, which is a more accurate translation of the Japanese word *Seiso*.

Therefore, the first opportunity to maximize success when implementing a basic 5S program is for the facilitator to clearly explain the definitions and use words that resonate with the employees. Some companies have decided to use the 5C model (clear out, configure, clean and check, conformity, customize and practice), which is very similar to 5S but has a more accessible vocabulary for English speakers to digest.

The next step in maximizing a basic 5S program is to study the company's infrastructure and decide how 5S can best fit into the existing improvement structure. This should be followed with constant but brief communications explaining the 5S initiative to the workforce. Several formats should be considered, such as e-mail, electronic bulletin boards, and articles in the company newsletter.

The leadership team should be trained in the overall concept, and employees directly involved should be taught in each area of 5S. For example, in the first phase, Sort, one of the main objectives is to discard unnecessary items. Employees should understand the criteria for making this decision. In the next step, one of the main objectives is called Set in Order, which means to place things in the right places. Will a color-coding system be used, or will a system be used; where the items most frequently accessed will be placed in the most convenient area? In the Shine stage, piles are revisited, reexamined, and often cleaned or refurbished. Once again, what are the requirements? For example, art items may be managed in a certain way. Chemicals may have specific safety criteria.

Educating employees in the Standardization and Sustain Phase may be facilitated by workshops, but they may also be satisfied with solid, easy-to-understand documentation. For example, in Standardization, employees could be introduced to a schematic showing visual controls and be invited to discuss areas of risk. In the Sustain stage, employee training may consist of frequent updates on the system's success through the company newsletter or targeted e-mails.

One way to maximize the success of a 5S program is to ensure each employee has the appropriate amount of education. This would also include those facilitating the project. In addition, facilitators and leaders of the 5S effort should have a strong understanding of project management and deployment plans.

The best way to gain buy-in to a 5S program is to start with a pilot that shows results. Select a small or neglected area that can show benefits within one week of implementation. For example, all companies have a supply room or filing systems that could use a quick facelift. Cleaning up the supply closet is a simple way to show the benefits of the 5S program visually.

Before implementing an enterprise-wide implementation, develop a complete rollout plan and discuss it with all parties involved. Then, once the rollout begins, collect best practices for future projects.

12.4 Close-Out Activities

Most of the close-out activities necessary in a process improvement project are the same as in any project. The difference between project management close-out and process improvement close-out is that process improvement should contain the sustainability of the process. In best-case scenarios, this would also include continuous improvement. Informing all parties (employees, vendors, etc.) that the project has been completed involves:

- Recording best practices
- Updating documentation

However, every project is different. Close-out activities may vary. Knowing this information as early as the Define Phase can help the project manager understand how to include these activities in the project plan. In today's business environment, sustainability is essential to long-term success. Therefore, process improvement is crucial in achieving sustainable growth and development. This chapter post will explore the top five reasons why sustainability matters in process improvement.

Sustainability contributes to:

- Reducing costs
- Conserving resources
- Improving employee morale
- Reducing waste
- Increasing efficiency

12.4.1 Sustainability Reduces Cost

Sustainability is an essential factor to consider when improving processes. By focusing on sustainability, businesses can reduce their costs significantly overall. In addition, implementing sustainable practices in process improvement can help companies save money by reducing energy consumption, cutting waste, and making more efficient use of resources.

For example, by investing in renewable energy sources, businesses can simultaneously decrease their energy bills and help the environment. Additionally, companies can save money on materials and equipment by using less or replacing them with more efficient models. Reducing waste is also essential for cost savings, as it can help businesses avoid buying unnecessary items and reduce disposal fees.

When businesses focus on sustainability during process improvement, they save money and contribute to a healthier environment and a better future for everyone. In addition, by investing in sustainability, companies can reduce costs while contributing to their local community's health and well-being.

12.4.2 Sustainability Conserves Resources

As companies look to improve their processes, they often find ways to reduce the resources used. This is especially important when it comes to preserving our natural resources and conserving energy and water. Implementing sustainable practices can help businesses reduce the environmental impact of their processes and save valuable resources.

By reducing resource consumption, businesses can reduce costs and become more efficient. In addition, by focusing on sustainable solutions, companies can create value for their customers and protect the environment simultaneously. For example, a company may purchase renewable energy sources or implement energy efficiency measures to reduce its use. By utilizing these strategies, a business can reduce costs, improve its bottom line, and be more environmentally friendly.

It is also essential for businesses to consider their processes' effect on the environment. Sustainable solutions can help reduce pollution, waste, and other negative environmental impacts of process improvement. By focusing on sustainable solutions, businesses can ensure they are taking steps to protect the environment while improving their processes.

Overall, sustainability is an essential factor to consider in process improvement. It can help businesses conserve valuable resources, reduce costs, increase efficiency, and be more environmentally conscious. By focusing on sustainable solutions, companies can ensure they positively impact the environment while improving their processes.

12.4.3 Sustainability Improves Employee Morale

It's no secret that a workplace environment that promotes sustainability can have a positive impact on employee morale. Studies have shown that when employees know the company's commitment to sustainability, it boosts their enthusiasm for the organization and their job. This increased enthusiasm can lead to higher engagement in their work and, ultimately, improved productivity.

Moreover, sustainability initiatives help employees feel more connected to the mission and purpose of the organization, allowing them to take pride in their contribution to the greater good. This sense of purpose, in turn, leads to a feeling of fulfillment in the workplace.

Employees who understand their organization's commitment to sustainability will likely have higher job satisfaction and greater loyalty to the company. It is essential to recognize that when an organization takes measures to be more sustainable, it demonstrates care and respect for its employees, which can profoundly affect their morale.

12.4.4 Sustainability Reduces Waste

When it comes to process improvement, sustainability is critical to reducing waste. By utilizing processes and technologies that are energy efficient and environmentally friendly, companies can reduce their environmental impact. For example, a manufacturing plant can improve its function by utilizing energy-saving technologies such as energy-efficient lighting and air conditioning systems. This will not only reduce the amount of energy used but also reduce the amount of waste produced. Additionally, improved process control and automation can reduce material wastage and scrap generation. Companies can also reduce their environmental footprint by utilizing recyclable materials and employing green practices such as reusing and repurposing products. By reducing waste, companies can save money and reduce their environmental impact.

12.4.5 Sustainability Increases Efficiency

When looking at process improvement, it is essential to consider how it can increase efficiency. By making processes more sustainable, businesses can make their operations more efficient and productive. Sustainability helps to reduce energy usage, which saves money and decreases the amount of waste produced. Sustainability can also improve systems and processes that create more efficient workflows.

For example, using renewable energy sources such as solar or wind power can help businesses save on energy costs and reduce the amount of waste generated from fossil fuels. This allows companies to spend less on energy and invest more in productivity. Furthermore, investing in green technology can help reduce waste by decreasing the number of materials used in production. This can help businesses save on costs and improve their environmental impact.

Sustainability also leads to more efficient product design and development. By using more sustainable and renewable materials, businesses can reduce the resources needed for production, leading to cost savings and better performance. Additionally, companies can use advanced technologies such as 3D printing and artificial intelligence to streamline product development and testing, reducing the resources used and improving performance.

Finally, sustainability can lead to improved customer service. Sustainable practices such as reducing energy consumption and waste production can reduce costs and better performance, improving customer satisfaction and loyalty. This can help businesses maintain competitive advantages and remain profitable in the long run.

In conclusion, sustainability has a significant impact on efficiency and process improvement. Businesses can save money by reducing energy consumption and waste production while increasing efficiency. Additionally, investing in green technologies can further reduce the resources needed for production and improve performance. Finally, incorporating sustainable practices into customer service can improve customer satisfaction and loyalty, giving businesses a competitive edge in the marketplace.

12.5 Discussion

1. What are the critical activities in this phase?
2. List the tools typically used in this phase.
3. What are some examples of toll gate questions in this phase?
4. What are the main components of a transition plan?
5. How would a control chart be used in this phase?
6. Summarize your thoughts (three to four paragraphs) on the purpose of the Control Phase.
7. Why would you mention a 5S model in this phase?
8. Why would a Failure Mode Effects Analysis (FMEA) be helpful in this phase?
9. Why would it be essential to ensure that all standard operating procedures have been updated?
10. What similarities does the Control Phase have to close out a regular project?

Chapter 13

Summary of DMAIC

DMAIC is an acronym for five interconnected phases: Define, Measure, Analyze, Improve, and Control. It is a Six Sigma business philosophy that employs a client-centric, fact-based approach to reducing variation to dramatically improve quality by eliminating defects and, as a result, reducing cost.

In the Define Phase, a team and its sponsors agree on the project and what it should accomplish. The outcome is:

- A clear statement of the intended improvement (Project Charter)
- A high-level map of the processes (Suppliers, Inputs, Processes, Output, and Customers [SIPOC])
- A list of what is essential to the customer (Critical to Quality [CTQ])

The tools commonly used in this phase include:

- Project charter
- Stakeholder analysis
- SIPOC process map
- Voice of the Customer
- Affinity diagram
- CTQ tree

The Measure Phase builds a solid understanding of existing process conditions. The outcome is:

- A good understanding of where the process is today and where it needs to be in the future

DOI: 10.4324/9781003397649-15

- A solid data collection plan
- An idea of how data will be verified

The tools commonly used in this phase include:

- Prioritization matrix
- Process cycle efficiency
- Time value analysis
- Pareto charts
- Control charts
- Run charts
- Failure Mode and Effects Analysis (FMEA)

The Analyze Phase develops theories of root causes, confirms the theories with data, and identifies the root cause(s) of the problem. The outcome of this phase is:

- Data and process analysis
- Root cause analysis
- Being able to quantify the gap opportunity

The tools commonly used in this phase include:

- 5 Whys Analysis
- Brainstorming
- Cause-and-Effect diagram
- Affinity diagrams
- Control charts
- Flow diagram
- Pareto charts
- Scatterplots

The primary purpose of the Improve Phase is to demonstrate, with facts and data, that the solutions solve the problem.

The tools commonly used in this phase include:

- Brainstorming
- Flowcharting

- FMEA
- Stakeholder analysis
- 5S method

The Control Phase ensures that the problem does not recur and that the new processes can be further improved.

The tools commonly used in this phase include:

- Control charts (covered in the Measure Phase)
- Flow diagrams (covered in the Analyze Phase)
- Charts to compare before and after, such as Pareto charts (covered in the Measure Phase)
- Standardization

The Control process involves quality and statistical concepts that have existed for decades. However, the advent of quality control software makes the process simple enough for anyone to perform.

Variation is everywhere, and it degrades consistent, good performance. Valid measurements and data are required foundations for constant, breakthrough improvement.

A standard improvement model such as DMAIC provides teams with a road map. The DMAIC is a structured, disciplined, rigorous approach to process improvement consisting of the five phases mentioned, where each step is linked logically to the previous and subsequent phases.

Other benefits of using the DMAIC model often include the following:

- Better safety performance
- Effective supply chain management
- Better knowledge of competition and competitors
- Use of standard operating procedures
- Better decision-making
- Improved project management skills
- Sustained improvements
- Alignment with strategic vision and values
- Increased margins
- Greater market share
- Fewer customer complaints

All steps of the DMAIC should be followed for optimum results.

13.1 Define

Spending time in this phase is crucial and necessary to determine the objective, like all problem-solving methodologies. This phase is also valuable in understanding the intent of the project.

Leaving this phase with a strong Statement of Work or Project Charter is essential. This ensures that everyone involved in the project works from the same playbook.

13.2 Measure

For several reasons, getting a clear as-is picture of the process in its current state is imperative. The first is the Measure Phase, which creates the baseline of the success measurements later in the process. The second is that the process may be doing better than initially thought. Returning to the Define Phase and choosing a different project might be better. Third, if the process is broken and needs repair, the information gleaned from the Measure Phase will form a strong business case for the change.

Data is the cornerstone of any successful business. From the minor details of a product's cost to the broadest understanding of a customer's behavior, data helps organizations understand and improve their operations. Therefore, organizations must take the time to measure their operations before making any significant changes.

This information can be beneficial when deciding how to make changes or adjustments.

13.3 Analyze

The analysis is the process of breaking down a problem or cycle into its parts to understand better how it works. It involves examining a situation or system, looking at all the components that make up the whole, and understanding how they interact.

The analysis is essential to any process improvement project, as it helps identify problems and find solutions. By thoroughly analyzing a process or system, organizations can identify areas where improvements can be made and determine the best action. The analysis allows organizations to understand better the strengths and weaknesses of their processes and any potential threats or opportunities for growth. Analysis can only occur with understanding the current state captured in the Measure Phase.

Knowing what is happening in the current state will often lead to a quick analysis of the problem and obvious solutions. However, at other times the issue or current state needs detailed study and analysis. The DMAIC model promotes several analyzing tools and concepts to determine the proper solutions.

13.4 Improve

The Improve Phase in the DMAIC model aims to take the solutions identified in the Analyze Phase and use them to improve a process, product, or service.

This phase involves creating, evaluating, and implementing solutions to improve product or service quality. During this phase, teams work to develop and test potential solutions that are expected to result in significant performance improvements. Improvement is where piloting can be done.

The bottom part of Improve is about creating and executing a project plan. By using essential project management techniques, progress can be accomplished and documented.

13.5 Control

Control is an often overlooked but essential step in the DMAIC process. It is the last step, but it is the key to ensuring that the improvements made in the previous actions are sustainable.

Control involves setting up measurements and criteria to determine whether the upgrades have succeeded. It also establishes processes to maintain, monitor, and improve the new approach over time. Finally, control helps to ensure that the new method consistently delivers the desired results.

If you want to improve your business operations, the DMAIC methodology could be an effective tool. It is a five-phase process that helps organizations identify problems, analyze root causes, and develop solutions to improve processes and products. Here are some key steps to help you successfully implement the DMAIC methodology into your business:

1. Establish a project team: A successful DMAIC implementation requires input from multiple departments. Include customer service, operations, finance, and technology representatives. The team should also have a facilitator responsible for guiding the group and ensuring the process is followed.
2. Define the problem: Before implementing DMAIC, it is essential to define the problem clearly. This should include an assessment of current customer needs and expectations, potential impacts on customer satisfaction or profitability, and any existing organizational goals or standards.
3. Identify potential solutions: After the problem has been clearly defined, the project team should brainstorm possible solutions. This should be done through brainstorming sessions and research into industry best practices.
4. Develop an action plan: Once the potential solutions have been identified, the project team should develop an action plan. This plan should include timelines, milestones, resource requirements, and measures of success.
5. Execute the plan: The final step is to execute the action plan. During this phase, it's important to track results and measure progress against milestones. If necessary, adjust the plan as needed to ensure objectives are met.

By following these steps, your organization can successfully implement DMAIC and create positive changes in your business operations. DMAIC is a powerful tool for process improvement, and when used correctly can lead to greater customer satisfaction, improved efficiency, and higher profits.

When using the DMAIC methodology, organizations should have the right tools to properly define, measure, analyze, improve, and control their processes. Additionally, each step should be carefully monitored to ensure accuracy and efficiency. Finally, organizations should develop a plan for implementing their solutions and evaluating the results.

By following the DMAIC process, businesses can optimize their processes and performance, reduce waste and defects, and create more value for their customers. The benefits of utilizing this process include improved customer satisfaction, better operational efficiency, higher profitability, and improved employee morale.

13.6 Discussion

Here is a collection of questions asked in previous chapters:

1. Briefly define the phases of the DMAIC model.
2. List the CTQ requirements for a project you are working on or have worked on.
3. What steps participate in a data collection plan?
4. What is value stream mapping?
5. What is the difference between CTQs and CTQ definitions?
6. What is the purpose of a SIPOC?
7. What is Measurement Systems Analysis?
8. List the various types of benchmarking.
9. List some of the charts used in SPC.
10. What is hypothesis testing?

INTERNATIONAL IMPLEMENTATION OF PROCESS IMPROVEMENT PROGRAMS

III

Introduction

This section will provide several additional Lean Six Sigma tools that may resonate with particular cultures. These tools complement the seven quality improvement tools and other tools covered in Section II within the DMAIC (Define–Measure–Analyze–Improve–Control) model. This section also examines leadership and change management (CM) topics. These subjects must be considered when implementing process improvement programs and initiatives internationally.

Leadership and management are generally managed as separate roles in the United States. In other countries, the lines may be blurred. The International Lean Six Sigma (ILSS) practitioner must be equipped to both lead and manage the process improvement effort. Team building, for example, is a concept that has been introduced previously in many countries. Therefore, many traditional management and leadership tools to build teams must be more adaptable. For a process improvement effort to be successful, a certain amount of teamwork is required. The ILSS practitioner must rely on implementation while respecting the cultural norms of that particular country.

DOI: 10.4324/9781003397649-16

CM is a structured approach to transitioning organizations, individuals, and teams to a desired future state. There is a strong argument that actual change agents should be reporting to the executive level of leadership; however, this is rarely the case internationally. In addition, how change is managed, in general, varies. Therefore, it becomes necessary for the ILSS practitioner to become a CM professional.

In some companies or countries, there may be designated CM professionals. The title of the person managing the CM functions may not necessarily reflect this responsibility. For example, we refer to CM professionals as Champions in the Lean Six Sigma environment. Identifying CM professionals in the organization and forming a positive relationship is essential.

Most process improvement professionals believe training is needed to ensure that process improvement is executed and sustained. The ILSS practitioner is often expected to create and deliver the entire Lean Six Sigma program.

The ILSS practitioner must be prepared to build, deliver, and present successful training plans and curricula. For example, training plans may refer to one workshop, whereas training curriculum usually refers to a group of classes.

For the ILSS practitioner to be successful, a great deal of thought should be given to leadership, team building, CM, and training models. However, this section also offers a Quick Start Guide for the ILSS practitioner who must implement a Lean Six Sigma program quickly due to market constraints.

Chapter 14

Additional Lean Six Sigma Tools

Every industry has process improvement tools that are specific to that business. When using the Define–Measure–Analyze–Improve–Control (DMAIC) model, it is possible to include industry-standard tools within the DMAIC framework.

For example, in a scientific project, you may very well take advantage of some of the standard LSS tools, such as:

- 5 Whys
- FMEA
- PDCA

As a scientist, you may embrace Value Stream Mapping used in the Lean Six Sigma approach. Value stream mapping is a powerful process improvement tool that can help you identify and eliminate waste in your scientific procedures. By mapping out the steps of a process from start to finish, you can identify inefficiencies and opportunities for improvement.

But you can use a tool such as the 8D method. It is one of the popular tools used in scientific processes. The method's name derives from the eight disciplines practitioners use to solve a problem.

The eight steps of the 8D method include the following:

1. Form a team: Establish a cross-functional team of people with various areas of expertise who will work together to solve the problem.

DOI: 10.4324/9781003397649-17

2. Define the problem: Identify and describe the situation that needs to be solved.
3. Containment: Take action to contain the problem and prevent it from spreading or causing additional issues.
4. Root cause analysis: Determine the root cause(s) of the problem.
5. Corrective action: Develop and implement a corrective action plan to address the root cause(s).
6. Verification: Verify that the corrective actions taken are practical.
7. Preventative action: Identify and implement measures to prevent the problem from occurring again.
8. Closure: Once the problem is resolved, close the project and communicate the findings and solutions to the appropriate stakeholders.

The 8D method is a powerful tool used in scientific settings to address various problems, including product defects, process failures, and safety concerns. Its structured approach allows practitioners to systematically identify and address issues, leading to more effective problem-solving and process improvement.

Another thought about Lean Six Sigma tools, in general, is that a scientist or scientific environment may find more use for Statistical Process Control (SPC) than someone who is improving an office building. Although SPC is promoted as a robust LSS tool, it uses statistical analysis to identify and control variations in the process. SPC may also be a critical factor in improving a medical device. Still, for improving the construction of an office building, the LSS used Program Evaluation and Review Technique (PERT) more easily. PERT is a valuable tool for improving the construction process. This tool, likewise, may be used by a scientist, but it could be more prevalent in the construction industry.

However, a tool such as Building Information Modeling (BIM) is separate from the LSS toolbox in the construction industry. BIM is a 3D model-based process that involves the creation and management of digital representations of the physical and functional characteristics of a building. The DMAIC model is a construct that can use industry-standard tools and capitalize on one tool more than the others, depending on the project.

There are several other tools and ideas that Lean Six Sigma uses that have been more or less absorbed into the body of knowledge but were outside the original history of Lean or Six Sigma. These tools are accepted as standard LSS tools.

Most have been discussed in previous chapters. The goal of the International Lean Six Sigma practitioner should be memorizing only some of the means or reciting the body of knowledge. Instead, international Lean Six Sigma practitioners should increase their awareness of the many tools available and their tool purposes.

The dynamics of using these tools are generally mapped out in simple step-by-step instruction guides. Many LSS tools can work as stand-alone process improvements for simple improvements that only merit doing part of the project.

Memorizing the mechanics of a tool is less valuable than the awareness of what tools are available to solve a particular problem. Also, understanding how the company culture will embrace a specific tool should be a consideration for the ILSS practitioner.

Lean Six Sigma uses many tools that number the topics with a memory device. Some have already been covered, such as the 5 Whys and the 7 Tools of Quality. Here are more examples:

- 3 Ps
- 6 Ms
- 6 Ws

Both the 3 Ps and the 6 Ms are helpful when building a fishbone diagram to label the large bones of the fish to help the brainstorming effort. The 3 Ps and 6 Ms are also good to review during the Improve Phase of the DMAIC to ensure all bases have been covered. The 3 Ps and 6 Ms are also excellent for developing a process map or determining measurements.

The 3 Ps consider the topics in three categories: People, Process, and Product/Service. The 6 Ms are Machines, Methods, Materials, Measurements, Mother Nature (Environment), and Manpower (People).

The 3 Ps and the 6 Ms can be used to mistake-proof a project plan by reconsidering these areas before rollout. They may also be used to produce categories for fishbone analysis.

The 6 Ws are often used in the Define Phase of the DMAIC model when working with the scope and again on the project plan in the Improve Phase to ensure everything is noticed. The 6 Ws are:

- WHAT: What will you make?
- WHY: Why will we do this?

- WHERE: Where will this happen?
- WHO: Who will do this?
- WHEN: When will the project start/stop?
- WHICH: Which approach will you take?

As discussed earlier, the body of knowledge for Lean Six Sigma continues to grow. However, some of the popular tools that should be reviewed and studied include:

- Activity Network Diagram
- Box Plots or sometimes called Box and Whisker Plots
- Delphi Technique
- Gantt Chart
- Matrix Diagram
- PERT
- Prioritization Matrix
- Quality Function Deployment (QFD, or House of Quality)
- Stem-and-Leaf Plot

14.1 Activity Network Diagram

This is a way of representing activities and dependencies involved in a complex project. There are several versions of an Activity Network Diagram, the two main types being PERT and Critical Path Method (CPM). Both methods show precedence relationships explicitly.

The Activity Network Diagram displays interdependencies between tasks using boxes and arrows. Arrows pointing into a task box come from its predecessor tasks, which must be completed before the job can start. Arrows pointing out of a task box go to its successor tasks, which cannot begin until at least this task is complete.

Activity diagrams are also referred to as PERT or CPM.

PERT was developed primarily to simplify the planning and scheduling of large and complex projects. It was designed for the US Navy Special Projects Office in 1957.

The CPM is a project modeling technique developed in the late 1950s. CPM calculates the longest path of planned activities to the end of the project and the earliest and latest that each activity can start and finish without making the project longer.

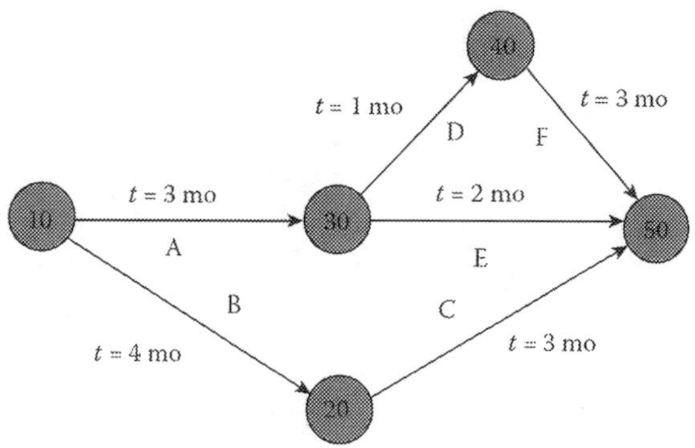

Figure 14.1 CPM/PERT diagram.

CPM is commonly used with all projects, including construction, aerospace and defense, software development, research projects, product development, engineering, and plant maintenance.

The steps involve:

1. A list of all activities required to complete the project.
2. The time (duration) each activity will take to complete.
3. The dependencies between the activities.
4. Developing a diagram.

Figure 14.1 is an example of the basic CPM/PERT format.

14.2 Box Plots

Box plots are a convenient way of graphically depicting groups of numerical data using five areas:

- The slightest observation (sample minimum)
- Lower quartile (Q1)
- Median (Q2)
- Upper quartile (Q3)
- Most considerable statement (sample maximum)

A box plot may also indicate observations that may be considered outliers. Finally, box plots represent relatively small data sets (Figure 14.2).

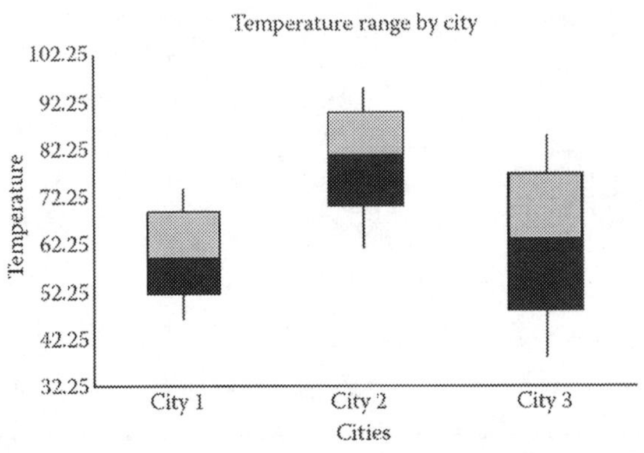

Figure 14.2 Box plot.

14.3 Delphi Technique

The RAND Corporation developed the Delphi technique in the late 1960s as a forecasting methodology. Later, the US government enhanced it as a group decision-making tool.

The tool works formally or informally, in large or small contexts, and reaps the benefits of group decision-making while insulating the process from the limitations of group decision-making. The process involves much ranking and reranking based on criteria and constraints.

The Delphi method is a structured communication technique, originally developed as a systematic, interactive forecasting method that relies on a panel of experts. Delphi is based on the principle that forecasts (or decisions) from a structured group of individuals are more accurate than those from unstructured groups. The term collective intelligence has indicated this.

The Delphi technique is used when some degree of confidentiality should exist, or participants are not comfortable formally giving feedback on a topic. Delphi is also a more formalized approach to gaining consensus.

The procedure is as follows:

- Pick a facilitation leader.
- Select a panel of experts.
- Identify a straw man criterion list.
- The panel ranks the criteria.
- Rerank the criteria.
- Identify project constraints and preferences.
- Rank projects by constraint and preference.

- Analyze the results and feedback to the panel.
- Rerank the projects until they stabilize.

14.4 Gantt Chart

This is a chart showing the work breakdown structure represented in bars. The vertical axis shows the activities, and the horizontal axis shows the time.

14.5 Matrix Diagram

A diagram is used to analyze the associations between two groups of ideas. It is a simplified version of QFD.

14.6 Program Evaluation and Review Technique

PERT is a graphical method (often computerized) for managing large projects.

This tool is an excellent tool to use when there is a high degree of uncertainty regarding the completion time of many activities. It takes into consideration the following factors:

- Optimistic time estimate: an estimate of the minimum time an activity will require.
- Most likely time estimate: an estimate of the standard time an activity will require.
- Pessimistic time estimate: an estimate of the maximum time an activity will require.

14.7 Prioritization Matrix

These are used to help prioritize decisions.

A Prioritization Matrix is a technique used to achieve consensus about an issue. The matrix helps rank problems or issues. Points are assigned a numerical value based on importance. Criteria discussed by the group determine the number.

14.8 Quality Function Deployment (Also Called QFD or House of Quality)

QFD is a method used to relate the characteristics that customers value to the specific features and specifications of the product. QFD is similar to the Matrix Diagram but contains more features.

14.9 Stem-and-Leaf Plot

A stem-and-leaf plot is similar to a histogram but uses decimal places to build up the bars. The advantage of this is that the plot contains all of the original data.

In summary, industry-standard tools can be utilized in the DMAIC framework. However, the International Lean Six Sigma practitioner may also find that specific tools are used more on particular projects than others. The point of the tools, and additional tools, in the Lean Six Sigma process improvement effort, is to help that phase of the DMAIC model.

14.10 Discussion

1. How would a project manager use the 3 Ps model?
2. Where would the 8D model be the most effective?
3. In what phases of the DMAIC model would the 6 Ws be useful?
4. Box plots visually represent what concept?
5. When would it be appropriate to use the Delphi technique?
6. Why are Gantt charts so popular?
7. How is a PERT different from a WBS (work breakdown structure)?
8. What is one of the most common outputs of a QFD?

Chapter 15

Quick Start Guide

Instructional Systems Design (ISD) can provide the framework you need to design, develop, and implement a successful program. ISD is a comprehensive process used to analyze, design, develop, implement, and evaluate effective instructional programs, such as process improvement initiatives.

However, sometimes it is necessary to implement Lean Six Sigma quickly. For example, your team members may need a Lean Six Sigma or a process improvement background. For example, you may have people working on different phases that need to get the gist of what they are doing in real time. So, this Quick Start Guide is intended to allow the International Lean Six Sigma (ILSS) practitioner to jump-start the improvement journey process immediately if training is a component.

Process improvement is about making things better, faster, or more cost-effective. International Lean Six Sigma practitioners develop a mindset. Another word for "better" is "quality." Whereas faster and more cost-effective are generally more appealing to the boss or client, quality sometimes requires an expense. This expense can be articulated and mitigated often by mentioning the Cost of Poor Quality (COPQ).

One thing to keep in mind is that everything isn't a project. Some activities are just good ideas or simple tasks that must be implemented. Lean Six Sigma tools can make the process better, faster, and more cost-effective, but it isn't necessary to employ a full-blown process improvement model.

What makes a good Lean Six Sigma project? First and foremost, the proposed project needs to be able to project a return on investment (ROI) or cost savings. Typically, the ROI, or cost savings, will be immediate in Lean Six Sigma projects. If COPQ is used as the proposal for a project, it needs to be outlined in detail.

DOI: 10.4324/9781003397649-18

Once a decision has been made to move forward with a project, a project charter needs to be prepared. At a minimum, the alliance should contain the following components:

- Reasons for undertaking the project
- Objectives and constraints of the project
- Directions concerning the solution
- Identities of the main stakeholders

After the charter has been accepted, the Define–Measure–Analyze–Improve–Control approach may be applied.

DEFINE: Everyone should agree on the project's goal, projected timeline, and projected project benefit.

The core "Define" activities should include the following:

- Project Name and Purpose
- Completing Project Charter (Required)
- Developing a High-Level Process Map (Required)
- Identifying Process Owner, Champion, Team
- Defining Customers and Requirements (Critical to Quality [CTQ])
- Aligning Goals with Business Initiatives
- Determining Projected ROI

Tools that will help in this phase include:

- Brainstorming
- Project Charter Template
- Graphing Software/House of Quality
- Stakeholders' Analysis
- Suppliers, Inputs, Process, Output, and Customers (SIPOC) Diagram/ Voice of the Customer (VOC) Gathering
- Historical Data
- ROI Formulas and Cost/Benefit Analysis

MEASURE: Get a clear snapshot of what is happening today.

The core "Measure" activities should include the following:

- Designing a Detailed Process Map
- Collecting Data

- Measuring the data using some measurement tool, such as
  - Scorecard
  - ROI
  - Sigma
  - Benchmarking
  - Industry metrics

Tools that will help in this phase include:

- Online Sigma Calculator
- Benchmarking Guides or Reference Material
- Observation
- Finding out what is Critical to Quality (Critical to Success)
- Making sure the measurement system is accurate

ANALYZE: Analyze the data to discover variation, variance, root cause, and the impact of these activities on the project.

The core "Analyze" activities should include the following:

- Defining performance objectives
- Identifying value-added and non-value activities
- Determining the root cause
- Checking for correlation

Tools that will help in this phase include:

- Voice of the Customer
- Voice of the Employee
- Voice of the Process
- Voice of the Business
- Historical Data
- Seven Quality Tools
  - Fishbone
  - Flowchart
  - Check Sheets
  - Pareto Chart
  - Histogram
  - Scatter Diagram
  - Control Chart
- The 5 Whys

IMPROVE: Suggest a solution, implement, and evaluate it.

The core "Improve" activities should include:

- Listing Potential Solutions
- Ranking Solutions
- Selecting Solution
- Piloting the Idea
- Double-Checking Results
- Rolling Out
- Evaluating and Correcting

Tools that will help in this phase include:

- Brainstorming
- Decision Matrix
- Strength–Weakness–Opportunity–Threat (SWOT) analysis on solutions
- Capability Studies
- Pilot, Simulation, or Focus Group
- Failure Mode Effects Analysis
- Project Management Software
- Evaluation Plan or Template

CONTROL: Verify the ROI, benefits, cost saving/cost avoidance, and plan for sustainability.

The core "Control" activities should include:

- Verifying Benefit
- Documenting Procedures to Standardize
- Rewriting/Updating Standard Operating Procedures or Policies
- Transition Plan

Tools that will help in this phase include:

- Online Sigma Calculator
- ROI or Cost-Saving Formula
- Control Plan Template
- Transition Plan Template

Remember that this chapter is intended as a quick start approach when training is necessary immediately.

Of course, the more that is known about the Lean Six Sigma methodology and tools, the higher the rate of success, but learning can work in tandem with doing the first project.

Indeed, as an ILSS practitioner, if you have time to develop a more in-depth program, you should consider adopting the principles of ISD. This was mentioned at the beginning of the chapter. More training and knowledge is almost always better than less.

15.1 Discussion

1. What are the major tools and activities your industry might use in Define?
2. What are the major tools and activities your industry might use in Measure?
3. What are the major tools and activities your industry might use in Analyze?
4. What are the essential tools and activities your industry might use in Improve?
5. What are the essential tools and activities your industry might use in Control?

Chapter 16

Leadership Challenge

Spending time educating the workforce on how to engage in process improvement has extreme merit. However, strong leadership is necessary for the best intentions to stay within the goal.

Leadership is critical to any successful project, and Lean Six Sigma projects are no different. Knowing how to effectively lead a Lean Six Sigma initiative is essential to ensuring the project's success and achieving the desired outcomes.

Even using the Define–Measure–Analyze–Improve–Control (DMAIC) model as a construct, strong leadership is needed in the areas of:

- Defining the project
- Building the team
- Creating and executing the project plan
- Evaluating the success of the project plan

In defining the project, the leadership should consider the benefits of Lean Six Sigma, including waste reduction, improved quality, and increased efficiency. With these benefits in mind, the team should determine what process or area of the business will be the project's focus.

Once the project scope is defined, the leadership team should work with subject matter experts to map the process and identify potential areas for improvement. This mapping process will help the team understand the process flow, identify areas of inefficiency or waste, and create a baseline for measuring progress.

DOI: 10.4324/9781003397649-19

The success of any Lean Six Sigma project heavily relies on the skills and expertise of the team members. The leader is responsible for building a team that can effectively work toward achieving the project goals. Here are some tips on building a strong Lean Six Sigma team:

1. Define the Roles and Responsibilities: Before assembling the team, clearly define the roles and responsibilities of each team member. This will help everyone understand their contributions and focus on their tasks.
2. Choose the Right People: Selecting the right people for the project team is crucial. It would help if you had individuals with the necessary skills, expertise, and commitment to succeed in their roles. In addition, it's essential to choose people who can work together cohesively and support each other throughout the project.
3. Train the Team: Even if your team members are experts in Lean Six Sigma methodologies, they may need additional training. Offer training sessions and workshops to ensure the team understands the project objectives and methods well.
4. Foster Open Communication: Good communication is essential for the success of any project. As the team leader, create an environment that encourages open communication. This will help to identify problems early and work together to find solutions.
5. Provide Support and Encouragement: Leading a Lean Six Sigma project can be challenging, and team members may sometimes feel overwhelmed. However, providing support and encouragement throughout the project is essential as a leader. Celebrate milestones and successes and be there to offer help when needed.

Once the team has been assembled and the project scope has been defined, the next step is to create a project plan. The project plan is a roadmap that outlines how the project will be executed and managed. The following are some critical steps involved in creating an effective project plan for a Lean Six Sigma project:

1. Establish Goals and Objectives: The first step is to establish the goals and objectives of the project. What are you trying to achieve with the project? What is the expected outcome? What is the timeline for completion? These questions need to be answered and documented in the project plan.

2. Identify Deliverables: The next step is identifying the specific deliverables needed to achieve the project objectives. For example, if the project aims to reduce defects in a manufacturing process, the deliverables could include a defect analysis report, a root cause analysis report, a process improvement plan, and a new standard operating procedure.
3. Define Tasks and Activities: Once the deliverables have been identified, the next step is to define the tasks and activities required to produce each deliverable. This involves breaking each deliverable into smaller, manageable tasks and determining the dependencies between tasks.
4. Develop a Work Breakdown Structure: A work breakdown structure (WBS) is a hierarchical chart that breaks down the project into smaller, more manageable components. This allows for better planning, scheduling, and control of the project.
5. Estimate Resources and Timeframes: Once the tasks and activities have been defined, the next step is to estimate the resources (people, equipment, materials) required to complete each task and the timeframe for each job. This information can then be used to develop a detailed project schedule.
6. Establish a Communication Plan: Communication is critical to the success of any project. A communication plan should be developed to ensure all stakeholders are informed of the project's progress, issues, and risks. The program should outline who will communicate what information, how often, and through what channels.
7. Define Risk Management Strategies: The project plan should include strategies for managing risks that may arise during the project. This includes identifying potential hazards, assessing their likelihood and impact, and developing mitigating or managing processes.

Once the Lean Six Sigma project plan is in place, it's time for the team to execute it. This is where strong leadership is essential. A good leader guides their team, provides resources and support, and ensures everyone works toward the same goal.

One of the critical components of successful project execution is effective communication. The leader must communicate regularly with team members, stakeholders, and management. They must provide updates on the project's progress, address any issues, and keep everyone informed of what's happening.

Another critical aspect of project execution is monitoring progress. The leader should track the project's progress against the project plan, ensuring that everyone is working on their assigned tasks and that everything is on schedule. If there are any delays or issues, the leader should work with the team to identify the cause and find a solution.

The team leader should also be focused on quality. Lean Six Sigma reduces waste, improves processes, and delivers quality results. The leader should ensure that everyone on the team is focused on these goals and always striving for continuous improvement.

Finally, it's essential to recognize and celebrate achievements. The Lean Six Sigma process can be challenging, and it's important to acknowledge the hard work and dedication of the team. Celebrating milestones and successes can help keep morale high and motivate the team to work toward the ultimate goal.

Once the Lean Six Sigma project has been completed, evaluating the project's success is essential. This helps you identify areas of improvement and ensures that the project is aligned with your business goals.

Analyzing the data is one of the most critical steps in evaluating a project. First, the data should be compared with the original project goals and objectives to see if the desired results were achieved. Additionally, any changes in the organization's performance or operations should be examined to see if the project had a significant impact.

It's also essential to gather feedback from the project team and stakeholders. This feedback will help you identify potential improvement areas for future projects. Furthermore, you can evaluate how well the team worked, what worked well and what didn't, and what could be done differently.

The project's final results should also be communicated to the organization. This helps build excitement around the project's successful completion and inspires other teams to embark on their Lean Six Sigma projects.

Ultimately, evaluating the project is vital in the Lean Six Sigma process. It helps you measure the project's impact, identify areas of improvement, and ensure that the project has helped the organization move closer to achieving its overall business goals. In addition, by evaluating the project, you can create a continuous improvement culture that will benefit your organization in the long run.

Lean Six Sigma recognizes the analytical business processes that must occur but balances that approach with acknowledging that people are the drivers. Other process methodologies would agree; however,

Lean Six Sigma emphasizes the role of the leader along with understanding change management and team dynamics. Change management is discussed in the next chapter.

The history of leadership, the types of leadership styles, and an appreciation for great leaders still have a place in what is known as Lean Leadership.

The leadership styles used in business began getting attention in the early 1900s. Over the decades, these styles have been repackaged and renamed. The four types initially given the most respect because of research performed included:

- Bureaucratic
- Charismatic
- Democratic
- Reactive

According to the most popular research, bureaucratic leaders are structured and follow established procedures. Charismatic leaders lead by inspiration. Democratic leaders are concerned with consensus. Reactive leaders make decisions immediately without considering feedback from other employees.

In 1939, a group of researchers led by psychologist Kurt Lewin identified only three leadership styles. This work was based on studying groups of children and is still highly respected today. The children were assigned to one of the following groups:

- Authoritarian
- Participative
- Laissez-faire

The autocratic leader provides clear expectations, and there is an apparent division between leader and follower. The participative or democratic leader offers guidance to group members, but this type of leader also participates in the group, allowing input from other group members. The laissez-faire leader delegated most tasks to the members of the team.

Lewin's research indicated team members were the most productive in autocratic environments but more creative in participative environments. However, his research also stated that the least effective and innovative environments were the groups designated as laissez-faire.

Lewin's research deemed the democratic leadership style as the most effective. He believed that although autocratic leadership appeared to offer the most productivity, it was the leadership style most likely to be abused. However, Lewin also thought authoritarian leadership was effective when the deadlines did not allow for group decision-making or when the leader demonstrated that they were the most knowledgeable team member.

All research on leadership styles initially promoted the idea that everyone had a specific type. Much merit was given to the notion that good leaders must identify their core style to be enlightened and expand their leadership abilities. However, newer thinking is based on situational leadership. This means that the leadership style would be dependent on the actual situation.

Leadership styles have been expanded to include the following:

- Relation-oriented leader
- Servant leader
- Transformational leader
- Task-oriented leader

Relation-oriented leaders are also referred to as people-oriented leaders. In this style, the leader tries to support and mentor the team members instead of setting the supreme direction.

Servant leaders have become a popular theory. This leader only officially acts as a leader but takes a more informal approach and makes decisions collectively by consulting with the team. It is similar to democratic leadership. However, most literature indicates that this type of leadership is more sensitive than the democratic leader. This leader is concerned about how people feel and why they voted the way they did instead of simply making consensus-based decisions.

Transformational leaders motivate the team, allowing them to adopt a particular change. It is similar to charismatic leadership, but the focus is not on the leader's traits or popularity.

Task-oriented leaders are known for focusing on what the team needs to achieve. This leader is similar to result-oriented leaders but is more aware of the needs and welfare of the team members.

Most current leadership research suggests that all leaders must be more engaged to lead teams in the right direction. In addition, leaders need to function as a catalyst for change.

The article "Leaders Asleep at the Wheel" states that it is no mystery why so many leaders are asleep at the wheel and not as fully engaged in the leadership process.

Nowadays, it is typical for the best and the brightest to opt for opportunities that offer more life balance. Ten years ago, a bevy of baby boomers emerged, excited about the prospects of entering senior leadership roles. A decade later, the bloom is off the rose. The entire do-more-with-less philosophy is partially to blame. Equally to blame, however, is the fact that the culture changed. Leaders are expected to listen, be open, and seek differing opinions.

Intelligent individuals who want to lead get with the program and understand the new culture. Unfortunately, some still have yet to learn these new principles. Consequently, there need to be more qualified people to manage all the leadership roles available. Unfortunately, the void is often filled by people without the innate ability to lead and those without formal leadership training.

These leaders are "asleep at the wheel." They are sometimes difficult to identify because they are almost always swamped. Being asleep at the wheel does not mean that they are lethargic or lazy. Their hectic schedule often causes them to miss the big picture. It becomes about finishing projects as opposed to finishing projects right. The process becomes unimportant.

Leaders asleep at the wheel are sure they are more intelligent than the rest of us. They know what we need and want without asking. They talk a lot about listening but rarely do. This occurs frequently, even in some of the more minor leadership roles. These leaders need more vision. They honestly believe that they are in touch with the very pulse of their community. Because they are so sure they are right about everything, they miss the obvious. They may represent their position as the voice of a particular organization or an entire industry.

Leaders who are asleep at the wheel are not totally to blame. The life-balance scenario is very appealing. Plenty of people want to work or serve their organization. However, they want to avoid being in charge. This means many leadership decisions need to be revised. Unfortunately, this makes the leader feel more powerful, and even the slightest criticism can be interpreted by the leader as a significant threat. This results in people realizing that speaking up may have consequences.

Even our churches are suffering from leaders who are asleep at the wheel. A recent *Wall Street Journal* article reported that members are ostracized or shunned by their congregations because they question the pastor or ask to see the church's financial records. Thus, it is often tempting to sit back and let the other person drive, even though it is dangerous.

The Enron financial fiasco that became known in 2001 is a perfect example of leaders asleep at the wheel. Although it will be a point of debate for many years to come as to who was responsible for the debacle, many department leaders need to pay more attention. They had been encouraged not to worry by their supervisors. They were receiving compensation at a level that must surely mean they were doing the right thing. Instead, no one questioned the situation, and those who did were deemed ungrateful or unworthy.

There are thousands of examples where businesses lost out or went under because leadership was asleep at the wheel. Consider a recent example with CompUSA. CompUSA started a customer loyalty program called The CompUSA Network. Rewards were earned for purchases. However, management leadership needed to promote the program properly, and it was suspended. Customers who liked the program were infuriated. This lack of leadership attention contributed to the closing of 126 stores.

Former FEMA director Mike Brown was not listening when he responded too slowly to the urgent requests for help associated with Katrina. Embarrassing e-mails revealed that he was sure he had the situation under control. But unfortunately, he was asleep at the wheel.

Leaders asleep at the wheel rush to judgment, misuse their resources, and repeatedly use failure-prone tactics to make decisions. They need help to change things independently or see the situation differently. As good team members, everyone must be prepared to speak up, ask questions, and hold our leaders accountable.

Lean Six Sigma leaders seek "mission-critical projects," and they provide management the energy and horsepower to free up resources. Still, more than that, Lean Six Sigma leaders have the vision to "imagine the future." An effective Lean Six Sigma leader identifies high-potential employees and understands the value of training.

Leadership is an essential quality that all project managers are presumed to possess, but the amount of actual ability is variable. Some come by it naturally as a result of inherited qualities. Others may benefit from formal leadership development. Leadership development refers to any activity that enhances the quality of leadership.

A critical skill for leaders is the ability to manage their learning. The first step is to conduct a self-assessment. Leadership development is a continuous process, not an annual event. Therefore, adapting leadership styles to each person's needs and not being afraid to collect input from others is crucial.

The personal attributes and character of leaders are varied. The particular competencies (knowledge, skills, and abilities) a person needs to lead at a specific time in an organization depend on various factors. However, most people will agree that a good leader should possess common sense and judgment.

How an organization is structured often dictates the leadership role in a Lean Six Sigma project. For example, organizations that favor matrix management can positively and negatively affect the Lean Six Sigma leader. In this type of company, a link between senior management functions and self-contained work cells is sometimes maintained through a matrix structure in which personnel assigned to roles are deployed temporarily to the cells. This approach supports specialization's advantages while facilitating coordination within cells.

This arrangement takes work to run. As a result, the managers of the various work cells may compete with their counterparts for the services, such as quality control and maintenance. In addition, managers of functions may be concerned that temporary personnel assignments to cells may become permanent. A consensus on the ideal solution has yet to emerge. However, some continuity of staffing may be needed for the project's success, and permanent assignments may impair the ability of the functions to maintain specialized knowledge.

As noted earlier, the new Leaner tools focus on continuous improvement as a guiding principle. The road to quality is paved with minor incremental improvements. Significant sweeping changes seldom work. As this country moves its business style from control to management to leadership, the people doing the work can most identify changes necessary to improve quality. Leadership must listen and implement changes rather than direct them.

Lean Six Sigma leaders are encouraged to think in a new way and may be involved in any of the following activities:

- Acting as a catalyst
- Asking the right questions
- Creating a responsive project solution
- Developing options and alternatives
- Discovering and exposing ideas

- Effecting timely decision-making
- Establishing effective and efficient project start-up
- Establishing team ownership
- Expediting decision-making
- Facilitating the design team
- Identifying and clarifying the organizational structure
- Improving communication
- Integrating customers into the total team
- Orienting the total team to a mutual goal
- Providing a framework by which to benchmark project success
- Reaching design consensus
- Synthesizing ideas
- Testing options and alternatives
- Uncovering opportunities
- Understanding total requirements

In Western corporate organization models, leadership issues must align with vertical integration, horizontal diversification, growth by merger, acquisition, and shareholder interests. Lean Six Sigma encourages working in tandem rather than against the business system.

Successful Lean Six Sigma leadership efforts are generally linked to the following:

- Individual learner characteristics
- The quality and nature of the leadership development program
- Genuine support from the leader's supervisor

Leadership development differs in Lean Six Sigma because specific leadership programs focus on the leader's story, such as the personal attributes desired in a leader, expected ways of behaving, and ways of thinking or feeling. Instead, Lean Six Sigma leadership focuses more on developing leadership as a process. This includes the social influence process, interpersonal relationships, and team dynamics. The advantage of this approach is that a person who may not feel like a natural leader may be more comfortable learning a process than changing their overall personality. Lean Six Sigma leadership is also very flexible and supports changing strategy when necessary.

Leaders play a critical role during change implementation. Effective leadership will reduce the adverse reaction to change.

A leader must understand the dynamics in companies with a Project Management Office (PMO) since all projects will be monitored through this entity.

Typically, the accepted functions of a PMO are:

- To provide support and guidance to managers in project implementation.
- To introduce the proper process and evolve a suitable methodology to develop acceptable standards.
- To design training programs to prepare the team members to perform their assigned tasks efficiently.
- Continuous monitoring of project progress and mentoring the team members.
- To select, introduce, and oversee the use of appropriate software tools.
- To constitute a panel of program managers and train them to run multiple interrelated projects.
- Timely resource allocation to complete work within specified time limits.

In summary, strong leadership is vital in defining the project scope of a Lean Six Sigma initiative. By carefully identifying the business problem, establishing clear goals and objectives, and using data to support decision-making, the project is set up for success.

16.1 Discussion

1. What does acting as a catalyst mean to a leader?
2. What is the difference between being a manager and a leader?
3. Give examples of leadership styles.
4. What are some of the newer leadership styles?
5. What is significant about the research done by Kurt Lewin?

Chapter 17

Change Management

Change management is essential to achieving success in any organization. It manages the organizational change process and ensures it runs smoothly. Change is inevitable in any organization. However, it can be a daunting task for employees and management alike. In today's fast-paced business world, change is more prevalent than ever before, which is why businesses need to adopt the best practices of change management.

Change management is a structured approach to transitioning organizations, individuals, and teams from a current state to a desired future state. However, when change management became popular in the business community, everyone needed clarification. All processes of improvement require change. Therefore, the International Lean Six Sigma practitioner must understand the various methods.

Amazingly, change management models have a massive constructive collaboration with process improvement. Many models are specifically process-related.

Although all change management models must consider both people and the process side of change, an excellent place to start is by dividing the most popular change management models into two categories:

- Primarily Process-centric models
- Primarily People-centric models

There are many change models, but here is a summary of the most popular ones that can be incorporated into the Lean Six Sigma strategy.

DOI: 10.4324/9781003397649-20

17.1 Primarily Process-Centric Change Management Models

All change management models have people and process concerns. However, these seven are more assertive on the process side and include the following:

- Plan–Do–Check–Act (PDCA)
- Awareness, Desire, Knowledge, Ability, and Reinforcement (ADKAR—Prosci Model)
- Kotter 8 Steps
- Lewin's Change Model
- McKinsey 7S Framework
- Governance, Structure, and Systems (GSS) Change Management
- The DMAIC process itself

17.1.1 Plan–Do–Check–Act (PDCA)

Plan–Do–Check–Act (PDCA) is a great place to begin because this model is actively used in Lean Six Sigma. The PDCA is recognized as a four-step model for process improvement, but it can also be used as a four-step model to work with change.

It is a simple methodology that can keep things on track. The standard business management process of *Plan-the-Work* and then *Work-the-Plan* is prevalent.

The PDCA originated with Dr. Edwards Deming circa 1950 in Japan. In 1986 Deming wanted to emphasize the importance of reflecting on the metrics and began referring to the model as Plan–Do–Study–Act, highlighting the "study" piece of the model.

Moving forward, the terms PDCA and PDSA are both used. PDSA is often the methodology used in pharmaceuticals, biotech, and general medical environments.

For the International Lean Six Sigma (ILSS) professional specifically in charge of a change management process, the PDCA or PDSA may be the easiest route.

There is no specific process to become certified in PDCA/PDSA; however, a person authorized in any of the Lean, Six Sigma, or Lean Six Sigma would be expected to understand and use this model.

17.1.2 Awareness, Desire, Knowledge, Ability, and Reinforcement (ADKAR)

ADKAR® is an acronym for the five phases of a model developed by the founder of Prosci, Jeff Hiatt: Awareness, Desire, Knowledge, Ability, and Reinforcement.

The appeal to the ILSS professional is that ADKAR, like PDCA (discussed above) and DMAIC (Define–Measure–Analyze–Improve–Control), offers a phased approach that can be used in either a circular or waterfall approach.

The first phase of the ADKAR model is *Awareness*. Creating awareness often involves education.

The second phase of the ADKAR model is *Desire*. Sometimes awareness alone is not sufficient. The theory is that people will only change if they want to. On the surface, this may appear fundamental. But some informal change models depend on fear to make the change, so creating the desire, instead of fear, is vital. Anxiety can be perceived or real. Starting a desire may mean creating a clearer vision than was communicated in the first phase, awareness.

The third phase of the ADKAR model is *Knowledge*. This is where the goals are created, as well as the strategy. Increasing knowledge involves more communication and sometimes additional training.

The fourth phase of the ADKAR model is *Ability*. Most advocates of the ADKAR model believe this phase requires support, permission to fail, training on the specific tasks of team members, and celebrating successes.

The fifth and final phase of the ADKAR model is *Reinforcement*. This involves developing a sustainability plan. The reinforcement phase is natural for ILSS professionals who use the DMAIC model because many of the components in the "C" phase of the DMAIC are the same. However, ADKAR addresses the people's side more strongly.

In addition to the fifth phase of the ADKAR model, Reinforcement, having constructive interaction with the fifth phase of the DMAIC, Control, there are other similarities that the ILSS professional can capitalize on during the process.

Due to homogeneity, tools used in the DMAIC model may be used in the ADKAR model.

DEFINE and AWARENESS, for example, are trying to understand the need to change or improve processes.

MEASURE and DESIRE aim to look at the current state to determine the next step. Although MEASURE in the DMAIC is more committed to this concept than DESIRE is in ADKAR, the necessity of understanding what is happening NOW to impact future change is apparent.

Analyses in the DMAIC compared to Knowledge in the ADKAR model depend on determining the optimum solution based on data and information. IMPROVE (DMAIC) compared to ABILITY (ADKAR) both require communication and education.

And as mentioned previously, REINFORCEMENT in ADKAR shares the need to sustain the change or process improvement, much like CONTROL in the DMAIC. Many practitioners will argue that DMAIC focuses on the change with the process or product, whereas ADKAR focuses on the people. But focusing on both is imperative for any change management or process improvement model.

17.1.3 Kotter's 8 Steps

Kotter's 8-Step Change Model is a simple step-by-step process easy to follow and understand. It is easy to follow. Here are the summarized steps:

1. Create urgency
2. Form a coalition
3. Create a vision for change
4. Communicate the vision
5. Remove obstacles
6. Create short-term wins
7. Build on change
8. Anchor the changes

17.1.4 Lewin's 3-Stage Model of Change

Lewin's model is one of the more accessible and easy-to-understand change models to understand but is very powerful in practice: Unfreeze, Change, Refreeze.

17.1.5 McKinsey 7-S Model Framework

The McKinsey Model is based on a company's organizational structure. It is comprised of Seven "Ss." The "S" designation represents hard and soft criteria to impact change. They include:

- Strategy
- Structure
- Systems
- Style
- Shared Values
- Skills
- Staff

17.1.6 Governance, Structure, and Systems (GSS) Change Management Model

Change can include anything from technological advancements to shifting business strategies and reorganizations. GSS Change Management ensures that changes are integrated successfully, avoiding disruptions and ensuring employees understand the new processes and workflows.

Implementing GSS Change Management requires an organization to create a framework and a set of guidelines to follow when implementing new changes. These guidelines help employees navigate changes smoothly and ensure that there is a structured process in place to deal with change.

GSS Change Management involves breaking down changes into smaller manageable segments and identifying the affected individuals or departments. Once these areas have been identified, the implementation process can begin with a clear plan of how the changes will be communicated and training will be conducted. This process is essential in minimizing resistance and increasing the adoption of new changes.

GSS Change Management is all about establishing clear objectives, processes, and protocols for handling organizational changes. With this approach, it is easier to evaluate the impact of changes on employees, customers, and the business as a whole. In short, GSS Change Management is the key to successfully integrating new changes into an organization while minimizing disruption and resistance.

At its core, GSS Change Management is about managing the people, processes, and systems affected by a change. This includes identifying potential roadblocks, addressing concerns from stakeholders, and ensuring that the change is communicated effectively to everyone involved. With proper GSS Change Management, even the most well-intentioned changes can succeed, leading to wasted time, money, and resources.

One of the critical benefits of GSS Change Management is that it helps to minimize risk. By taking a structured, organized approach to change direction, organizations can identify potential issues before they become significant problems. This allows them to address concerns early on and make necessary adjustments to ensure that the change is successful.

Summarized the steps in the GSS process include:

1. Set clear goals and objectives: Define what you want to achieve through change management and how it will contribute to the overall success of your organization.
2. Identify the scope of change: Identify the specific areas that require change management and focus on those. This will help you to prioritize and allocate resources appropriately.
3. Develop a change management plan: A plan should outline the activities required to initiate, implement, and sustain the change. It should include a communication strategy, training programs, and measures for monitoring progress.
4. Engage stakeholders: Successful change management requires the buy-in and support of all stakeholders. Involve them in the planning process and communicate the benefits of the change to build enthusiasm and support.
5. Implement the change: Execute the plan, monitor progress, and make necessary adjustments. Again, communication and training are essential during this stage to ensure all stakeholders are on board and can effectively implement the change.
6. Evaluate the results: Evaluate the effectiveness of the change management process and the results achieved. This will help you identify areas for improvement and build on successes for future change management initiatives.

17.1.7 Using the Define–Measure–Analyze–Improve–Control (DMAIC) Approach as Change Management Model

A fascinating facet of the DMAIC model is that it can be used to understand and manage change. For example, the top five reasons people resist change are:

1. They don't understand the change.
2. They think you are trying to fix something that is not broken.
3. They don't understand your logic.
4. They feel they don't have a choice.
5. They feel the change is not sustainable.

These objections align well with the DMAIC approach. Although not intended as a model for buy-in, many of the tools in each phase can be used independently to achieve this condition.

The Define Phase of the DMAIC model uses several tools to ensure the person doing the project and the sponsor understands what should happen next. This allows people to understand the change better.

The Measure portion of the DMAIC model is all about depicting the current state in a non-bias manner. The tools typically used in this phase can help your audience understand the need for change.

The Analyze stage of the DMAIC model shows your logic. For example, why did you pick the solutions you did and some of the other choices? Tools used in this phase can help you articulate to your audience the logic behind it.

Once the practitioner is in Improve, ideas are put forth, and a discussion occurs before the final decision to move forward is made. This decision is completed well before putting the project plan into action. So, if your audience feels roped into a particular choice, many tools are used in Improve to achieve consensus.

There are other reasons for people to refrain from buying into your change or ideas. However, the last of the top five conditions is that they don't believe it is sustainable. Things will go back to the way they were. The Control Phase of the DMAIC model is about documenting sustainability.

It is also wise to introduce any change appropriate through the DMAIC phases to allow everyone to adapt. One advantage of using the DMAIC (Define–Measure–Analyze–Improve–Control) methodology is that the model clearly states that ideas must be piloted before rollout. This helps with the resistance factor. Successful pilots demonstrate the probability of success and reduce the fear factor. It is often said that successful change occurs when support is earned, and execution is emphasized.

The Measure Phase of the DMAIC is also crucial in the change management effort. Helping employees understand the current state of a process lessens speculation. When a project manager initially takes reliable and valid measurements and shares the current state with the employees, project managers can introduce a simple comparison chart when the change is realized. This is where we were. This is where we are today. Buy-in is not an issue because the process improvement is apparent. However, when the project manager needs to validate the current state, employees often need clarification about why the change is necessary.

Change management anxiety can also contribute to participants believing they do not have enough time to implement the change. Lean Six Sigma, again, positions itself as a program that will help increase time and focus resources. Lean Six Sigma has several simple tools that can be implemented immediately to make things work faster.

A strong argument is that true change agents should report to the executive leadership level. However, in some companies, change management is managed through the human resources department. Although there are better situations than this, if the company is invested in this idea, it would help the project manager to align with change leaders in the human resources department.

The topic of change management is often covered in Human Resource Management programs. Change management (CM) professionals with a background or education in essential project management have a clear advantage. Being well versed in an improvement methodology like Six Sigma is a bigger plus. CM professionals presenting a business case with a compelling return on investment will be respected. A valid handle on cost/time estimates, analytical thinking processes, and fact-based strategies will open doors.

Understanding and using statistics to convey thoughts raise the bar on necessary conversations such as:

- Legal compliance related to change management
- Developing a recruiting and retention strategy
- Performance management
- Job design
- Knowledge management
- Human resource information systems
- Strategic, operational, and administrative issues

The role of the CM professional is typically divided into three main categories—strategic, operational, and administrative. In today's world, CM professionals are expected to act with confidence in all three types. Six Sigma methodologies provide a framework for confidently capturing and presenting information in all three areas.

CM professionals may benefit from using Six Sigma concepts in many other ways. First, the Six Sigma methodology provides a solid path to implementing new projects. Second, learning to use the statistical information promoted in Six Sigma allows the CM professional to make better, more informed decisions. Third, studying Six Sigma principles improves communication with project managers, technical staff, and executive management.

CM professionals responsible for health and safety issues will benefit from applying the Six Sigma methodology to high-risk environments. Six Sigma forces the practitioner to study the existing system. This may lead to identifying potential dangers. Whereas many safety programs focus on satisfying lengthy compliance agendas, they need to position employees to consider the impact or identify future risk issues.

One area in which the CM professional can be a strong contributor is designing metrics. It is necessary to distinguish which metrics genuinely add value to the organization. Measuring for measurement's sake is time-consuming and contributes to waste. To determine which metric should be used, it is imperative to understand the strategic initiatives of the department and the organization. Being familiar with strategic initiatives is critical to many human resource processes, such as performance reviews, job descriptions, and employee orientation. Six Sigma models all depend on proper measurement systems, and the CM professional may have already compiled valuable data that can be used in these metrics.

Internal benchmarking is an area that many CM professionals understand. Internal benchmarking involves comparing a specific operation within the organization to another operation. Although the two functions do not need to be precisely the same, they must be similar. This process knowledge is beneficial to the Six Sigma project team. For example, identifying critical-to-quality factors is identical to placing items critical to employee satisfaction. Another popular Lean Six Sigma model, SIPOC (Supplier, Inputs, Process, Output, and Customer), could be a better stretch for CM professionals. The recruiting process must identify these areas to implement a successful program.

CM professionals are also astute at documenting best practices. This is another area where understanding the process is as important as understanding the subject matter. Even in a structured Six Sigma project, it is common for internal best practices to remain unidentified. This is usually because methods for communicating best practices do not exist. To be successful, organizations must implement a process that promotes and rewards the sharing of ideas.

Scorecards may be an area that the CM professional has experience designing. Scorecards are an accepted way to keep track of business success. A successful business scorecard would promote a balance between long- and short-term goals, between financial and nonfinancial measures, and between internal and external perspectives. Implementation of a scorecard system requires translating the vision into operational or financial goals. Although the CM professional may have yet to gain experience enterprise-wide, most are skilled at doing this type of measurement for their departments.

This experience benefits projects that use a scorecard system because there must be a commitment to a vision, a process, and a communication plan to share with employees. The same competencies that allow a project manager to improve the quality and bottom-line results may backfire without the necessary people skills.

First, it may be difficult for a CM professional to get the training necessary to be successful. There may need to be a budget or a desire to educate administrative support staff formally.

Other areas that are a natural fit for a CM professional trying to gain Six Sigma experience include developing Six Sigma retention strategies and creating job descriptions. Although promoted in Six Sigma, developing a rewards and recognition program rarely has a severe process owner. CM professionals need to seek out opportunities to become involved. A proactive approach will be noticed and appreciated. Although Six Sigma requires formal education and training, hands-on experience will make the concepts easier to digest.

CM professionals also have the opportunity to use skills such as change management and leadership development. Acting as a resource or coach for Black Belts encountering team-related problems will quickly build credibility. Sometimes the CM professionals are positioned better to consult with sponsors, leaders, and champions than the project manager.

Introducing Lean Six Sigma into an organization is a significant change that will profoundly affect a broad group of stakeholders. Managers and employees at many levels of the organization will be asked to engage in new behaviors. Those leading other initiatives may see Six Sigma as a source of competition for resources, executive attention, and executive power. In addition, there may be confusion over how Lean Six Sigma fits within many ongoing corporate programs such as CMMI (Capability Maturity Model Integration) or ISO (International Organization for Standardization). Finally, improvement only happens with a plan.

Most executives will state that people are their most important resource. Therefore, the change management group should adopt quality initiatives and continuous improvement programs. The CM professional can help determine which functions to measure and which metrics to be used. This can provide education on applying realistic benchmarking and compiling a workable scorecard. The CM professional can help reduce uncertainty and anxiety surrounding Six Sigma and be a valuable resource to the Six Sigma team.

CM professionals interested in studying and utilizing the Six Sigma methodology are an asset to any company. They can improve processes in their department, serve as a role model, and assist in larger company projects.

One of the most challenging situations in CM is the concept of resistance. Several models of resistance identify where resistance will be most likely. However, one of the pluses of the Bridges Change Management Theory is that this work identifies four states of mind that individuals may experience during the transition process:

1. Denial: In the initial stages of transition, people often go through denial. They refuse to accept that the change is happening and try to cling to the old ways of doing things. This state of mind is common when people feel overwhelmed and unsure of how to move forward.
2. Resistance: The next state of mind is resistance, where people start to acknowledge that change is happening but actively resist it. They may argue against the change or become defensive. This resistance is often due to fear of the unknown or feeling a loss of control.
3. Exploration: The third state of mind is exploration, where people start to look for new ways of doing things. They may explore different approaches to change and become more curious about what is happening. This stage is essential for building resilience and preparing for the next phase of the transition.
4. Commitment: The final state of mind is commitment, where people embrace the change and are willing to move forward. They have accepted that the old ways of doing things are no longer relevant and are ready to adapt to the new working methods.

In Lean Six Sigma, CM is front and center. The Lean Six Sigma International Practitioner needs to learn to deal with change. Fortunately, there are a variety of CM models that have proven successful. Being familiar with two or more of these approaches can benefit the ILSS practitioner because it allows for pivoting if one model doesn't work. Being familiar with different types of resistance is also beneficial. A robust change management model and a strategy to manage resistance will save the ILSS practitioner much frustration.

In summary, successful implementation of change management in Lean Six Sigma requires a structured approach that engages stakeholders, communicates effectively, and provides ongoing evaluation and adjustment. Organizations can unlock their full potential and achieve long-term success by prioritizing change management and investing in the process. The structured approach chosen by the ILSS practitioner depends on the company's culture, mission, vision, and work commitment.

The benefits of considering what change management approach is the best to use include better resource management, improved communications, reduction of risk, increased agility, and greater employee satisfaction.

17.2 Primarily People-Centric Change Management Models

As an important reminder, all change models address people and processes. However, these three models focus more on the people's side.

- Nudge Theory
- Bridges Change Management Theory
- Kübler-Ross Method

17.2.1 Nudge Theory

Nudge Theory utilizes small, subtle changes to influence people's behavior and ultimately encourage them to make decisions that benefit their organization.

Nudge Theory is a behavioral economics concept that suggests that people can be influenced to make certain decisions based on subtle and indirect suggestions rather than being told what to do outright. This theory argues that the most effective way to achieve desired behaviors is to nudge individuals toward them rather than using heavy-handed tactics like incentives or penalties.

Nudge Theory is based on the premise that people often make irrational decisions and can be influenced by the context in which they are made.

Therefore, by changing the environment or framing a decision differently, it's possible to guide people toward making better choices.

17.2.2 Bridges Change Management Theory

This model offers a practical and comprehensive approach to successfully navigating change, focusing on understanding the emotional response to change and adapting to it.

The heart of the Bridges model is that change involves a transition process different from the change itself. Change is an external event that happens to us, while transition is an internal process that we go through to adapt to the change. Bridges identify three stages of change that individuals and organizations typically go through:

1. Endings: This stage involves letting go of the old ways of doing things and saying goodbye to the past. Endings can be difficult and emotional, as people may feel a sense of loss, grief, or uncertainty.
2. Neutral Zone: This stage is characterized by ambiguity, experimentation, and exploration. It is a time of limbo where people still need to fully commit to the new way of doing things and may need clarification about the future.
3. New Beginnings: This stage involves fully embracing the new reality and moving forward with confidence and commitment. It is a time of creativity, productivity, and growth.

The Bridges model also identifies three phases of transition that individuals typically go through:

1. Letting go: acknowledging and releasing the old way of doing things.
2. Moving through navigating the ambiguity and uncertainty of the neutral zone.
3. Coming embracing the new way of doing things and moving forward purposefully.

A common factor with nearly all change management initiatives is resistance. Generally, people resist changing out of fear of losing something at a personal level. Therefore, the project manager may need to assure employees that Lean Six Sigma is a tool, not a replacement, for processes the employee currently controls.

17.2.3 Kübler-Ross Model

Grief and change are two everyday experiences in life, and understanding how to manage them is essential. In 1969, psychiatrist Elisabeth Kübler-Ross introduced the Five Stages of Grief concept in her book *On Death and Dying*. Since then, the Kübler-Ross model has been adapted for use in the field of change management, with the stages of grief being used to understand and plan for the emotional reactions to organizational change.
The five phases of grief, according to the model, are:

1. Denial
2. Anger
3. Bargaining
4. Depression
5. Acceptance

Using the Kübler-Ross Model for Change promotes working with the Change curve and understanding where productivity can fall. The theory also provides helpful suggestions on how to deal with each area.

17.3 Discussion

1. What are the characteristics of a good change management agent?
2. Why is understanding change management so important in Lean Six Sigma?
3. What are some components of creating a solid change management solution?
4. Should change be introduced all at once or incrementally?
5. What Lean Six Sigma concepts can help manage change in general?

Chapter 18

Training Modules: Using Instructional Systems Design for Lean Six Sigma Training

The chances of implementing and sustaining process improvements are increased as employees become more aware of how to apply Lean Six Sigma to their projects. Often, the International Lean Six Sigma (ILSS) practitioner effectively accelerates this effort by performing the role of trainer, mentor, or champion.

In some situations, the ILSS practitioner may be assigned a team and be expected to perform the role of a project manager, trainer, and educator.

The ILSS practitioner may realize that the team needs more training to be effective. In this scenario, the strategy is straightforward. The first step is to do a gap analysis and determine which essential skills are necessary but not present in the team. The second step is to design brief training or coaching sessions involving selected group members. Since the training/coaching, in this case, is limited to the specific process improvement being considered, sessions are generally intended to be short and informative. There may be an expectation that a team member completes some directed self-study.

However, an ILSS practitioner may also be responsible for leading the entire LSS training effort or internationally expanding an existing LSS program. Therefore, ILSS practitioners must be prepared to build, deliver, and present successful training plans and curricula. For example, training plans may sometimes refer to one workshop, whereas generally, a training curriculum always refers to a program of classes or activities designed to meet a particular learning goal.

DOI: 10.4324/9781003397649-21

Instructional Systems Design (ISD) is an accepted set of training development models. There are several well-established ISD training models used to build a training curriculum. In addition, ISD training models are used to determine learning needs, success criteria, and metrics for evaluation.

The most popular ISD training model is Analysis–Design–Development–Implementation–Evaluation (ADDIE). Many LSS tools may be applied to the ADDIE model. ADDIE is also highly detailed, making it better, faster, and more cost-effective for the ILSS practitioner new to developing training plans.

18.1 The ADDIE Model

18.1.1 Analysis

The Analyze phase is the foundation for all other stages of instructional design. During this phase, the training statement is constructed, which determines the high-level training goal. A needs, job, and task analysis is performed to do this. The outputs of this phase include the instructional purposes and a list of tasks to be instructed. These outputs will be the inputs to the Design phase.

18.1.2 Design

The Design phase involves using the outputs from the Analyze phase to plan a strategy for developing the instruction. During this phase, an outline is created on how to reach the goals determined during the Analyze phase and expand the instructional foundation. Some elements of the Design phase may include writing a target population description, conducting a learning analysis, writing objectives and test items, selecting a delivery system, and sequencing the instruction.

18.1.3 Development

The Development phase builds on both the Analyze and Design phases. This phase aims to generate lesson plans and lesson materials. During this phase, instruction is developed, as well as all media used in education and any supporting documentation. Currently, it may also include e-learning materials.

18.1.4 Implementation

The Implementation phase refers to the actual delivery of the instruction, whether classroom, laboratory, or computer-based. The purpose of this phase is the effective and efficient delivery of education. This phase must promote the student's understanding of the material, support the student's mastery of objectives, and ensure the student's knowledge transfer from the instructional setting to the job.

18.1.5 Evaluation

This phase measures the effectiveness and efficiency of the instruction. Evaluation should occur throughout the instructional design process—within degrees, between phases, and after implementation.

There are two types of evaluation in the ADDIE model: formative and summative.

Formative Evaluation is ongoing during and between phases. This type of evaluation aims to improve the instruction before the final version is implemented.

Summative Evaluation usually occurs after the final version of instruction is implemented. This type of evaluation assesses the overall effectiveness of the education. In addition, data from the Summative Evaluation is often used to make decisions about the instruction, such as whether to purchase an instructional package or discontinue.

Like Lean Six Sigma's Kaizen Event, ADDIE offers a Rapid Prototyping process. For the Lean Six Sigma practitioner who must roll out training quickly, Rapid Prototyping should be considered. This approach is not novel to ISD models but also appears in design-related domains, including software design, architecture, transportation planning, and product development. In addition, the ADDIE phases are shortened when applied to Rapid Prototyping.

When engaging in this method, however, the following items must still be considered:

- Resources
- Policy development
- How sessions will be conducted
- Online training

Resources can be a primary constraint to any training program. The questions to answer regarding resources may include the following:

- Who is qualified to teach these instruction sessions?
- Do they need extra training?
- Can multiple sessions be taught?
- Do you have space/resources (i.e., computers) for the instruction session, or will you need to hold the instruction session in the classroom?
- Is your management supportive of this type of interaction with the faculty?

The training session strategy should be divided into three categories:

- Before
- During
- After

Before the first session, perform a simple pretest to assess the student's knowledge online, if possible. Be sure to have a copy of the course outline available.

During the session, perform introductions. Provide an overview of what to expect that day. Try to incorporate active learning techniques and teach critical-thinking skills. While it may be tempting to lecture to the group, try to use techniques involving the student's process.

After the last session, administer a simple posttest. If the class is being taught with a type of certification involved, an additional test may be required. The posttest or review determines how much follow-up will be necessary for the student. If appropriate, also provide an evaluation form.

18.2 Training Plans

A training plan is often built into the process using a model such as ADDIE. A training plan benefits the person managing the effort and those involved in writing any associated curriculum. Since the training plan may need to be reviewed or presented, the best approach is to have a program summary available during the process. A detailed schedule will help the ILSS practitioner mistake-proof. When presenting the project in meetings, a shorter version should be available.

To create a summary plan that contains the essential elements, the following should be considered:

- General information
- Training approach
- Evaluation

General information would cover items such as purpose, scope, and overview. If the presentation or paper is being presented to an audience that needs to have core knowledge of that department or entity, then a brief history should also be included. The primary curriculum should be presented in the form of an outline. Technical training programs should provide a list of abbreviations or acronyms. This information would appear in this section if a needs analysis were performed before making the training decision.

Training approach would start with training requirements or prerequisites and the roles and responsibilities of those involved in the program. This should be followed by handouts explaining the schedule or proposed schedule of events.

Evaluation should clearly explain the evaluation strategy and the metrics used to determine the program's success. In addition, an explanation should accompany any complex metrics.

18.3 E-Learning

Computer-based learning can be a great way to introduce an employee to the main concepts, provide follow-up training, or develop an entire course. Today, computer-based learning has always been challenging to create. For example, if the goal is primarily to deliver a lecture or set of instructions followed by a quiz, presentations with voice-over can be made in Microsoft PowerPoint. It is also easy to record a session or do a webinar. On the other hand, a more robust e-learning approach is needed. In that case, several e-learning authoring packages will allow the user to build and deploy a particular program.

The newest of all trends, online live learning, is becoming increasingly popular. Better and more stable technology allows the student to directly interface with a live instructor in real time. The instructor can see and hear the student and vice versa.

There are several things unrelated to the technology that should be considered. First, each course should have a specific objective. Content should meet this objective. If the content doesn't contribute to the goal, it should be eliminated from that module. Many courses tend to offer too much information. This is more tempting when designing an e-learning course. Avoid information overload. Keep slides simple and related to only one concept. Avoid colors or slide transitions that might tire the viewer. Avoid sending the student to various hyperlinks to complete their learning objectives.

The problem in using e-learning in other countries is not generally related to content but to graphics. Visual representations are often processed differently by different cultures.

18.4 Training Manuals

A training manual is a specific instruction book explaining how to perform tasks.

Manuals sometimes need clarification with training materials provided in the training session. The material in the training manual should be considered a separate document and focus on instructions for a particular activity. The training session often contains topics associated with buy-in. This is optional in the training manual. Training manuals have been developed using the quick sheet or cheat sheet method, summarizing critical factors on a single laminated page. This allows for quick reference and is very effective.

The purpose of a training manual is to provide a reference guide. Online training manuals and e-books allow the student to search for information faster.

18.5 Adult Learners

Adult learners are referred to in the United Kingdom as mature learners who usually approach learning differently from younger learners. They are more self-guided in their learning.

They require learning "to make sense"—they will not perform a learning activity, for example, just because the instructor requests that it be done.

Adults learn best when the following requirements are met:

- Purposeful learning
- Involved with other adult learners
- Build upon past knowledge, skills, and experience
- Adults share past learning with each other
- Individuals learn in an environment of respect

18.6 Training in Different Cultures

In the United States, most employees are trained to work on a schedule. Other cultures may not be as defined in their daily schedules. Successful ILSS practitioners stay attuned to these different perceptions of time. The ILSS practitioner will want to schedule more flexible meetings and other work-related events. There are various methods of training, which can be divided into cognitive and behavioral approaches. Mental processes include lectures, demonstrations, and discussions. Behavioral techniques include games, case studies, and role-playing. They are determining which type of training best suits the culture is crucial.

Defining the country's cultural standing when referring to power, individualism, collectivism, and masculinity versus femininity should be researched. For example, some countries put more emphasis on group communication rather than individual decisions. Remember the three stages of culture shock: optimism, frustration, and gradual improvement of mood and satisfaction.

When designing training, it is helpful to remember the four components:

- Awareness of one's cultural worldview
- Attitude toward cultural differences
- Knowledge of different cultural practices and worldviews
- Cross-cultural skills

Total Quality Management (TQM) is the foundation of all process improvement programs, including Lean Six Sigma. The basic principles for TQM are to

- Satisfy the customer
- Satisfy the supplier
- Continuously improve the business processes

Understanding how a particular culture relates to the TQM philosophy will be valuable when rolling out a general process improvement initiative. This is true, even if no formal training component is involved in the project.

Ensuring that culture understands and embraces the basic theories of TQM will provide a strong foundation. Other concepts include understanding:

- Internal and external customers
- Critical-to-quality factors
- Internal and external suppliers

History owes the emphasis on process improvement training to W. Edwards Deming. He believed that personal and quality training was necessary for successful process improvement. Before globalization and technological advances became important, competitive pressures were typically much lower. As a result, companies were delighted with focusing their quality efforts on the production process alone. This required little training other than the training for the task the employee was required to perform.

Deming went to Japan after World War II and began working with prominent Japanese businesses on their quality initiatives by providing education and training on Statistical Process Control. By improving quality, companies in Japan decreased expenses and increased productivity and market share. After learning Deming's techniques, companies such as Toyota, Fuji, and Sony saw great success.

Joseph Juran, who also did significant work in Japan, promoted the concept that everyone is trained in quality. In addition, Juran advocated quality teams and trained members of the group. Much of the primary material promoted by Deming and Juran still provides solid material for workshops and may be used as discussion items.

It should be noted that developing a training plan or training curriculum is only one facet of building a Lean Six Sigma department or company. However, other considerations must be discussed. For example, what types of projects should be selected? What will be the measures of success? Will a team decide if an LSS project meets the requirements? If the ILSS practitioner is requested to build an LSS program, this entails more than simply training the workforce.

In summary, ILSS practitioners can increase their capabilities related to training by familiarizing themselves with various approaches to building, delivering, and presenting training plans and curricula. When developing training plans, choosing a suitable model that works with the culture receiving the training is essential. In most cases, the ADDIE model will be sufficient. However, for an ILSS practitioner new to the process, relying on the works and philosophies of Edwards Deming and Joseph Juran will provide reputable introductions to training modules that will be universally respected.

Lean Six Sigma continues to evolve. In *Lean Six Sigma: Practical Bodies of Knowledge*, the assertion is that Lean Six Sigma comprises several bodies of knowledge related to business. Other process improvement programs and essential business education progress as well. However, the critical difference with Lean Six Sigma is that the tools are constantly adapted and modified. When government becomes involved in the core critical thinking and thought needed to use these tools successfully, their organizations begin looking at things through a continuous improvement lens.

Adopting Lean Six Sigma is becoming increasingly necessary when considering issues facing local, state, and federal governments closing budget gaps.

18.7 Discussion

1. What components should be considered when developing an international training program?
2. What is ISD?
3. What is ADDIE?
4. Why is ADDIE popular with ILSS practitioners?
5. What factors should be considered when building e-learning programs unrelated to technology?
6. What is the typical difference between training materials and a training manual?
7. What main items should be addressed in a training plan?
8. What are the three principles of TQM?

LEAN SIX SIGMA APPLICATIONS

Introduction

Various industries either focus on or support different Lean Six Sigma functions. Therefore, this section will cover the following sectors:

Healthcare
Medical Devices
Artificial Intelligence
Innovative Thinking and Design

DOI: 10.4324/9781003397649-22

Chapter 19

Lean Six Sigma in Healthcare: Medical Facilities

When we think about medical facilities, it is natural to visualize brick-and-mortar hospitals. The popularity of Telemedicine expands that vision. In addition, Lean Six Sigma may be used in support services, hospice, and preventative medicines.

Other hospital-like entities to consider include:

- Mental Health Facilities
- Long-term Care
- Rehabilitation Centers
- Specialty Clinics
- Home Health

The Joint Commission is a US-based organization accrediting most United States healthcare organizations and programs. In addition, international chapters accredit medical services around the world.

The Joint Commission plays a crucial role in healthcare quality improvement, and they have advocated for using the Lean Six Sigma methodology in healthcare organizations for several years now. They believe that Lean Six Sigma can help healthcare organizations improve the quality of care they provide to patients and reduce costs.

According to the Joint Commission, Lean Six Sigma is a data-driven methodology that focuses on improving processes and eliminating waste to

DOI: 10.4324/9781003397649-23

achieve better outcomes. It combines two methods: Lean, which focuses on eliminating waste and improving efficiency, and Six Sigma, which focuses on reducing variation and defects.

The Joint Commission recognizes that healthcare organizations face many challenges, including rising costs, increasing service demand, and pressure to provide high-quality care. By adopting Lean Six Sigma, healthcare organizations can identify inefficiencies and streamline processes, leading to improved outcomes and reduced costs.

Implementing Lean Six Sigma in healthcare organizations has proven to have numerous benefits, including:

1. Improved patient outcomes: Lean Six Sigma reduces errors and improves efficiency, leading to better patient outcomes. By eliminating waste and streamlining processes, healthcare providers can focus on delivering high-quality care to their patients.
2. Increased employee satisfaction: Lean Six Sigma encourages teamwork and collaboration, which can lead to increased job satisfaction for healthcare employees. In addition, by empowering employees to take ownership of their work and make improvements, they are more likely to feel engaged and invested in the organization's success.
3. Reduced costs: Eliminating waste and unnecessary processes can lead to significant cost savings for healthcare organizations. By identifying and addressing inefficiencies, Lean Six Sigma can help healthcare providers deliver high-quality care while reducing costs.
4. Improved patient experience: Lean Six Sigma methodology v. Healthcare organizations can provide a better overall patient experience by identifying and addressing patient concerns.
5. Improved communication: Lean Six Sigma encourages open communication and transparency, which can lead to better collaboration among healthcare providers. By breaking down silos and fostering communication, healthcare organizations can collaborate more effectively to deliver high-quality care.

Overall, implementing Lean Six Sigma in healthcare organizations can lead to improved quality of care, increased efficiency, and reduced costs. In addition, by empowering employees and focusing on the needs of patients, healthcare providers can work together to deliver the best possible outcomes for their patients.

There are a variety of Lean Six Sigma tools that can help healthcare organizations achieve this goal and improve patient outcomes. The most popular tools are:

- Process Mapping: Process mapping involves creating a visual representation of the steps in a healthcare process. This tool is used to identify bottlenecks, redundancies, and waste in operations, allowing healthcare professionals to streamline procedures and improve patient outcomes.
- Root Cause Analysis: Root cause analysis is a technique used to identify the underlying cause of problems in healthcare processes. By determining the root cause of a problem, healthcare professionals can implement targeted solutions rather than just treating the symptoms.
- Value Stream Mapping: Value stream mapping is a Lean Six Sigma tool used to visualize the entire process flow from start to finish. This tool helps healthcare professionals identify opportunities for improvement in the overall process and eliminates waste, resulting in better patient outcomes.
- Control Charts: Control charts monitor a process over time and detect any changes or trends. By monitoring and analyzing data using control charts, healthcare professionals can identify patterns that might otherwise go unnoticed and take action to address issues before they become significant problems.

Other health accreditation or compliance organizations in the United States also follow many Lean Six Sigma practices including:

- Health Facilities Accreditation Program (HFAP)
- National Committee for Quality Assurance (NCQA)
- Community Health Accreditation Program (CHAP)
- Accreditation Commission for Health Care (ACHC)
- Healthcare Quality Association on Accreditation (HQAA)
- The Compliance Team, Inc.
- Accreditation Association for Ambulatory Health Care (AAAHC)

The Health Facilities Accreditation Program is headquartered in Chicago. HFAP is a nationally recognized authority by the Centers for Medicare and Medicaid Services. HFAP provides accreditation programs for hospitals, clinical laboratories, ambulatory surgical centers, office-based surgery, and critical access hospitals. In addition, HFAP accredits mental health and physical rehabilitation centers. HFAP also provides certification for primary stroke centers.

The National Committee for Quality Assurance manages voluntary accreditation programs for individual physicians, health plans, and medical groups. It is headquartered in Washington, DC.

The Community Health Accreditation Program was the first body created in the United States to evaluate community-based healthcare organizations. It is headquartered in Washington, DC, and has regulatory authorization to survey agencies providing home health and hospice services. In 2006, they were granted authority over Home Medical Equipment.

The Accreditation Commission for Health Care was set up in 1985 by home care health providers to create an accreditation option more focused on small providers' needs. In November 2006, the Centers for Medicare and Medicaid Services approved ACHC to accredit suppliers of durable medical equipment, prosthetics, orthotics, and supplies (DMEPOS).

The Healthcare Quality Association on Accreditation is an HME accreditation company that streamlines accreditation with web-based tools and individualized coaching.

The Compliance Team, Inc. is headquartered in Philadelphia, Pennsylvania. In 2006, The Compliance Team, Inc. was formally granted authority as an accrediting body for all durable medical equipment (DME) types. DME includes respiratory, mobility, wound care, orthopedics, prosthetics, orthotics, diabetic, and incontinence supplies. DME point-of-service providers have a pharmacy, home care, podiatrists, and orthopedic surgeons.

The Accreditation Association for Ambulatory Health Care, located in Skokie, Illinois, is an organization that accredits ambulatory health care organizations, including surgery centers, office-based surgery centers, endoscopy centers, and college student health centers.

There are many international accreditation and compliance organizations. For example, the United Kingdom Accreditation Forum is an accreditation organization in the United Kingdom. In India, the National Accreditation Board for Hospitals and Health Providers is the primary organization in that country. Australia uses the Australian Council on Health Standards International. In addition, some countries have their accreditation, such as New Zealand (Quality Health New Zealand) and France (Haute Autorité de Santé).

One of the most significant advantages of Lean Six Sigma is its ability to streamline processes. This is particularly important in healthcare, where delays or inefficiencies can have serious consequences. By identifying and eliminating process waste, Lean Six Sigma can significantly reduce waiting times, minimize errors, and improve patient outcomes.

Lean Six Sigma for healthcare is a structured approach that allows healthcare organizations to measure the impact of their quality improvement efforts and make data-driven decisions. This can lead to sustained improvements in healthcare quality over time.

The Joint Commission encourages healthcare organizations to adopt Lean Six Sigma by providing resources, education, and support. They offer online courses and workshops to teach healthcare professionals about Lean Six Sigma and how to implement it in their organizations. They also provide accreditation and certification to organizations that meet their standards for quality and safety.

Lean Six Sigma is a continuous improvement methodology. It is not a one-time fix but a process designed to evolve and improve constantly. This means that Lean Six Sigma can help healthcare professionals stay on top of new challenges and continually improve the quality of care they provide.

Chapter 20

Lean Six Sigma and the Medical Device Industry

The medical device industry is one of the fastest-growing industries internationally with an estimated worth of $400 billion. A medical device is a product used for medical purposes in patients, diagnosis, therapy, or surgery. This industry has become a sound and reliable career choice for the International Lean Six Sigma (ILSS) practitioner.

The U.S. Food and Drug Administration (FDA) has recognized three classes of medical devices based on the level of control necessary to assure the safety and effectiveness of the device:

- Class I—General Controls
- Class II—General Controls with Special Controls
- Class III—General Controls with Premarket Approval

Class I—Class I medical devices are required to have the least amount of regulatory control. Examples of Class I devices include elastic bandages, examination gloves, and handheld surgical instruments. Class I devices rarely require any premarket controls.

Class II—Class II medical devices are subject to special controls.

Special controls include items such as labeling requirements, mandatory performance standards, and postmarket evaluation. Examples of Class II devices include powered wheelchairs, infusion pumps, and surgical drapes.

 DOI: 10.4324/9781003397649-24

Class III—Class III medical devices need premarket approval. They are generally devices that improve or sustain human life. Examples include implantable pacemakers, pulse generators, HIV diagnostic tests, automated external defibrillators, and most implants.

Lean Thinking, Six Sigma, and Lean Six Sigma are valuable in gathering the documentation necessary to determine device class, optimize the device, and create and sustain improvements.

The ILSS practitioner should be aware of other classification systems such as those promoted by the European Union and European Free Trade Association. There are four classifications under this system ranging from low to high risk. Compliance with ISO 13485 is often seen as the first step in achieving compliance with European regulatory requirements. ISO 13485 is the ISO (International Organization for Standardization) standard for medical devices.

Knowledge of ISO 13485, Quality Management System for Medical Devices, is essential for the ILSS practitioner. This standard specifies the requirements necessary to meet customer needs on a consistent basis. As a reminder, ISO 9001 is the standard that is most commonly used to demonstrate a commitment to the overall quality system.

Interestingly, ISO 13485 adds additional requirements to ISO 9001 while eliminating others. For example, a fundamental difference is that ISO 9001 requires an organization to demonstrate continual improvement, whereas ISO 13485 requires only that the quality system is implemented and maintained. The ILSS practitioner should be aware that although ISO 13485 is a stand-alone standard, companies certified in ISO 13485 are generally also certified in ISO 9001.

As with all ISO standards, a qualified third-party certification body, known as a registrar, is required to start an ISO 13485 Quality Management System program. This registrar or another registrar will also audit the program to ensure continued compliance. The ISO 13485 standard represents a great set of guidelines for medical device companies, whether or not the organization decides to become formally certified. For the ILSS practitioner who is charged with discovering process improvement opportunities, this standard also serves as an idea map.

ISO 13485 requires a systematic approach to quality control, supported by ample quality procedures along with continual improvement. This includes more than corrective and preventive action, although attention to this area is very important to maintain certification. The US FDA regulates the design, manufacturing, packaging, labeling, storage, and delivery of medical devices. The laws normally require "manufacturers" to implement a quality system that meets Quality System Regulations (QSR) found in 21 CFR (Code of Federal Regulations) Part 820. This QSR is commonly referred to as current Good Manufacturing Practice (cGMP). ISO 13485, by design, meets this criterion. FDA inspectors may audit cGMP compliance.

Typically, the benefits listed for certification with ISO 13485 include:

- Customer satisfaction
- Reduced operating costs
- Improved stakeholder relationships
- Legal compliance
- Improved risk
- Proven business credentials

ISO 13485 provides a valuable framework for Research and Development (R&D) departments. ISO 13485, true to other ISO standards or best practices, does not dictate or support a methodology that must be followed to achieve requirements. Most business philosophers would agree that you can't really govern the creative process. Lean Thinking methodology offers a structure for the R&D department but allows for flexibility.

There are also specific requirements for security for certain medical devices. Most notable is incorporating radio-frequency identification (RFID) into the device. Two types of RFIDs were approved in 2004 by the FDA. The first type is the SurgiChip tag, an external surgical marker that is intended to minimize the likelihood of wrong-site, wrong-procedure, and wrong-patient surgeries. The second type of RFID medical device is the implantable radio-frequency transponder system for patient identification and health information.

RFID technology generally recognizes the four components of information security, which also meets ISO security standards as well as International Electrotechnical Commission regulations. These components are:

- Confidentiality
- Integrity
- Availability
- Accountability

Often, the medical device industry will address home medical equipment as its own category. The devices are used by private facilities or by family members. The term used to refer to this equipment is *durable medical equipment* (DME). DME is intended to withstand repeated use by the patient or caregiver and is appropriate to use in the home.

Examples of DMEs include respiratory, mobility equipment, wound care, orthopedic, prosthetics, orthotics, diabetic, and incontinence supplies. DME point-of-service providers can include pharmacy, home care, podiatrists, and orthopedic surgeons. Another term, durable medical equipment, prosthetics, orthotics, and supplies (DMEPOS), is also used although DME is sometimes used as an umbrella term to include these additional considerations. This information may be of interest to the ILSS practitioner working in Lean health, covered in the previous chapter. FDA and Medicare regulations exist for the purposes of reimbursement for approved DMEs. Additional examples of DMEs include the following:

- Air purifiers
- Artificial limbs
- Crutches
- Respiratory assistance devices
- Walkers
- Wheelchairs

Some equipment, such as oxygen, is also FDA regulated and must be prescribed by a physician before purchase, whether reimbursed or not. Technically, a physician is allowed to recommend a supplier for the home medical equipment.

The DME supplier is obligated to perform certain functions when providing home medical equipment. These include:

- Proper delivery and setup of the equipment
- Ensuring the home environment is suitable and safe for proper usage of the equipment
- Training the patient, family, and caregivers on the proper usage and maintenance of the equipment
- Informing the patient and caregiver of their rights and responsibilities
- Providing periodic maintenance services (e.g., refilling oxygen, servicing equipment, etc.)

There are many obvious opportunities in the medical device industry for the ILSS practitioner. In both Lean Thinking and ISO 13485, there are measuring and analyzing needs that can be facilitated by using the Define–Measure–Analyze–Improve–Control (DMAIC) process. DMAIC tools are also essential in documenting the process as well as developing a plan for sustainability.

Chapter 21

From Efficiency to Intelligence: Unleashing the Power of Lean Six Sigma in AI

21.1 Introduction

In the modern world, implementing Lean Six Sigma processes is becoming increasingly crucial for businesses to remain competitive. This is especially true when it comes to Artificial Intelligence (AI). By combining the principles of Lean Six Sigma with AI, businesses can gain a robust set of tools to drive efficiency, cost savings, and increased innovation. In this chapter, we'll explore the potential of Lean Six Sigma in AI and discuss how organizations can harness its power.

21.2 What is AI?

AI is a rapidly evolving field that aims to create intelligent machines capable of performing tasks that typically require human intelligence. AI systems are designed to learn from data, recognize patterns, make decisions, and even engage in natural language interactions.

At its core, AI is all about developing algorithms and models that can mimic human intelligence. It encompasses various technologies such as machine learning, natural language processing, computer vision, and

DOI: 10.4324/9781003397649-25

robotics. These technologies enable AI systems to analyze massive amounts of data, learn from it, and make predictions or actions based on that learning.

Machine learning, a subset of AI, is essential in today's AI landscape. It focuses on building models that can learn from data and make predictions or decisions without being explicitly programmed. Through iterative processes, these models can improve their performance over time and become more accurate in their predictions.

Natural language processing is another crucial aspect of AI that focuses on enabling computers to understand, interpret, and generate human language. It allows AI systems to comprehend and respond to human queries or commands, making them more user-friendly and accessible.

Computer vision is another field of AI that enables machines to perceive and interpret visual information, just as humans do. This technology has applications in various domains, such as facial recognition, object detection, and autonomous driving.

AI has the potential to revolutionize industries across the board. From healthcare and finance to manufacturing and transportation, AI systems can automate mundane tasks, optimize complex processes, and unlock new levels of productivity and efficiency. They can analyze massive amounts of data in real time, identify trends and anomalies, and provide valuable insights to support decision-making.

Integrating Lean Six Sigma principles with AI opens up even more possibilities. Lean Six Sigma can help businesses identify wasteful activities and eliminate defects, while AI can provide the tools and algorithms to automate and optimize these processes. Together, they form a powerful constructive collaboration that can drive efficiency, cost savings, and increased innovation.

In the next section, we will delve into the potential of combining Lean Six Sigma and AI and discuss this powerful combination's specific benefits and applications. Stay tuned!

21.3 The Potential of Combining Lean Six Sigma and AI

The potential of combining Lean Six Sigma and AI is genuinely exciting. Businesses can achieve remarkable results by leveraging the power of Lean Six Sigma's process improvement methodologies with the advanced capabilities of AI. This combination allows organizations to optimize their processes, reduce waste, and enhance overall efficiency, leading to significant cost savings and increased productivity.

One of the key advantages of integrating Lean Six Sigma with AI is the ability to streamline processes. AI systems can automate repetitive tasks and analyze vast amounts of data at a speed and scale that humans cannot match. By implementing AI technologies, businesses can reduce manual effort and human error, resulting in faster and more accurate processes. This, in turn, enables organizations to streamline their operations and allocate resources more effectively.

Another area where the combination of Lean Six Sigma and AI excels is reducing waste and increasing efficiency. Lean principles help identify and eliminate non-value-added activities, while AI can further automate and optimize these processes. By leveraging AI's predictive and prescriptive analytics capabilities, businesses can identify inefficiencies and bottlenecks in real time, enabling them to make data-driven decisions and continuously improve their processes.

Another significant benefit of combining Lean Six Sigma with AI is improving quality control. AI systems can analyze large datasets to identify patterns and anomalies, allowing organizations to detect quality issues early on and take corrective actions promptly. This ensures consistent quality, helps prevent defects, and reduces the likelihood of customer complaints or recalls.

Furthermore, integrating AI with Lean Six Sigma can enhance decision-making capabilities. AI systems can analyze complex datasets and provide valuable insights to support strategic decision-making. By combining these insights with the structured problem-solving approach of Lean Six Sigma, businesses can make more informed decisions and develop innovative solutions that drive growth and competitiveness.

Overall, the potential of combining Lean Six Sigma and AI is vast. It empowers businesses to optimize processes, reduce waste, improve quality, and make data-driven decisions. This combination can transform industries and drive businesses toward operational excellence. As organizations continue to harness the capabilities of AI and embrace Lean Six Sigma methodologies, they can stay ahead of the competition and thrive in the modern world.

21.3.1 Streamlining Processes with AI and Lean Six Sigma

Streamlining processes is crucial for any business looking to maximize efficiency and reduce waste. The combination of AI and Lean Six Sigma can be a significant change when it comes to streamlining processes.

AI technologies, such as machine learning and natural language processing, can automate repetitive tasks and analyze massive amounts of data, enabling businesses to streamline operations and allocate resources more effectively.

Lean Six Sigma methodologies, on the other hand, provide a structured framework for identifying and eliminating non-value-added activities in a process. By combining the power of AI and Lean Six Sigma, businesses can leverage AI's capabilities to optimize further and automate processes identified by Lean Six Sigma as wasteful or inefficient.

One way in which AI and Lean Six Sigma can streamline processes is through automation. AI systems can take over repetitive and mundane tasks, freeing employees to focus on more value-added activities. For example, AI-powered customer support chatbots can handle basic customer queries and support, reducing the need for human intervention and speeding up response times. This not only improves efficiency but also enhances the overall customer experience.

Another way in which AI and Lean Six Sigma streamline processes is through data analysis. AI systems can analyze vast amounts of data in real time, identifying trends and patterns that may be difficult for humans to spot. By using AI to analyze data collected through Lean Six Sigma processes, businesses can gain valuable insights into process inefficiencies and make data-driven decisions to optimize those processes. This enables companies to improve their operations and increase efficiency continually.

Additionally, AI can help businesses identify bottlenecks in processes and suggest improvements. By analyzing data and monitoring the performance of different process stages, AI systems can identify areas where efficiency can be improved and recommend process enhancements. These recommendations can be integrated into the Lean Six Sigma framework, allowing businesses to streamline their processes based on AI-driven insights continuously.

In summary, combining AI and Lean Six Sigma offers a powerful toolset for streamlining processes. AI technologies automate repetitive tasks, analyze data at scale, and provide valuable insights, while Lean Six Sigma methodologies provide a structured framework for identifying and eliminating waste. By leveraging these tools, businesses can achieve remarkable results in process optimization, efficiency, and resource allocation, giving them a competitive edge in today's fast-paced business landscape.

21.4 Reducing Waste and Increasing Efficiency with AI and Lean Six Sigma

In today's fast-paced business landscape, reducing waste and increasing efficiency are critical for success. And when it comes to achieving these goals, the combination of AI and Lean Six Sigma is a significant change. By leveraging AI's capabilities and integrating them with the structured problem-solving approach of Lean Six Sigma, businesses can achieve remarkable results in streamlining their processes and driving efficiency.

AI technologies, such as machine learning and natural language processing, have the power to automate repetitive tasks and analyze vast amounts of data. This allows businesses to streamline their operations and allocate resources more effectively. For example, AI-powered chatbots can handle basic customer queries, freeing employees to focus on more value-added activities. This not only improves efficiency but also enhances the overall customer experience.

But AI doesn't stop at automation. When combined with Lean Six Sigma methodologies, AI can identify and eliminate non-value-added activities, further optimizing processes. AI can provide valuable insights into process inefficiencies by analyzing data collected through Lean Six Sigma processes. This allows businesses to make data-driven decisions and continuously improve their operations. With AI's ability to analyze data in real time, companies can identify trends and patterns that may be difficult for humans to spot, leading to more accurate and efficient decision-making.

Furthermore, AI can help identify bottlenecks in processes and suggest improvements. By monitoring the performance of different process stages, AI systems can pinpoint areas where efficiency can be improved and make recommendations for process enhancements. These recommendations can be seamlessly integrated into the Lean Six Sigma framework, allowing businesses to streamline their processes based on AI-driven insights continuously.

The combination of AI and Lean Six Sigma offers a powerful toolset for reducing waste and increasing efficiency. By leveraging AI's automation capabilities and data analysis prowess, businesses can optimize their processes, allocate resources more effectively, and make more informed decisions. This leads to cost savings and increased productivity and gives companies a competitive edge in today's rapidly evolving business landscape.

21.5 Improving Quality Control with AI and Lean Six Sigma

Improving quality control is a critical aspect of any business. It ensures that products and services meet the highest standards and that customers are satisfied with their experience. Regarding quality control, combining AI and Lean Six Sigma can be a significant change. By leveraging AI's capabilities and integrating them with the structured problem-solving approach of Lean Six Sigma, businesses can achieve remarkable results in enhancing quality control.

AI technologies such as machine learning and computer vision can analyze large datasets and identify patterns or anomalies. This is particularly valuable in quality control, where detecting defects or deviations from desired specifications is crucial. AI can quickly and accurately identify quality issues that may be difficult for humans to spot, enabling organizations to take prompt corrective actions.

Additionally, AI can help businesses automate quality control processes. For example, in manufacturing, AI-powered vision systems can inspect products on the production line for defects, ensuring that only high-quality items reach the market. This improves efficiency and reduces the risk of defective products reaching customers, leading to higher customer satisfaction and loyalty.

Furthermore, AI can support proactive quality control by predicting potential quality issues before they occur. By analyzing historical data and identifying patterns, AI systems can provide early warnings of potential quality issues, allowing organizations to take preventive measures. This predictive capability can significantly reduce the likelihood of defects, customer complaints, and costly recalls, saving businesses time and money.

Integrating Lean Six Sigma with AI in quality control also enables businesses to make data-driven decisions. Lean Six Sigma provides a structured framework for collecting and analyzing data, while AI provides the tools to analyze vast amounts of data and extract meaningful insights. This combination allows businesses to identify the root causes of quality issues, understand process variations, and develop targeted solutions to improve quality control.

Integrating AI and Lean Six Sigma in quality control empowers businesses to detect defects, automate processes, predict quality issues, and make data-driven decisions. This combination not only improves product and service quality but also reduces costs, enhances customer satisfaction, and strengthens competitiveness in the market. By embracing the power of AI and Lean Six Sigma in quality control, businesses can ensure that they deliver exceptional products and services to their customers.

21.6 Enhancing Decision-Making with AI and Lean Six Sigma

In today's rapidly changing business landscape, making informed decisions is crucial for success. This is where the combination of AI and Lean Six Sigma can truly shine. By integrating the power of AI with the structured problem-solving approach of Lean Six Sigma, businesses can enhance their decision-making capabilities and drive growth and competitiveness.

AI can analyze massive amounts of data and extract valuable insights. It can identify trends, patterns, and anomalies that may be difficult for humans to spot. With AI's advanced analytics capabilities, businesses can better understand their operations, customers, and market trends. This allows for more informed decision-making, as leaders can rely on data-driven insights rather than intuition or past experiences.

By integrating AI with Lean Six Sigma, businesses can take decision-making to a new level. Lean Six Sigma provides a structured framework for collecting and analyzing data, while AI offers the tools and algorithms to analyze and interpret that data. They enable organizations to make data-driven decisions based on accurate and timely information.

Moreover, AI can help businesses identify and assess the risks and opportunities associated with different decisions. By leveraging predictive analytics and scenario modeling, AI systems can simulate various scenarios and predict the possible outcomes of other choices. This enables businesses to assess the risks and benefits before making a final decision, reducing uncertainty and improving overall decision quality.

Additionally, AI can provide real-time insights and recommendations, empowering leaders to make faster and more agile decisions. AI-powered dashboards and visualizations can present data in a user-friendly format, allowing decision-makers to grasp the key insights and take appropriate action quickly. This real-time decision support can be invaluable in today's fast-paced business environment, where timely action can make a significant difference.

In summary, enhancing decision-making with AI and Lean Six Sigma allows businesses to make more informed, data-driven decisions. By leveraging AI's data analytics capabilities and integrating them with the structured problem-solving approach of Lean Six Sigma, organizations can gain valuable insights, assess risks and opportunities, and make faster, more agile decisions. This ultimately leads to better outcomes, improved performance, and a competitive edge in the market. As businesses continue to embrace the power of AI and Lean Six Sigma in decision-making, they will be better positioned to navigate the challenges and seize the opportunities of the modern business landscape.

Chapter 22

Lean Six Sigma in Innovative Thinking and Design

Design thinking is a problem-solving approach that has revolutionized innovation and creativity across industries. At the same time, Lean Six Sigma has established itself as a highly effective method for quality management and process improvement. These two approaches might seem distinct, but when used together, they can create powerful results.

Innovation and design thinking are crucial to businesses' success. However, incorporating innovation into the product development process can be challenging. That's where Lean Six Sigma comes in. Lean Six Sigma is a methodology used for process improvement and operational excellence, often used in manufacturing and service industries. However, its principles can also be applied to innovation and design.

Design thinking is a user-centric approach to product development to create products and services that meet the user's needs. It is a highly collaborative approach emphasizing understanding users, ideation, prototyping, and testing. The goal of design thinking is to create solutions that are not only useful but also desirable and emotionally resonant.

When combined, Lean Six Sigma and Design Thinking can offer a comprehensive approach to innovation. Design thinking helps teams generate new ideas, while Lean Six Sigma helps them implement those ideas in a way that minimizes errors and waste.

By using Lean Six Sigma's DMAIC process (Define–Measure–Analyze–Improve–Control) in design thinking, teams can identify inefficiencies in the design process and develop a plan to improve them.

DOI: 10.4324/9781003397649-26

For example, using the Define Phase, teams can clearly define the problem they want to solve, ensuring they use their resources wisely to solve the wrong problem. Then, in the Analyze Phase, teams can gather data about user needs and pain points to inform their ideation and prototyping process. Finally, the Control Phase can help ensure the new product or service meets the required quality standards.

International innovative design has become a popular topic in the medical device, semiconductor, and aerospace industries. However, creative design or thinking can benefit many process improvement projects. Therefore, the International Lean Six Sigma (ILSS) practitioner should know the concept.

The term *design innovation* has yet to have a universally agreed-upon definition in process improvement. The expression may be used to optimize products, processes, or services. It is also used when referring to the invention process. Usually, the term means creative ways to design and think based on a solid understanding of best practices used in that particular industry. The approach is agile, but the design or thinking is rooted in scientific or business imperatives.

Innovative design is best understood by first reviewing basic design concepts, which include:

- Designing workflow around value-added activities
- Performing work where it makes the most sense
- Providing a single point of contact for customers and suppliers
- Considering any handoff as an opportunity for error

Textbooks sometimes explain an innovative design process as two separate phases: (1) the Creative Phase and (2) Execute Phase. In the Creative Phase, the activities would be

- Finding the opportunity
- Connecting to the solution
- Selecting the solution

In the Execution Phase, the activities would be

- Making the solution user-friendly
- Getting the product to market

In Lean or Six Sigma environments, *design innovation* is frequently mentioned in Design for Six Sigma (DFSS) discussions. It is also used when addressing a Russian best practices document and database known as the *Theory of Inventive Problem Solving* (TRIZ). The most accepted DFSS is the Define–Measure–Analyze–Design–Verify (DMADV) model. This model replaces the last two phases of the Define–Measure–Analyze–Improve–Control (DMAIC) with a Design and Verify Phase. The DMADV model is commonly used when developing a new product but may also be used for service initiatives. In this model, innovative design would take place in the Analyze Phase but would be built in the Design Phase. Verifying, in the DMADV model, means optimizing. TRIZ, discussed later in this chapter, provides, along with additional information, a list of methods used for successful product improvement. Innovative design or thinking centers on the ability to choose, apply, and optimize these models.

Because *innovation* has become a widespread global word, the ILSS practitioner should clarify the definition. For example, the title Innovative Thinking was used for a three-year project supported by Intelligent Energy Europe. Seven countries in the European Union worked together to achieve joint commitments within the communities for sustainable development through energy efficiency and renewable energy. Sometimes, the term is used as an adjective to mean “new” or “novel.” Agile programming is an innovative approach to software development.

Information technology (IT) often plays a primary role in innovative design projects. For the ILSS practitioner who is not well versed in this area but has identified that the project will require more than the standard interface with IT, a review of the Information Technology Infrastructure Library (ITIL) may be helpful. ITIL is a set of practices that aligns IT services with business needs. ITIL has five volumes, and although it is optional for a process improvement professional to understand the information in-depth, a clearer understanding of the technology involved will be beneficial. Keep in mind that innovation is not driven by technology; instead, innovators use technology to find innovative solutions.

Edwards Deming believed that approaching innovation required a solid understanding of the following:

- What materials will be required and at what cost?
- What are the possible methods of production?

- What new people need to be hired?
- What changes in the equipment will need to be made?
- What supervisors need to be trained?
- What is the cost of production and marketing?
- How will the company know if the customer is satisfied?

Most process improvement professionals will agree that innovative design is more than thinking outside the box. Peter F. Drucker, an influential management consultant, believed that creative design possibilities quickly become apparent by carefully observing the environment. In addition, Drucker believed that by paying attention to changes in the industry and marketplace, opportunities for innovative thinking are ongoing. Drucker also believed that analyzing human perception and global demographics could contribute to creative design. This thought supports the idea that subject matter experts best provide innovative design activities.

Many briefs about innovative design begin with a conversation about innovative or creative thinking. Innovative thinking can be divided into inspiration, ideation, and implementation. The typical steps used in innovative thinking are closely related to other problem-solving models and include the following:

- Defining the problem
- Gathering and synthesizing the data
- Framing the possibilities
- Brainstorming
- Building a prototype and testing
- Rolling out the solution

Global companies engaged in design innovation often work with TRIZ. TRIZ is a problem-solving method based on logic and data. It is used in system and failure analysis. Internationally, TRIZ is commonly used as one of the source documents for Six Sigma processes, project management, and risk management systems. It contains

- A practical methodology
- Toolsets
- A knowledge base
- Model-based technology

TRIZ enthusiasts have a saying that roughly translates to "Someone, someplace, has already solved this problem or one very similar. Creativity is about matching and adapting the right solution to this particular problem." In the United States, it is close to the saying, "Don't reinvent the wheel."

Primary findings of TRIZ include the following:

- Problems and solutions are repeated across industries and sciences.
- Patterns of technical evolution are also repeated across industries and sciences.
- Innovations used outside the field may be applied to other areas.

Modifications of TRIZ include:

- SIT (systematic inventive thinking)
- ASIT (advanced systematic inventive thinking)
- USIT (unified structured inventive thinking)
- JUSIT (Japanese version of unified, systematic inventive thinking)
- TRIZICS (a methodology for the systematic application of TRIZ)

In TRIZ, the word *modification* is used frequently and understood in broad terms. Usually, modification in TRIZ means a change in a particular subject, such as color or structure. A typical example used when explaining this concept is as follows:

Question: What is the modification of the water?
Answer: Ice.

TRIZ believes that contradictions are gateways to modifications and, later, innovation. A contradiction arises when two mutually exclusive demands or requirements are put on the same object or system.

TRIZ promotes the use of 40 principles. These are the 40 inventive principles that have been used in hundreds of thousands of patents.

At this writing, there are no official TRIZ textbooks or training programs that are universally accepted. A body of knowledge is being developed by a group of TRIZ subject matter experts, including Lyubov Kozhevnikova, Oleg Gerasimov, Alexander Kislov, Alexander Gasanov, Isak Bukhman, Zinovy Royzen, Boris Zlotin, and Alla Zusman in association with Altshuller Institute for TRIZ Studies.

The main goals of the TRIZ Body of Knowledge include:

- Identifying the basic concepts, components, and tools of TRIZ.
- Fostering further advancement of TRIZ by improving the understanding of its fundamentals.
- Providing an objective basis for the certification of TRIZ specialists minimizes disputes concerning the requisite knowledge mandatory for specialist certification of one level or another.

Once a body of knowledge is accepted, a formal certification program will likely be developed.

Design for Six Sigma (DFSS) is also known as Design for Lean Six Sigma (DFLSS).

DFSS is a model used when a product or service needs to be created. Technically, the DMAIC methodology is used for process improvement. This means a process must be in place for the model to function. However, many proponents of the DMAIC model believe otherwise and find the DMAIC model suitable to create a new product or service and improve an existing process.

DFSS is a model that capitalizes on Six Sigma tools. DFLSS also uses Six Sigma tools but incorporates facilities for speed and a focus on reducing waste. As noted earlier, the most common DFSS model is the DMADV. The primary tools used in this model include Quality Function Deployment, Failure Mode Effect Analysis, and Design of Experiment.

The first three phases of the DMADV model—Define, Measure, and Analyze—are handled the same way as the phases in the DMAIC model.

DMADV is almost always applied to product development or optimization compared to service-related improvements. The DMADV model relies on material from sources such as TRIZ or product specifications in the Design Phase. The detailed attention given to the first three phases makes DMADV an innovative tool for the ILSS practitioner. The information gained by the ILSS practitioner, who may not be an expert in the area, is often powerful enough to allow the ILSS practitioner to participate as a full partner in the Design Phase. Usually, the Design Phase is commonly outsourced to a third party.

Innovative thinking can result from several factors, such as inspiration or association. Many design innovations are purely accidental. Many scholars believe that creative thought is something that happens unprovoked. Most believe that the ability to think creatively can be encouraged and developed.

Creativity is an essential part of process improvement. Innovative thinking builds on these basic principles:

- Build on the recognition that creativity is vital for process improvement success.
- Increase awareness of the existence of different approaches to creativity.
- Provide some ideas for creative approaches that can help in process improvement efforts.

Innovative thinking means fostering fresh thinking. It involves collaborative skills. It means building a capacity for original thinking and using it with business methodology and practices.

The quickest way for ILSS practitioners to increase their creative thinking skills is to review the knowledge bodies affecting Lean Six Sigma. Lean Six Sigma is not solely dependent on Six Sigma and Lean Thinking. Over the years, other bodies of knowledge have been incorporated. Innovative thinking requires research to increase understanding of facts and best practices that affect process improvement and a particular industry.

Reviewing these bodies of knowledge contributes to the innovative approach. These bodies also work as a catalyst for new ideas.

They include the following:

- Quality Body of Knowledge (Q-BoK)
- Business Analysis Body of Knowledge (BABOK)
- International Institute of Business Analysis (IIBA)
- Project Management Body of Knowledge (*PMBOK® Guide*)
- Business Process Reengineering (BPR)
- Measurement Systems Analysis
- Business Finance and Basic Accounting Principles
- Change Management
- Leadership Development
- Organizational Development

Significant additions to the above bodies of knowledge that the ILSS practitioner should consider include the following:

- PRINCE2
- ISO 9000
- ISO 13053 (Six Sigma)

- ISO 12500 (Project Management)
- ITIL
- TRIZ
- Malcolm Baldrige National Quality Award (MBNQA)

A quality Body of Knowledge is a collection of outlines and documents maintained by the American Society for Quality (ASQ). These outlines are used for general information, reference, and study for various ASQ certifications. ASQ was the first to establish an industry-recognized body of knowledge for Six Sigma. The Q-BoK contains a Six Sigma Green Belt body of knowledge and a Black Belt Six Sigma body of knowledge.

The IIBA maintains the Business Analysis Body of Knowledge. It supports six knowledge areas:

1. Business analysis planning concerns which business analysis activities are needed. This includes identifying the stakeholders.
2. Elicitation is obtaining requirements from the stakeholders.
3. Requirements management and communication deals with contradicting requirements, needs changes, and communication with stakeholders.
4. Enterprise analysis defines the business need and solution scope.
5. Requirements analysis is the progressive elaboration of requirements into something that can be implemented.
6. Solution assessment determines which solution is best, identifies any modifications that need to be made to the resolution, and assesses whether the solution meets the business needs.

The BABOK provides a framework that describes the areas of knowledge related to business analysis. The BABOK is intended to describe and define business analysis as a discipline rather than clarify the responsibilities of a person.

First published in 2005 by the IIBA, it was written to serve the project management community. The IIBA has created the Certified Business Analysis Professional (CBAP), a designation awarded to candidates who have successfully demonstrated their expertise in this field. This is done by detailing hands-on work experience in business analysis through the CBAP application process and passing the IIBA CBAP examination.

The Project Management Body of Knowledge is maintained by the Project Management Institute. All process improvement programs recognize that essential project management must be in place before process improvement may begin.

The *PMBOK® Guide* supports nine knowledge areas:

1. Integration Management
2. Scope Management
3. Time Management
4. Cost Management
5. Quality Management
6. Human Resource Management
7. Communications Management
8. Risk Management
9. Procurement Management

The *PMBOK® Guide* also promotes that the following phases are necessary for a successful project:

- Initiating
- Planning
- Executing
- Monitoring and Controlling
- Closing

Business Process Reengineering is an approach intended to elevate the efficiency and effectiveness of an existing business process. BPR is also known as Business Process Redesign, Business Transformation, and Business Process Change Management. BPR supports the following methodologies for process improvement:

- Process Identification
- Review Update As-Is State
- Design to Be
- Test and Implement to Be

Measurement Systems Analysis is a science that considers selecting the correct measurement. Studying the measurement interactions and assessing the measurement device is also part of the mix. Are measures reliable and valid? What is the measurement uncertainty?

Statistics is the science of effectively using numerical data relating to groups of individuals or experiments. Six Sigma and Lean have always included statistics when measuring and analyzing data. The new Lean Six Sigma practitioner has to make these studies more digestible for everyone involved. More emphasis is placed on choosing the right software and ensuring the statistics are valid.

Business Finance is essential for the new Lean Six Sigma practitioner. A project's buy-in and continued support cannot be based solely on statistical data. Choosing the right return-on-investment formula and measuring project success using financial terms have become essential. Accounting is counting the number of assets, calculating the profit generated, and understanding the cash flow and how money is spent.

Change Management has a variety of meanings depending on the area. However, all areas of change management play a role in the success of the ILSS practitioner. These areas include the following:

- Project Management refers to a process of formally introducing and approving changes.
- Information Technology Service Management is a discipline used by IT professionals.
- People Change Management is a structured approach to change individuals, teams, organizations, and societies.

Leadership Development traditionally has focused on developing leadership ability. In a Lean Six Sigma organization, these methods are imperative to the success of Lean Six Sigma Black Belts and Master Black Belts. Prosperous leadership development, in general, is linked to an individual's ability to learn, the quality of the program, and the genuine support the leader has from their supervisor. Leaders play a crucial role in building a successful ILSS organization. There are four main areas of responsibility for leadership related to process improvement. They include the following:

- Choosing the suitable projects
- Choosing the right people
- Following the proper methodology
- Clearly defining roles and responsibility

Organizational Development is a body of knowledge and practice that enhances performance and individual development. Today's organizations operate in a rapidly changing environment. Therefore, one of the most vital assets in an organization is the ability to manage change.

There needs to be a specific standard outlining the things necessary for successful organizational development, but most professionals in this field rely on the works of William Bridges. Bridges was one of the leading thinkers in change management and personal transition. Themes throughout Bridges' career encourage recognizing the various phases of change. The most popular are Freezing, Changing, and Refreezing.

PRINCE2 was discussed more in-depth in Chapter 2, Introducing Lean Project Management. PRINCE2 (PRojects IN Controlled Environments 2) is a structured project management method endorsed by the UK government as the project management standard for public projects. The methodology encompasses the management, control, and organization of a project. PRINCE2 is also used to refer to the training and accreditation of authorized practitioners of the method who must complete specific requirements to obtain certification.

ISO 9000 is a family of standards and best practices related to quality management systems and designed to help organizations ensure that they meet the needs of customers and other stakeholders. The standards are published by the International Organization for Standardization (ISO) and contain eight management principles intended to be deployed enterprise-wide in an organization. They include the following:

- Principle 1: Customer focus
- Principle 2: Leadership
- Principle 3: Involvement of people
- Principle 4: A process approach
- Principle 5: System approach to management
- Principle 6: Continual improvement
- Principle 7: Factual approach to decision-making
- Principle 8: Mutually beneficial supplier relationships

ISO 12500 (Project Management) is the ISO standard that outlines international guidelines for project management.

ISO 13053 is the new standard for Six Sigma that outlines the international standards used to implement a Six Sigma program.

ITIL is a set of best practices for IT service management that focuses on aligning IT services with business needs. ITIL is published in a series of five core publications, each of which covers an Information Technology System Management life cycle.

The "library" itself continues to evolve. The five volumes of information are as follows:

1. Service Strategy
2. Service Design
3. Service Transition
4. Service Operation
5. Continual Service Improvement

It isn't easy to perform any enterprise-wide process improvement without relying on IT. Even ILSS practitioners without an IT background benefit from familiarizing themselves with this documentation. This is especially true for Volume 5, which is dedicated to continuous improvement.

There are three levels of certification for ITIL: Foundation Certificate, Practitioners Certificate, and Managers Certificate. ITIL is a registered trademark of the UK Government's Office of Government Commerce.

TRIZ explained more in-depth earlier in this chapter, is a set of 40 principles that contribute to innovative design. These principles may be found in Section V, International Lean Six Information and Reference Material.

22.1 Malcolm Baldrige National Quality Award

In the early 1980s, many industry and government leaders saw that a renewed emphasis on quality was no longer an option for American companies but a necessity. The MBNQA was established. Named for Malcolm Baldrige, the Secretary of Commerce under the Reagan administration, until recently, this program was partially supported by the US government. Many factors of the Baldrige Award have become common quality goals in American businesses.

The program promotes the following principles:

1. Leadership: How upper management leads the organization and how the organization leads within the community.
2. Strategic planning: How the organization establishes and plans to implement strategic directions.
3. Customer and market focus: How the organization builds and maintains strong, lasting customer relationships.

4. Measurement, analysis, and knowledge management: How the organization uses data to support critical processes and manage performance.
5. Human resource focus: How the organization empowers and involves its workforce.
6. Process management: The organization designs, manages, and improves critical processes.
7. Business/organizational performance results: How the organization performs regarding customer satisfaction, finances, human resources, supplier and partner performance, operations, governance, and social responsibility, and how it compares to its competitors.

The ILSS practitioner should be aware that new roles may exist in projects involving innovative design that are generally not part of the Lean Six Sigma infrastructure. The ILSS practitioner should consider this staff as subject matter experts and process owners. These roles include, but are not limited to, the following:

- Chief Architect
- Chief Analyst
- Chief Engineer

If the ILSS practitioner is following the DMAIC model, the Chief Architect should be involved in most of the decision-making involved in managing the project. The Chief Analyst should be heavily involved in the Measure, Analyze, and Control Phases. Finally, the Chief Engineer will primarily be engaged in the Analyze and Improve Phases.

For the ILSS practitioner specifically asked to create a model for innovation, the Watermark–Creation–Enhancement–Application (WCEA) Model for Innovation is easy to use and digest. SSD Global developed the WCEA model as a model that could capitalize on DMAIC tools. More information on this model is available in Section V, International Lean Six Sigma Areas of Competency and Resource Materials.

In today's rapidly changing business environment, innovation has become a critical competitive advantage for organizations looking to stay ahead. Many organizations are leveraging design thinking and Lean Six Sigma methodologies to achieve this. Combined, these methodologies can provide a robust framework for innovation, as they bring together the creative mindset of design thinking and the rigorous data-driven approach of Lean Six Sigma.

Here are some of the key benefits of combining Lean Six Sigma with design thinking:

1. Better problem-solving: Design thinking is focused on solving complex problems by putting users at the center of the process. Lean Six Sigma, on the other hand, focuses on improving processes and eliminating waste. By combining the two, organizations can achieve a holistic approach to problem-solving, addressing both the user experience and the underlying process inefficiencies.
2. More efficient and effective innovation: By leveraging Lean Six Sigma tools and techniques, organizations can streamline their innovation processes, reducing waste and improving efficiency. This can help teams get to market faster with higher-quality products and services.
3. Enhanced customer experience: By putting the user at the center of the innovation process, organizations can create products and services tailored to their needs. This can lead to improved customer satisfaction and loyalty, helping organizations to retain their customer base and grow their business.
4. Improved data analysis: Lean Six Sigma is data-driven, focusing on analyzing data to identify patterns and trends. By integrating this approach into the design thinking process, organizations can ensure that their innovation efforts are grounded in data and evidence, increasing the likelihood of success.
5. More innovative solutions: Design thinking encourages teams to explore a wide range of ideas and solutions without getting stuck on the first solution that comes to mind. Lean Six Sigma, focusing on continuous improvement, encourages teams to refine and optimize solutions over time. By combining these two approaches, organizations can create more innovative and practical solutions to complex problems.

Combining Lean Six Sigma with design thinking can give organizations a robust framework for innovation, helping them create more efficient, effective, and customer-centric products and services. The key is to ensure that the two methodologies are integrated seamlessly, leveraging the strengths of both approaches to drive results.

In summary, understanding the principles of design thinking and Lean Six Sigma and how they can be combined is crucial for organizations to improve their product development process. By combining these methodologies, organizations can develop products that meet user needs while minimizing inefficiencies and waste in the design process.

INTERNATIONAL LEAN SIX SIGMA AREAS OF COMPETENCY AND RESOURCE MATERIALS

V

Introduction

When implementing Lean Six Sigma principles, many organizations focus on improving processes and eliminating waste. These are undoubtedly important aspects of the methodology, but, at the same time, one crucial element should not be ignored: competency models. These models define the skills, knowledge, and behaviors required to implement Lean Six Sigma successfully. Without a strong foundation of competencies, organizations may struggle to achieve their desired results and sustain improvement over time.

Understanding Lean Six Sigma is essential to comprehend the role of competency models. Lean Six Sigma aims to streamline processes, improve efficiency, and enhance overall performance. It involves a systematic approach to problem-solving and data-driven decision-making. On the other hand, competency models provide a framework for identifying and developing the competencies needed to implement Lean Six Sigma effectively.

By understanding Lean Six Sigma and its underlying principles, organizations can better appreciate the importance of competency models. These models help identify the specific skills and behaviors individuals and teams need to possess to succeed in Lean Six Sigma projects. Without a clear understanding of these competencies, organizations may struggle to achieve their desired results

DOI: 10.4324/9781003397649-27

and sustain improvement over time. Competency models guide organizations to assess and develop their employees, ensuring they have the necessary skills and knowledge to drive successful Lean Six Sigma initiatives.

Competency models play a vital role in successfully implementing Lean Six Sigma. These models act as a roadmap for organizations, guiding them in identifying and developing the skills and behaviors necessary for practical Lean Six Sigma projects. By having explicit competency models in place, organizations can ensure that their employees have the capabilities to drive improvement and achieve desired results.

Competency models help organizations assess the current skill levels of their employees and identify any gaps that need to be addressed. They also provide a framework for training and development programs, allowing organizations to enhance the competencies of their workforce. By aligning these competencies with the principles and goals of Lean Six Sigma, organizations can build a strong foundation for continuous improvement.

Competency models are a vital component of Lean Six Sigma, providing organizations with a clear framework to develop the necessary skills, knowledge, and behaviors for success. Organizations may struggle to achieve their desired results and sustain improvement without competency models.

A robust competency model is essential for successfully implementing Lean Six Sigma. It serves as a roadmap for organizations, providing a clear framework for developing the skills, knowledge, and behaviors necessary for practical Lean Six Sigma projects.

In the real world, competency models have significantly impacted the success of Lean Six Sigma initiatives. Countless organizations have implemented these models and witnessed remarkable results. One success story involves a manufacturing company that was struggling with high levels of defects and customer complaints. By implementing a competency model, they could identify their workforce's skills and knowledge gaps. They enhanced their employees' competencies through targeted training and development programs, resulting in improved process efficiency and significantly reduced defects. Another success story comes from a healthcare organization facing long wait times and patient dissatisfaction. By implementing a competency model, they identified the necessary skills and behaviors for effective process improvement. With a focus on training and developing these competencies, they were able to streamline processes, reduce wait times, and improve patient satisfaction. These real-world success stories highlight the undeniable impact of competency models in Lean Six Sigma implementation. They demonstrate that organizations can achieve tangible and sustainable improvements by identifying and developing the right skills and behaviors.

Appendix One

A Brief History of Lean Six Sigma

Lean Six Sigma had to pivot during the pandemic, and there are many new milestones. This Appendix covers some of those events and gives the International Lean Six Sigma (ILSS) practitioner information that may be helpful if the future brings a similar crisis.

The COVID-19 pandemic has changed how we live, work, and do business. And Lean Six Sigma, the methodology focused on continuous improvement, was not spared. Yet, as companies worldwide faced unprecedented challenges, Lean Six Sigma practitioners found ways to adapt and drive positive change. The pandemic brought about new opportunities and accomplishments for the methodology, demonstrating its value in times of uncertainty.

One of the critical benefits of Lean Six Sigma is that it fosters a culture of continuous improvement. Encouraging employees to look for ways to optimize their work creates a mindset of resilience and agility. As a result, when faced with new challenges, employees can adapt quickly and develop innovative solutions, keeping the organization competitive.

During the pandemic, people used the Define–Measure–Analyze–Improve–Control (DMAIC) model and the Plan–Do–Check–Act (PDCA) model to navigate and manage projects. Data Collection, promoted by Lean Six Sigma, and themes such as mistake-proofing and visual management became more critical.

The International Lean Six Sigma (ILSS) practitioner may be engaged by audiences curious about the history of Lean Six Sigma. The following briefly describes Six Sigma, Lean, and Lean Six Sigma events. Napoleon Bonaparte said: "History is the version of past events that people have decided to agree upon." Indeed, our United States' history of Lean Six Sigma does not encompass all the significant contributions of the international community. Many thoughts and tools that have become part of the Lean Six Sigma fabric were not captured or recorded. This chapter attempts to summarize the things we do know.

Six Sigma was developed by Motorola in 1981 to reduce defects. During the 1980s, it spread to recognized companies, including General Electric and Allied Signal. Six Sigma incorporated TQM (Total Quality Management) and SPC (Statistical Process Control), expanding from a manufacturing focus to other industries and processes. Motorola documented more than $16 billion in savings. This was when many other companies decided to adopt the methodology. Naturally, the Six Sigma methodology has evolved. A core belief is that manufacturing and business processes share characteristics that can be measured, analyzed, improved, and controlled.

In 1988, Motorola won the Malcolm Baldrige National Quality Award (MBNQA) for its Six Sigma program. Six Sigma promotes the following concepts:

- Critical to Quality: Attributes of the most important to the customer
- Defect: Failing to deliver what the customer wants
- Process Capability: What the process can deliver
- Variation: What the customer sees and feels
- Stable Operations: Ensuring consistent, predictable processes to improve what the customer sees and feels
- Design for Six Sigma: Designing to meet customer needs and process capability

In 1999, GE reported $2 billion in savings attributable to Six Sigma in its 2001 annual report. They discussed the completion of more than 6000 Six Sigma projects and their probability of yielding more than $3 billion in savings, by conservative estimates. Other early adopters of Six Sigma include:

- Bank of America
- Honeywell
- Raytheon

- DuPont
- Brunswick Corporation
- Borusan
- EDS
- Shaw Industries
- Smith & Nephew
- Wildcard Systems
- Idex
- Starwood (Westin, Sheraton, Meridian)
- Bechtel

Six Sigma is a statistical measurement based on Defects per Million Opportunities (DPMO). A defect is defined as any nonconformance of quality. At Six Sigma, only 3.4 DMPO may occur. To use Sigma as a measurement, there must be something to count, and everyone must agree on what constitutes a defect. Regular distribution models look at 3 Sigma, which is essentially 6210 DPMO. Some processes are acceptable at lower Sigma levels; in many cases, 6 Sigma is considered ideal. Sigma (σ) is a symbol from the Greek alphabet used in statistics when measuring variability. The Six Sigma methodology measures a company's performance at the Sigma level. Sigma levels are a measurement of error rates. It costs money to fix errors; hence, saving this expense can be directly transferred to the bottom line.

Typical tools taught in Six Sigma include:

- Process Mapping
- Affinity Diagram or KJ (Kawakita Jiro) method
- Measurement System Analysis or MSA
- Pareto Chart
- SIPOC (Supplier-Input-Process-Output-Customer) Analysis
- Scatter Diagram or Scatterplot
- Quality Function Deployment or QFD, also known as House of Quality
- Ishikawa Diagram or Fishbone
- Failure Mode Effects Analysis or FMEA
- Failure Mode and Effects Criticality Analysis or FMECA
- Value Chain Map
- Histogram
- Control Plan

Lean manufacturing is a production practice that concentrates on the elimination of waste. It is based on the Total Production System, introduced originally by Toyota, and based on TQM principles. TQM capitalizes on the involvement of management, workforce, suppliers, and customers to meet or exceed customer expectations.

Originally, Lean identified the following as the worst forms of waste:

- Transportation
- Inventory (all components, work-in-progress, and finished product not being processed)
- Movement
- Waiting
- Overproduction
- Overprocessing
- Defects
- Skills

An easy way to remember the primary forms of waste is T-I-M W-O-O-D-S.

Eventually, Lean evolved to consider additional forms of garbage. Lean Thinking is designed to

- Shrink lead times
- Save turnover expenses
- Reduce setup times
- Avoid unnecessary expenses
- Increase profits

Lean focuses on getting the right things to the right place, time, and quantity while minimizing waste. Lean makes the work simple enough to understand, do, and manage. The very nature of Lean would suggest that it would be "wasteful" to spend time trying to understand manuals or complicated processes; thus, it is best to simplify the language.

Typical tools promoted in Lean include:

- 5S
- Error Proofing
- Current Reality Trees
- Conflict Resolution Diagram
- Future Reality Diagram

- Inventory Turnover Rate
- JIT—Just-in-Time theories
- Kaizen
- Kanban
- Lean Metric
- One-Piece Flow
- Overall Equipment Effectiveness
- Prerequisite Tree
- Process Route Table
- Quick Changeover
- Standard Rate or Work
- Takt Time
- Theory of Constraints
- Total Productive Maintenance
- Toyota Production System
- Transition Tree
- Value Added to Non-Value Added Lead Time Ratio
- Value Stream Mapping
- Value Stream Costing
- Visual Management
- Workflow Diagram

Lean Six Sigma began in the late 1990s. Both Six Sigma and Lean already started expanding to include service and manufacturing. Allied Signal and Maytag began experimenting with using both methodologies. Employees were cross-trained. Maytag was the first to recognize that Lean manufacturing and Six Sigma do not conflict with each other and are perfect complements. The US Army shares this thinking. Everyone involved in the movement to implement Lean Six Sigma saw the power of combining both toolboxes and attacking both defects and wastes. Many shared tools are apparent in both methodologies that reduce the learning curve.

Lean Six Sigma can be used in any industry, including finance, construction, government, health care, insurance, and hospitality. Lean Six Sigma is about increasing quality and profit. The new tools include methodologies based on teamwork as a principle. Process improvement is not linear; each component is handed off to another department or individual. Instead, each member of the process is involved in improving client satisfaction.

The new leaner tools focus on continuous improvement (CI) as a guiding principle. The road to quality is paved with minor incremental improvements. Significant sweeping changes seldom work. Leadership must listen and implement changes rather than direct the solutions. Some examples are:

- Improving Forecast Accuracy
- Reducing the Volume of Rejected Orders
- Improving Consumer Loan Cycle Time
- Reducing Engine Installation Times
- Eliminating Mistakes in an Operating Room
- Reducing Pharmacy Dispensing Error Rates
- Improving the Effectiveness of Employee Hazard Recognition
- Reducing Process Variation Costs Related to Manufacturing

Before examining Lean Six Sigma, CI programs should be explored. Most companies have some quality control programs. These programs may be formal or informal. Some programs have defined documents and manuals; other quality programs still need to be recorded or tracked. Quality is a large piece of continual improvement. All CI programs ask two questions: (1) Who are the customers? (2) What will it take to satisfy them?

Both Lean and Six Sigma endorse the PDCA model. PDCA stands for Plan, Do, Check, Act. This popular project management tool is easy to understand. It is also called the Deming Wheel or Deming Cycle.

- Plan: Identify an opportunity and plan for change.
- Do: Implement the change on a small scale.
- Check: Use data to analyze the results of the change and determine whether it made a difference.
- Act: If the change was successful, implement it on a broader scale and continuously assess the results. If the change does not work, begin the cycle again.

Both Lean and Six Sigma support the idea of CI. It is an ongoing effort to improve products, services, or processes. It can be an incremental improvement (over time) or a breakthrough improvement (all at once). Unfortunately, CI programs often need to be more proactive and are presented with a problem upfront. Within any problem-solving model, there are four steps to remember: Define the Problem, Generate the Solution, Evaluate and Select an Alternative, and Implement it.

Lean Six Sigma uses a set of quality tools that are often used in TQM. These tools, sometimes referred to as problem-solving tools, include:

- Control charts
- Pareto diagrams
- Process mapping
- Root cause analysis
- SPC

As noted throughout this book, Lean Six Sigma largely depends on the DMAIC (Define–Measure–Analyze–Improve–Control) model that Motorola developed and was later enhanced by General Electric.

- Define the process improvement goals consistent with customer demands and enterprise strategy.
- Measure the current process and collect relevant data for future comparison.
- Analyze the relationship of factors. Determine the relationship, and attempt to ensure all aspects have been considered.
- Improve or optimize the process based on the analysis.
- Control to ensure that any variances are corrected before defects occur.

Lean Six Sigma uses the tools above. It also uses the martial arts designations White, Yellow, Green, Black, and Master Black Belt to denote the level of expertise. The generally accepted belt designations are as follows:

- White Belts—individuals who have been given a basic orientation
- Yellow Belts—individuals trained in the primary application of Six Sigma management tools
- Green Belts—individuals who handle Lean Six Sigma implementation along with their other regular job responsibilities
- Black Belts—individuals who devote 100% of their time to Lean Six Sigma initiatives
- Master Black Belts—individuals who act in a teaching, mentoring, and coaching role

The roles, responsibilities, and education for Lean Six Sigma Green Belts and Black Belts are the most consistent. The significant difference between a Green Belt and a Black Belt is that Green Belts have a regular job where they apply process improvement via Lean Six Sigma. In contrast, Black Belts are engaged solely in process improvement efforts. Individual expertise must be blended with Lean Six Sigma tools and methods to be a successful Green Belt.

To be a successful Black Belt or Master Black Belt, an overall understanding of business, usually in combination with a Masters of Business Administration degree, is required. Information Technologists, who by nature must interface with various departments or individuals who own businesses, are often excellent candidates for Lean Six Sigma Black Belt studies. Both Black Belts and Green Belts need to understand essential project management properly.

Other roles in the Lean Six Sigma organization include sponsor, process owner, and cross-functional team. The sponsor is generally the person paying for the project. The process owner usually is responsible for the process's success, and the cross-functional team is the ideal team promoted by Lean Six Sigma—a group of multiple disciplines including functional expertise, finance, marketing, and operations.

The roles and responsibilities in Lean Six Sigma are still rooted in TQM. In a TQM effort, all members of an organization participate in improving processes, products, and services. TQM practices are based on cross-functional product design and process management. Other components related to Lean Six Sigma also covered in TQM include:

- Supplier relations
- Overall quality management
- Customer and employee involvement
- Information
- Feedback
- Committed leadership
- Strategic planning

The ILSS practitioner interested in better understanding the history of process improvement will benefit from studying material first presented within the TQM framework. Works by W. Edwards Deming and Joseph Juran are still prevalent today. Other significant authors include Kaoru Ishikawa, A.V. Feigenbaum, and Philip B. Crosby. Reviewing work by these authors will also assist the ILSS in their ability to be innovative thinkers.

Lean Six Sigma is a methodology that applies to every industry. It is equally relevant in manufacturing, healthcare, logistics, and service-based industries. During the COVID pandemic, Lean Six Sigma has been applied in various fields, from ramping up ventilator production to optimizing telehealth services. The results have been remarkable, with organizations reporting improved efficiency, better customer outcomes, and significant cost savings. This is true post-pandemic.

The COVID-19 pandemic has undoubtedly transformed the way we work and collaborate. With many employees forced to work from home and remote teams becoming the norm, Lean Six Sigma professionals have had to adapt to this new reality by finding innovative ways to facilitate continuous improvement efforts from afar. Thankfully, technology has played a pivotal role in enabling virtual collaboration, which has allowed teams to stay connected, share knowledge and insights, and drive process improvement efforts forward.

One of the critical tools that Lean Six Sigma practitioners have embraced during the pandemic is video conferencing. Platforms like Zoom, Skype, and Microsoft Teams allow team members to stay connected regardless of location. This has enabled teams to host virtual kaizen events (also known as Rapid Improvement Events), brainstorming sessions, and even Lean Six Sigma training programs without needing to be in the same room.

Beyond video conferencing, cloud-based software tools like Asana, Trello, and Jira have also become instrumental in enabling virtual collaboration. With these platforms, teams can share tasks, assign responsibilities, and track progress on improvement projects, all in real time. Additionally, digital whiteboards like Mural, Stormboard, and Lucidchart have also emerged as valuable tools to enable teams to collaborate visually and co-create process maps, value stream maps, and other necessary documentation.

Overall, virtual collaboration has allowed Lean Six Sigma professionals to maintain their continuous improvement efforts despite the challenges of the pandemic. While virtual collaboration may only replace in-person collaboration partially, it has indeed shown us that with the right technology tools, we can overcome many of the barriers to effective teamwork that we thought were insurmountable. Ultimately, Lean Six Sigma professionals can use this newfound knowledge to drive greater agility, innovation, and resilience in their organizations during and after the pandemic.

Appendix Two

Pandemic Proofing the Future with Lean Six Sigma

The pandemic of 2020 brought about a series of unprecedented challenges for businesses. While many organizations were forced to close their doors, those that could remain open had to change how they operated to survive drastically. One of the most effective tools to help businesses adapt and stay afloat during the pandemic has been Lean Six Sigma. Lean Six Sigma is a set of business improvement processes that combines lean manufacturing principles with Six Sigma quality management, allowing organizations to reduce waste, increase efficiency, and improve customer service.

The COVID-19 pandemic has disrupted the global economy, forcing businesses and industries to adapt quickly to an ever-changing landscape. As a result, many companies have had to pivot their strategies, streamline their operations, and find new ways to deliver customer products and services. In the face of such unprecedented challenges, Lean Six Sigma methodologies have become increasingly popular as an effective way to optimize processes and reduce waste.

Lean Six Sigma is a business management approach combining Lean manufacturing principles and Six Sigma quality control. It involves using data-driven analysis to identify areas of inefficiency and waste in a business process and then process mapping and statistical analysis techniques to eliminate or reduce these issues. The goal is to create a streamlined, efficient workflow that delivers products and services with the highest possible quality at the lowest possible cost.

The pandemic has highlighted the importance of this approach as businesses have had to adapt to a remote work environment, new safety protocols, and changing customer needs. By applying Lean Six Sigma principles to these new challenges, companies have maintained or even improved their operations in the face of disruption.

The pandemic has drastically changed how we work and for many businesses it has forced the implementation of remote work policies. While this can present many challenges, it has also opened up new opportunities for Lean Six Sigma process improvement.

Slight process improvement allows teams to collaborate and work together, even when not physically in the exact location. By using virtual communication tools, Lean Six Sigma practitioners can still facilitate process mapping, identify areas of waste, and develop improvement plans. The remote environment can also help teams focus on tasks and improve productivity.

However, the key to successful remote process improvement is effective communication. Leaders must ensure everyone is on the same page and that progress is made toward improvement goals. This requires consistent communication through video conferences, emails, and other virtual tools.

Another advantage of slight process improvement is working with teams from different locations or time zones. This allows for a broader perspective and access to a more comprehensive range of expertise.

The pandemic has brought about many changes in the business world, with organizations having to pivot their operations quickly to stay afloat. This is where Agile Methodology comes into play, providing a flexible approach to project management that allows for adaptation to changes.

Agile emphasizes teamwork, communication, and customer collaboration to achieve a common goal. With the pandemic requiring remote work and physical distancing, Agile teams have had to find new ways to work together and communicate effectively. Video conferencing and virtual collaboration tools have maintained the Agile principles of regular meetings and quick feedback.

One of the key benefits of Agile is its ability to manage changing requirements and circumstances. For example, with the pandemic, businesses have had to adapt rapidly to new market demands and changes in supply chains. Agile teams can respond quickly to these changes by continuously testing and refining their approach.

Another essential aspect of Agile is its emphasis on delivering value to customers. With the pandemic affecting customer behavior and needs, businesses have adjusted their strategies and products accordingly. By using Agile, organizations can keep a customer-centric approach at the forefront of their decision-making and quickly respond to changing customer needs.

When a crisis hits, it can be easy to focus on putting out the immediate fire rather than taking the time to identify and address the underlying cause. But it is vital to engage in root cause analysis for crisis management to truly pandemic-proof your business.

Root cause analysis is a structured approach to identifying the underlying factors contributing to a problem. Using this approach during a crisis, you can place the root cause and develop long-term solutions that address the underlying issue rather than just the immediate symptoms.

For example, if a supply chain disruption is causing delays in your product delivery, your immediate response may be to find a new supplier or expedite shipments. However, by conducting a root cause analysis, you may discover that the root cause needs more diversification in your supply chain and that developing a more robust supplier network is a more effective long-term solution.

During a crisis, root cause analysis can help you:

1. Identify the root cause of the problem rather than address the immediate symptoms.
2. Develop long-term solutions that prevent the issue from recurring in the future.
3. Improve organizational learning and decision-making by better understanding the causes and effects of crises.
4. Strengthen crisis management processes by identifying areas for improvement.

The pandemic has shown that businesses must be flexible and adaptable to survive. By utilizing Agile Methodology, organizations can be better prepared to oversee unexpected changes, collaborate effectively, and deliver value to customers in a rapidly changing landscape.

Slight process improvement has become essential to Lean Six Sigma during the pandemic. It enables teams to continue their work and drive process improvements, despite the challenges of remote work. As a result, businesses can stay agile and efficient, even during these unprecedented times.

By using Lean Six Sigma tools, such as the 5 Whys and Fishbone Diagrams, you can engage in root cause analysis even amid a crisis. These tools help you ask probing questions to uncover the underlying causes of a problem and map out the relationship between various factors to develop a comprehensive understanding of the issue.

By prioritizing root cause analysis in your crisis management processes, you can pandemic-proof your business by developing effective long-term solutions to crises and improving organizational learning and decision-making.

Appendix Three

Competency Models

To implement Lean Six Sigma effectively, it is crucial to have trained and competent individuals leading the efforts. This is where the concept of competency models comes into play. Competency models assess the knowledge, skills, and abilities required for different levels of Lean Six Sigma professionals, specifically Green, Black, and Master Black Belts.

Competency models are a crucial component in Lean Six Sigma training programs. They serve as a guideline for what knowledge, skills, and abilities are required for each level of certification. In addition, competency models help ensure that individuals possess the necessary competencies to effectively implement Lean Six Sigma principles in their workplace.

By outlining specific competencies, organizations can tailor their training programs to meet the needs of their employees. This can result in a more effective training program, as individuals are taught the necessary skills to succeed.

Competency models also provide a clear path for career progression. Employees can work toward achieving the competencies required for the next level of certification, motivating ongoing professional development. This can help to increase retention rates, as employees feel supported in their growth and development within the organization.

Moreover, competency models can help organizations measure the effectiveness of their training programs. By assessing individuals against the required competencies, organizations can identify gaps in their training program and make necessary adjustments.

This appendix covers the industry-standard competency models for:

- Lean Six Sigma Green Belt
- Lean Six Sigma Black Belt
- Lean Six Sigma Master Black Belt

Lean Six Sigma Green Belt Basic International Competency Model

The following criteria may be used for interview questions, testing, and practical application exercises for Lean Six Sigma Green Belts.

Ability to Define Lean Six Sigma

- Philosophy of Lean Six Sigma
- Overview of DMAIC (Define–Measure–Analyze–Improve–Control)
- Understand how Lean and Six Sigma work together

Ability to Explain the Roles and Responsibilities of Lean Six Sigma Participants

- Master Black Belt
- Black Belt
- Green Belt
- Yellow Belt
- White Belt
- Champion
- Executive
- Coach
- Facilitator
- Team member
- Sponsor
- Process owner

Be Able to Use the 7 Tools of Quality

- Fishbone
- Check sheet
- Flowchart

- Histogram
- Pareto Chart
- Scatter Diagram
- Control Chart

Exposure to Basic Project Management

- Project Charter
- Process Mapping
- Opening and Closing a project
- Basic project management tools

Describe the Impact That Lean Six Sigma Has on Business Operations

- Methodologies for improvement
- Theories of Voice of the Customer (VOC), Voice of the Business (VOB), Voice of the Employee (VOE), and Voice of the Process (VOP)

Ability to Identify and Explain Areas of Waste

- Excess inventory
- Space
- Test inspection
- Rework
- Transportation
- Storage
- Reducing cycle time to improve throughput
- Skills

For Hiring Managers

Green Belts are entry-level professionals in the Lean Six Sigma hierarchy. They are the ones who work on small projects, analyze data, and implement solutions in their specific areas of responsibility. The Green Belt certification program provides training in the DMAIC (Define–Measure–Analyze–Improve–Control) methodology and the use of essential statistical tools to identify and eliminate process variation.

Competency models for Green Belts define the skills, knowledge, and behavior required to become proficient in the DMAIC process. These models outline Green Belts' specific competencies to perform their job effectively. The competency model can serve as a guide for organizations to recruit, train, and evaluate the performance of Green Belts.

A competency model for Green Belts typically includes:

1. Analytical skills: The ability to analyze data, identify trends, and draw conclusions based on data analysis. This includes the use of statistical tools and techniques.
2. Process knowledge: Understanding the Lean Six Sigma methodology, the DMAIC process, and the ability to apply these principles in real-world situations.
3. Communication skills: The ability to communicate effectively with stakeholders at all levels, including team members, management, and customers.
4. Project management skills: Planning, executing, and controlling projects to achieve the desired outcomes.
5. Leadership skills: The ability to lead and motivate teams, drive change, and achieve buy-in from stakeholders.

A competency model for Green Belts can help organizations identify gaps in skills and knowledge and develop training programs to fill those gaps. It can also help identify high-potential employees who could be considered for more advanced training in Lean Six Sigma, such as the Black Belt or Master Black Belt programs.

Lean Six Sigma Black Belt Basic International Competency Model

Professional competency models are established to provide guidelines for determining expertise and knowledge in a particular area or subject.

The following criteria may be used for interview questions, testing, and practical application exercises:

Ability to Lead a DMAIC Project

- Complete understanding of the Define–Measure–Analyze–Improve–Control process
- Understand leadership responsibilities in deploying a Lean Six Sigma project
- Understand change management models
- Be able to communicate ideas

Ability to Describe and Identify Organizational Roadblocks and Overcome Barriers

- Lack of resources
- Management support
- Recovery techniques
- Change management techniques

Using Tools and Theories Such As

- Constraint management
- Team formation theory
- Team member selection
- Team launch
- Motivational management

Understand Benchmarking, Performance, and Financial Measures

- Best practice
- Competitive
- Collaborative
- Scorecards
- Cost of Quality/Cost of Poor Quality (COQ/COPQ)
- Return on Investment (ROI)
- Net Present Value (NPV)

Use and Understand the Following Lean Six Sigma Tools

- Check Sheets
- Control Charts (line and run charts) and be able to analyze typical control chart patterns
- Critical Path
- Fishbone
- Flowcharting
- FMEA
- Gantt Chart
- Histogram
- Pareto Chart
- PERT Chart
- Scatter Diagrams
- Spaghetti Diagrams
- Swim Lane Charts

- SWOT Analysis
- Tim Woods or the Eight Areas of Waste
- Value Stream Mapping (Basic)

Define and distinguish between various types of benchmarking, including best practices, Competitive, and Collaborative.

Define various business performance measures, including a Balanced Scorecard, Key Performance Indicators (KPI), and The Financial Impact of Customer Loyalty.

Define financial measures, such as Revenue Growth, Market Share, Margin, Cost of Quality (COQ)/Cost of Poor Quality (COPQ), Net Present Value (NPV), Return on Investment (ROI), and Cost-Benefit Analysis.

***

SSD Global supports that all process improvement programs are rooted in Total Quality Management (TQM) concepts and that process improvement begins with a firm understanding of project management basics as outlined in the Project Management Body of Knowledge (PMBOK® Guide). Lean Six Sigma and Master Black Belts should be well versed in these areas. SSD Global suggests that International Lean Six Sigma practitioners consider joining the Project Management Institute and the American Society for Quality.

SSD Global further supports that the newer and leaner Lean Six Sigma, which is based on Six Sigma with a heavy emphasis on Lean Manufacturing/Lean Thinking, has evolved to include other established bodies of knowledge. In addition to basic TQM and the PMBOK® Guide, successful Lean Six Sigma Black Belts and Master Black Belts should review, study, and monitor these different bodies of knowledge:

- Business Analysis Body of Knowledge (BABOK)
- Business Process Reengineering (BPR)
- Change Management
- Leadership Development
- Measurement Systems Analysis

Statistics

- Business Finance
- Organizational Development

Note: SSD Global supports that all process improvement programs are rooted in Total Quality Management (TQM) images. Process improvement begins with a firm understanding of project management basics as outlined in the Project Management Body of Knowledge (PMBOK® Guide). The International Lean Six Sigma Master Black Belt should be well versed in areas covered in these evolving documents. It is also suggested that International Lean Six Sigma Master Black Belts familiarize themselves with ISO 13053, ISO 12500, and PRINCE2® and keep updated on new releases associated with these documents.

For Hiring Managers: Black Belts are typically highly trained professionals within a company's Lean Six Sigma program. These individuals have demonstrated a strong understanding of the methodology and possess the skills to lead process improvement initiatives.

Competency models for Black Belts are focused on advancing their technical knowledge and their ability to apply that knowledge in practical scenarios. Therefore, Black Belt competency models should cover statistical process control, hypothesis testing, project management, and advanced analytical techniques.

Black Belts should also develop soft skills, such as leadership and communication. Competency models should also cover these skills essential for driving successful improvement initiatives.

One important aspect of Black Belt competency models is that they often vary depending on the industry in which the organization operates. Therefore, competency models must be tailored to the specific challenges and opportunities faced by the company to provide the most effective training and development opportunities for Black Belts.

A good competency model for Black Belts should include clear performance standards, training requirements, and career advancement opportunities. This ensures that Black Belts clearly understand what is expected of them and how they can continue to develop their skills and advance their careers.

Overall, competency models for Black Belts are essential for ensuring that companies have the best trained and most capable process improvement leaders. With a clear understanding of the knowledge and skills required to be successful in their role, Black Belts can help drive significant improvements in organizational efficiency, productivity, and profitability.

Lean Six Sigma Master Black Belt Basic Competency Model

Professional competency models are established to provide guidelines for determining expertise and knowledge in a particular area or subject. The following criteria may be used for interview questions, testing, and practical application exercises.

Ability to Identify and Lead a DMAIC Project

- Ability to teach and facilitate the Define–Measure–Analyze–Improve–Control process
- Demonstrate leadership in deploying a Lean Six Sigma project
- Deploy and monitor change management models
- Superior verbal and written presentation skills

Ability to Creatively Deal with Roadblocks and Overcome Barriers Related to

- Lack of resources
- Management support
- Recovery techniques
- Change management techniques

Teaching and Mentoring Knowledge of Tools and Theories to Include

- Constraint management
- Team formation theory
- Team member selection
- Team launch
- Motivational management

Prepare, Explain, and Evaluate Factors Related to Benchmarking, Performance, and Financial Measures

- Best practice
- Competitive
- Collaborative
- Scorecards
- Cost of Quality/Cost of Poor Quality (COQ/COPQ)
- Return on Investment (ROI)
- Net Present Value (NPV)

Use, Evaluate, and Explain

- Check Sheets
- Control Charts (line and run charts) and be able to analyze typical control chart patterns
- Critical Path
- Fishbone
- Flowcharting
- FMEA
- Gantt Chart
- Histogram
- Pareto Chart
- PERT Chart
- Scatter Diagrams
- Spaghetti Diagrams
- Swim Lane Charts
- SWOT Analysis
- Tim Woods or the Eight Areas of Waste
- Value Stream Mapping (Basic)

Develop, Delivery, and Evaluate Training Plans

- Design training plans
- Understand various training approaches
- Build curriculum
- Demonstrate success
- Ability to coach and mentor Black, Green, and Yellow Belts

Additional Design Criteria

- Business Performance Measures such as
  - Balanced scorecard
  - Key Performance Indicators (KPI)
  - Financial measures
    - Revenue Growth
    - Market Share
    - Margin
    - Cost of Quality (COQ)/Cost of Poor Quality (COPQ)
    - Net Present Value (NPV)
    - Return on Investment (ROI)
    - Cost-Benefit Analysis

For Hiring Managers: Master Black Belts (MBBs) are experts in Lean Six Sigma methodology and have attained the highest level of certification in this field. In addition, these individuals lead and guide other Lean Six Sigma professionals in an organization. As such, it is essential to clearly understand the competency models required to excel in this role.

The competency models for MBBs are focused on their ability to lead strategic improvement initiatives within an organization. MBBs are responsible for guiding the deployment of Lean Six Sigma projects across different departments and ensuring that projects align with the overall organizational goals. Additionally, they are accountable for coaching and mentoring other Lean Six Sigma professionals within an organization.

The following are the critical competency models required for MBBs:

1. Strategic thinking: MBBs must have a deep understanding of the organization's vision and goals and be able to align Lean Six Sigma projects with those goals. This requires the ability to think strategically and to be able to communicate complex concepts to others clearly and concisely.
2. Coaching and mentoring: MBBs must be able to coach and mentor other Lean Six Sigma professionals within an organization and help them to develop their skills and competencies. This requires strong interpersonal skills and the ability to build relationships with others at all levels of an organization.
3. Change management: MBBs must have a strong understanding of change management principles and be able to apply them to Lean Six Sigma projects. This requires the ability to anticipate potential obstacles to change and to develop strategies to overcome them.
4. Technical expertise: MBBs must have a deep understanding of Lean Six Sigma methodology and tools and be able to apply them in various situations. This requires ongoing learning and development and a commitment to staying up-to-date with new trends and best practices.

Having a clear understanding of the competency models required for MBBs is critical for organizations looking to deploy the Lean Six Sigma methodology effectively. In addition, by investing in developing their MBBs, organizations can ensure they have the right people to drive strategic improvement initiatives and achieve their goals.

Competency models are essential for the success of Lean Six Sigma training programs. They provide clarity on what is expected at each level of certification and enable organizations to tailor their training programs to the needs of their employees. With the right competencies, individuals can effectively implement Lean Six Sigma principles, driving positive organizational change and results.

Reference Materials

Lean Six Sigma Body of Knowledge Outline (SSD Global Version 4.0)

Summarized Version

The first entities attributed with blending Lean and Six Sigma were Allied Signal and Maytag, independently in 1999. At that time, it was referred to as "Lean and Six" as both Allied Signal and Maytag realized that the two methodologies complement one another. It was not until several years later that the term Lean Six Sigma became popular and only since 2004 has being certified as an International Lean Six Sigma Practitioner gained recognition as a solid industry certification.

Over the past decade Lean Six Sigma adopted many tools and ideologies that were not originally based in Lean or Six Sigma. The newer, leaner, Lean Six Sigma, has been improved to capitalize on any tools or thoughts that contribute to process improvement. In other words, Lean Six Sigma has become better, faster, and more cost-effective as a methodology. In its new form, it is the only methodology that works in tandem with other process improvement methodologies.

Although Six Sigma is the dominant methodology in Lean Six Sigma, which is heavily influenced by Lean Thinking, the new, more powerful Lean Six Sigma is actually comprised of several bodies of knowledge.

This document is an outline of the Lean Six Sigma Body of Knowledge (SSD Global Version 4.0). This body of knowledge is presented in four sections:

- Major Process Improvement Programs that Contributed to Lean Six Sigma (Section 1)

- Lean Six Sigma Knowledge (Section 2)
- Core Tools Used in Lean Six Sigma (Section 3)
- Implementation (Section 4)

1 MAJOR PROCESS IMPROVEMENT PROGRAMS THAT CONTRIBUTED TO LEAN SIX SIGMA

- 1.1 Primary Recognized Process Improvement Programs
  - 1.1.1 Total Quality Management (TQM)
  - 1.1.2 International Standards Organization (ISO)
  - 1.1.3 Capability Maturity Model Integrated (CMMI)
  - 1.1.4 Six Sigma
    - 1.1.4.1 Defect Reduction
    - 1.1.4.2 DMAIC Model
    - 1.1.4.3 DFSS Model
    - 1.1.4.4 Statistical Thinking
    - 1.1.4.5 Recognizing Individual Tasks within a Process and Assigning Major Causes of Variation
      - 1.1.4.5.1 Common Cause Variability
      - 1.1.4.5.2 Special Cause Variability
    - 1.1.4.6 Stabilize Processes
  - 1.1.5 Lean Manufacturing
    - 1.1.5.1 Waste Reduction/Elimination
    - 1.1.5.2 Speed
    - 1.1.5.3 Voice of the Customer/Employee/Business/Process
  - 1.1.6 Additional Methodologies and Bodies of Knowledge That Play a Role in Lean Six Sigma
    - 1.1.6.1 Total Quality Management (TQM)
    - 1.1.6.2 Quality Body of Knowledge (Q-BoK™)
    - 1.1.6.3 Business Analysis Body of Knowledge (BABOK®)
    - 1.1.6.4 Project Management Body of Knowledge (PMBOK® Guide)
    - 1.1.6.5 Business Process Reengineering (BPR)
    - 1.1.6.6 Change Management
    - 1.1.6.7 Leadership Development
    - 1.1.6.8 Measurement Systems Analysis
    - 1.1.6.9 Statistics
    - 1.1.6.10 Business Finance
    - 1.1.6.11 Organizational Development

2 LEAN SIX SIGMA

- 2.1 Systematic Approach to Reducing Waste and Eliminating Defects
  - 2.1.1 Statistical Thinking Blended with Voice of the Customer
  - 2.1.2 Better, Faster, More Cost-Effective Methods and Tools
  - 2.1.3 Uses DMAIC and DFSS Models
  - 2.1.4 Incorporates PDCA Model
- 2.2 Important Names in Lean Six Sigma
  - 2.2.1 Shewhart
  - 2.2.2 Deming
  - 2.2.3 Juran
  - 2.2.4 Baldrige
  - 2.2.5 Taguchi
  - 2.2.6 Goldratt
  - 2.2.7 Ishikawa
- 2.3 Basic Quality Concepts
  - 2.3.1 Customer Satisfaction
  - 2.3.2 Supplier Satisfaction
  - 2.3.3 Continuous Improvement
- 2.4 Quality Impact
  - 2.4.1 Prevention vs. Detection
  - 2.4.2 Inputs/Outputs
  - 2.4.3 Process
  - 2.4.4 Customer

3 CORE TOOLS AND KNOWLEDGE USED IN LEAN SIX SIGMA

- 3.1 Process Improvement
  - 3.1.1 Better Quality
    - 3.1.1.1 Cost of Quality
    - 3.1.1.2 Cost of Poor Quality
  - 3.1.2 Faster/More Efficiency
    - 3.1.2.1 Process Mapping to Eliminate or Reduce Steps
  - 3.1.3 Cost Impact
    - 3.1.3.1 Profit
      - 3.1.3.1.1 Return on Investment Formulas
      - 3.1.3.1.2 Cost Benefit Analysis
    - 3.1.3.2 Savings
      - 3.1.3.2.1 Cost Savings Calculations
      - 3.1.3.2.2 Cost Lower than Historical Cost
      - 3.1.3.2.3 Cost Lower than Projected Cost

3.1.3.3 Cost Avoidance
3.3.3.3.1 Reduce Future Costs
3.3.3.3.2 Avoid Compliance Issues
3.1.4 Business Systems vs. Business Processes
3.2 Popular Methods on Measuring Process Improvement
3.2.1 Return on Investment
3.2.2 Sigma Levels
3.2.3 Scorecard Approach
3.2.4 Industry Benchmarking and/or Metrics
3.3 Lean Six Sigma Tools
3.3.1 Seven Tools of Quality
3.3.1.1 Fishbone
3.3.1.2 Flowcharting
3.3.1.3 Check Sheets
3.3.1.3.1 Low Tech Tool to Gather Information
3.3.1.3.2 Toll Gate
3.3.1.4 Histogram
3.3.1.4.1 Frequency Diagram
3.3.1.4.2 Collecting Information
3.3.1.5 Pareto Chart
3.3.1.6 Scatter Diagrams
3.3.1.6.1 Intersection Points
3.3.1.6.2 Correlation Analysis
3.3.1.7 Control Charts
3.3.1.7.1 Line Charts
3.3.1.7.2 Run Charts
3.3.1.7.2.1 Attribute Charts
3.3.1.7.2.2 Variable Charts
3.3.1.7.3 Control Chart Patterns
3.3.2 Additional Charts and Graphs
3.3.2.1 Value Stream Mapping
3.3.2.1.1 Flowcharting Symbols
3.3.2.1.2 Value Stream Mapping Symbols
3.3.2.2 Gantt
3.3.2.3 PERT
3.3.2.3.1 Critical Path
3.3.2.4 Swim Lane Charts
3.3.2.5 Spaghetti Diagrams

- 3.3.3 Capitalizes on Structured Brainstorming Tools
  - 3.3.1.1 Tim Woods or the Eight Areas of Waste
  - 3.3.1.2 SWOT Analysis
  - 3.3.1.3 FMEA Thinking Process
  - 3.3.1.4 Fishbone Analysis
- 3.3.4 Miscellaneous Tools
  - 3.3.4.1 3 Ps
    - 3.3.1.4.1 People
    - 3.3.1.4.2 Product
    - 3.3.1.4.3 Process
  - 3.3.4.2 6 Ms
    - 3.3.4.2.1 Machines
    - 3.3.4.2.2 Methods
    - 3.3.4.2.3 Materials
    - 3.3.4.2.4 Measure
    - 3.3.4.2.5 Mother Nature
    - 3.3.4.2.6 Manpower
  - 3.3.4.3 6 Ws
    - 3.3.4.3.1 What
    - 3.3.4.3.2 Where
    - 3.3.4.3.3 Why
    - 3.3.4.3.4 Who
    - 3.3.4.3.5 When
    - 3.3.4.3.6 Which
  - 3.3.4.4 8 Ds—Short for the Eight Disciplines
    - 3.3.4.4.1 Establish the Team
    - 3.3.4.4.2 Describe the Problem
    - 3.3.4.4.3 Develop an Interim Containment Plan
    - 3.3.4.4.4 Determine Root Cause
    - 3.3.4.4.5 Choose Corrective Action
    - 3.3.4.4.6 Implement Action
    - 3.3.4.4.7 Prevent Recurrence
    - 3.3.4.4.8 Recognize the Team

3.4 The Define-Measure-Analyze-Improve-Control Model (DMAIC)

- 3.4.1 Define
  - 3.4.1.1 Core Activities
    - 3.4.1.1.1 Gaining Consensus on the Statement of Work

- 3.4.1.1.2 Completing the Project Charter
  - 3.4.1.1.2.1 Typical Project Charter Characteristics
    - 3.4.1.1.2.1.1 Name/Title
    - 3.4.1.1.2.1.2 Project Objectives
    - 3.4.1.1.2.1.3 Scope
    - 3.4.1.1.2.1.4 Deliverables
    - 3.4.1.1.2.1.5 Assumptions/ Constraints
    - 3.4.1.1.2.1.6 Project ROI or Cost Savings
- 3.4.1.1.3 Forming a Team
- 3.4.1.1.4 Identifying the Major and Minor Stakeholders

3.4.1.2 Essential Tools
- 3.4.1.2.1 Project Charter
- 3.4.1.2.2 Process Map
- 3.4.1.2.3 Cost Benefit Analysis
- 3.4.1.2.4 Return on Investment and/or Cost Savings Calculations
- 3.4.1.2.5 Stakeholders Analysis
- 3.4.1.2.6 Supplier-Input-Process-Output-Customer (SIPOC) Diagram
- 3.4.1.2.7 Critical to Quality (CTQ) Definitions
- 3.4.1.2.8 DMAIC WBS
- 3.4.1.2.9 Quality Function Deployment/House of Quality

3.4.2 Measure

3.4.2.1 Core Activities
- 3.4.2.1.1 Getting a Solid "As Is" Picture of the Current Situation
- 3.4.2.1.2 Determining the Right Blend of Hard and Soft Metrics
- 3.4.2.1.3 Measuring the Measurement System/ Measurement Systems Analysis
  - 3.4.2.1.3.1 Bias
  - 3.4.2.1.3.2 Linearity
  - 3.4.2.1.3.3 Stability

- 3.4.2.1.3.4 Repeatability
- 3.4.2.1.3.5 Reproducibility
- 3.4.2.2 Essential Tools
  - 3.4.2.2.1 Detailed Process Map
  - 3.4.2.2.2 Benchmarking
    - 4.4.2.2.2.1 Internal
    - 4.4.2.2.2.2 Competitive
    - 4.4.2.2.2.3 Functional
    - 4.4.2.2.2.4 Collaborative
    - 4.4.2.2.2.5 Generic
  - 3.4.2.2.3 Sigma Levels
  - 3.4.2.2.4 Return on Investment Calculations
  - 3.4.2.2.5 Failure Mode and Effects Analysis (FMEA)
  - 3.4.2.2.6 Industry Metrics
  - 3.4.2.2.7 Observation
  - 3.4.2.2.8 Gage R&R (repeatability and reproducibility)
  - 3.4.2.2.9 Data Collection Plans
  - 3.4.2.2.10 Scorecard
- 3.4.3 Analyze
  - 3.4.3.1 Core Activities
    - 3.4.3.1.1 Analyze Data
      - 3.4.3.1.1.1 Determine Root Causes
      - 3.4.3.1.1.2 Determine Correlations
      - 3.4.3.1.1.3 Identify Variations
      - 3.4.3.1.1.4 Determine Type of Data
        - 3.4.3.1.1.4.1 Attribute
        - 3.4.3.1.1.4.2 Variable
      - 3.4.3.1.1.5 Determine Data Characteristics
        - 3.4.3.1.1.5.1 Nominal
        - 3.4.3.1.1.5.2 Ordinal
        - 3.4.3.1.1.5.3 Interval
  - 3.4.3.2 Essential Tools
    - 3.4.3.2.1 Basic Statistics
      - 3.4.3.2.1.1 Measures of Central Tendency
        - 3.4.3.2.1.1.1 Mean
        - 3.4.3.2.1.1.2 Mode
        - 3.4.3.2.1.1.3 Media

3.4.3.2.1.2 Range
3.4.3.2.1.3 Variance
3.4.3.2.1.4 Variation
3.4.3.2.1.5 Correlation
3.4.3.2.1.5.1 Positive
3.4.3.2.1.5.2 Negative
3.4.3.2.1.5.3 No Correlation
3.4.3.2.2 Advanced Statistics in Projects Dealing with Safety or Very High Dollar Amounts
3.4.3.2.2.1 Process Capability
3.4.3.2.2.2 Probability Distributions
3.4.3.2.2.2.1 Exponential
3.4.3.2.2.2.2 Binomial
3.4.3.2.2.2.3 Poisson
3.4.3.2.2.2.4 Normal
3.4.3.2.2.2.5 Chi-Squared
3.4.3.2.2.3 Standard Deviation
3.4.3.2.2.4 Regression Analysis
3.4.3.2.3 Seven Tools of Quality
3.4.3.2.4 The Five Whys
3.4.3.2.5 Design of Experiments
3.4.3.2.5.1 Screening
3.4.3.2.5.2 Factorial Design
3.4.3.2.6 Chi Squared Test
3.4.3.2.7 Process Capability
3.4.4 Improve
3.4.4.1 Core Activities
3.4.4.1.1 Determine 3-5 Solutions
3.4.4.1.2 Gain Consensus on a Solution
3.4.4.1.3 Pilot Solution
3.4.4.1.4 Roll Out Solution
3.4.4.1.5 Evaluate for Process Improvement
3.4.4.2 Essential Tools
3.4.4.2.1 Decision Matrix /SWOT Analysis
3.4.4.2.2 Project or Execution Plan
3.4.4.2.3 Failure Mode Effects Analysis (FMEA)
3.4.4.2.3.1 To Double Check Core Activities on Project Plan
3.4.4.2.4 Evaluation Tools

- 3.4.5 Control
  - 3.4.5.1 Core Activities
    - 3.4.5.1.1 Verify Benefits
    - 3.4.5.1.2 Control Plan
    - 3.4.5.1.3 Transition Plan
  - 3.4.5.2 Essential Tools
    - 3.4.5.2.1 Measurement Tools
    - 3.4.5.2.2 Control Chart
    - 3.4.5.2.3 5S Model
    - 3.4.5.2.4 Environment Has a Better Opportunity of Sustaining Improvement
    - 3.4.5.2.5 Transition Plan Template
- 3.5 The Design for Six Sigma Model (DFSS)
  - 3.5.1 Primary Model Define–Measure–Analyze–Design–Verify
    - 3.5.1.1 Define (See DMAIC)
    - 3.5.1.2 Measure (See DMAIC)
    - 3.5.1.3 Analyze (See DMAIC)
    - 3.5.1.4 Design
      - 3.5.1.4.1 Core Activities
      - 3.5.1.4.2 Essential Tools
    - 3.5.1.5 Verify
      - 3.5.1.5.1 Core Activities
      - 3.5.1.5.2 Essential Tools
    - 3.5.1.6 Other Popular DFSS Models
      - 3.5.1.6.1 Identify–Define–Design–Optimize–Verify (IDDOV)
      - 3.5.1.6.2 Define–Customer–Concept–Design–Implementation (DCCDI)
- 3.6 Pre-DMAIC
  - 3.6.1 Plan–Do–Check–Act (PDCA) Model
    - 3.6.1.1 Problem May Be Better Suited to Easier Model
    - 3.6.1.2 May Not Have Time to Do DMAIC/DFSS
    - 3.6.1.3 May Be Used Prior to a DMAIC/DFSS for Justification
  - 3.6.2 The Sort–Straighten–Shine–Standardize–Sustain (5S) Model
    - 3.6.2.1 Sort
    - 3.6.2.2 Set-in-Order
    - 3.6.2.3 Shine
    - 3.6.2.4 Standardize
    - 3.6.2.5 Sustain

- 3.6.3 Strengths–Weakness–Opportunity–Threats (SWOT) Model
  - 3.6.3.1 Force Field Analysis
  - 3.6.3.2 Go/No Go Decision
  - 3.6.3.3 Risk
- 3.6.4 Martial Art Designations Are Used to Denote Levels of Expertise
  - 3.6.4.1 White Belt
  - 3.6.4.2 Yellow Belt
  - 3.6.4.3 Green Belt
    - 3.6.4.3.1 Tactical Responsibilities
    - 3.6.4.3.2 Applies Lean Six Sigma to Specific Job
  - 3.6.4.4 Black Belt
    - 3.6.4.4.1 Strategic Responsibilities
    - 3.6.4.4.2 Can Make Process Improvement in Any Department
    - 3.6.4.4.3 Aligning Projects to Company Goals and Initiatives
    - 3.6.4.4.4 Risk Analysis
    - 3.6.4.4.5 Closed Loop Assessment
  - 3.6.4.5 Master Black Belt
    - 3.6.4.5.1 Mentor
    - 3.6.4.5.2 Coach
    - 3.6.4.5.3 Facilitator/Teacher

- 3.7 Constraint Management
  - 3.7.1 Based on the Theory of Constraints (TOC)—Eliyahu Goldratt
    - 3.7.1.1 Types of Constraints
      - 3.7.1.1.1 Market
      - 3.7.1.1.2 Capacity
      - 3.7.1.1.3 Resources
      - 3.7.1.1.4 Suppliers
      - 3.7.1.1.5 Finance
      - 3.7.1.1.6 Knowledge or Competence
      - 3.7.1.1.7 Policy
  - 3.7.2 Exploiting Your Constraints
  - 3.7.3 Developing a Constraints Strategy

4 IMPLEMENTATION

- 4.1 Project Management Must Be in Place to Implement Process Improvement
  - 4.1.1 Project Management Basics
    - 4.1.1.1 Financial Management
      - 4.1.1.1.1 Budget
      - 4.1.1.1.2 Earned Value
    - 4.1.1.2 Risk Management
      - 4.1.1.2.1 Risk Analysis
      - 4.1.1.2.2 Risk Mitigation
    - 4.1.1.3 People Management
      - 4.1.1.3.1 Leadership
        - 4.1.1.3.1.1 Role of the Black Belt and Master Black Belt
        - 4.1.1.3.1.2 Project Selection
        - 4.1.1.3.1.3 Project Mentoring
        - 4.1.1.3.1.4 Project Critique
      - 4.1.1.3.2 Team Building
  - 4.1.2 Project Management Activities
    - 4.1.2.1 Planning
    - 4.1.2.2 Assessing Risk
    - 4.1.2.3 Allocation of Resources
    - 4.1.2.4 Acquiring Human and Non-Human Resources
  - 4.1.3 Project Management Primary Tools
    - 4.1.3.1 Project Charter
    - 4.1.3.2 Process Map
    - 4.1.3.3 Stakeholder's Analysis
    - 4.1.3.4 Responsibility and Accountability Document
    - 4.1.3.5 Work Breakdown Structure
    - 4.1.3.6 Gantt Chart
    - 4.1.3.7 PERT Chart
  - 4.1.4 Lean Six Sigma Martial Arts Designations
  - 4.1.5 Arguments Supporting Lean Six Sigma Implementation
  - 4.1.6 Speed
  - 4.1.7 Voice of the Customer (VOC) Emphasis
    - 4.1.7.1 Collection of Data
    - 4.1.7.2 Analysis of Data

4.1.7.3 Stakeholders
4.1.7.4 Translating into Customer Requirements
4.1.8 Recognition of Waste as a Defect
4.1.8.1 Areas of Waste
4.1.8.1.1 Transportation and Motion
4.1.8.1.2 Over Processing/Over Production
4.1.8.1.3 Defects
4.1.8.1.4 Skills
4.1.8.1.5 Waiting
4.1.8.2 Hidden Areas of Waste
4.1.8.2.1 Duplication of Reports
4.1.8.2.2 Duplication of Duties
4.1.9 Inexpensive to Implement
4.1.10 Used by Many Fortune 500 Companies
4.2 Team Building
4.2.1 Roles and Responsibilities
4.2.1.1 Initiating a Team
4.2.1.2 Team Performance Evaluation
4.3 Team Tools
4.3.1 Facilitation Techniques
4.3.2 Motivation
4.3.3 Team Building
4.3.4 Phases
4.3.4.1 Forming
4.3.4.2 Storming
4.3.4.3 Norming
4.3.4.4 Performing
4.4 Change Management
4.4.1 Conflict Management and Negotiation Tactics
4.4.1.1 Win/Win
4.4.1.2 Collaboration
4.4.1.3 Agreement
4.4.1.4 Empathy
4.4.2 Roadblocks to Improvement
4.4.2.1 Conflict
4.4.2.2 Change
4.4.2.3 Lack of Critical Thinking
4.4.2.4 Lack of Creative Thinking
4.4.2.5 Lack of Basic Project Management Skills

4.4.2.6 Communication
4.4.2.7 Motivation
4.5 Voices to Consider during Implementation
4.5.1 Voice of the Customer
4.5.2 Voice of the Employee
4.5.3 Voice of the Business (or Industry)
4.5.4 Voice of the Process

Lean Six Sigma Body of Knowledge (SSD Global Version 6.0)

Full Text Version

This document expands the concepts as outlined in the Lean Six Sigma Body of Knowledge (SSD Global Version 4.0) summary outline. The following information is repeated from the outlined version.

The first entities attributed with blending Lean and Six Sigma were Allied Signal and Maytag, independently in 1999. At that time, it was referred to as "Lean and Six" as both Allied Signal and Maytag realized that the two methodologies complement one another. It was not until several years later that the term Lean Six Sigma became popular and only since 2004 has being certified as an International Lean Six Sigma Practitioner gained recognition as a solid industry certification.

Over the past decade Lean Six Sigma adopted many tools and ideologies that were not originally based in Lean or Six Sigma. The newer, leaner, Lean Six Sigma, has been improved to capitalize on any tools or thoughts that contribute to process improvement. In other words, Lean Six Sigma has become better, faster, and more cost-effective as a methodology. In its new form, it is the only methodology that works in tandem with other process improvement methodologies.

Although Six Sigma is the dominant methodology in Lean Six Sigma, which is heavily influenced by Lean Thinking, the new more powerful Lean Six Sigma is actually comprised of several bodies of knowledge.

This body of knowledge is presented in four sections:

- Major Process Improvement Programs that Contributed to Lean Six Sigma (Section 1)
- Lean Six Sigma (Section 2)

- Core Tools and Knowledge Used in Lean Six Sigma (Section 3)
- Implementation (Section 4)

Section 1: Major Process Improvement Programs that Contributed to Lean Six Sigma

The Primary Recognized Process Improvement Programs

Total Quality Management (TQM)

Total Quality Management (TQM) is the foundation of most process improvement programs. The core TQM strategy is to embed the awareness of quality throughout the entire organization. Both Six Sigma and Lean Manufacturing/Thinking promote concepts and tools first introduced by TQM. TQM also means continuously improving processes and products as well as reducing waste. This is why TQM aligns closely with Lean Six Sigma.

The major difference between Lean Six Sigma and TQM is that the tools used in Lean Six Sigma are updated and less labor intensive. Generally the mission, goals, and philosophy of TQM are also represented in Lean Six Sigma.

Many TQM ideas and problem-solving tools can be traced back to the early 1920s, when statistical theory was applied to product quality control. The concept of applying mathematical and statistical models to improve product quality was further developed in Japan in the 1940s. This effort was led by Americans, such as W. Edwards Deming and Joseph Juran. Deming was responsible for popularizing the idea whereas Juran wrote much of the original literature.

Deming was a protégé of Dr. Walter Shewhart. Juran also studied with Shewhart. Shewhart is sometimes referred to as the father of statistical quality control. Shewhart's contribution to quality focuses on control charts, special/common cause variation, and analytical statistical studies. Shewhart's work also concentrates on Statistical Process Control (SPC). Often SPC is studied as a sub-set of TQM. SPC studies various charts and graphs to determine and monitor process capability.

Beginning in the 1980s a new phase of quality control and management began. The focus widened from quality of products to quality of all issues including service opportunities within an organization. It was determined that many of the same mathematical and statistical models used to identify, monitor, and evaluate the quality of products could also be applied in the service industry.

In 1988, a significant step in quality management was made when the Malcolm Baldrige Award was established by the President of the United States. This national award recognizes companies for their quality contributions. Malcolm Baldrige was responsible for bringing quality to the government during the Reagan Administration. The Baldrige Program's mission is to improve the competitiveness and performance related to quality.

The Baldrige Program was a direct result of the TQM movement and includes:

- Raising the awareness of performance excellence
- Providing organizational assessment tools and criteria
- Educating business leaders
- Recognizing national role models in quality

TQM is a set of management practices throughout an organization, geared to ensure that the organization consistently meets or exceeds customer requirements. In a TQM effort, all members of an organization participate in improving processes, products, and services. Quality initiatives are not limited to the Quality Department.

Modern definitions of TQM include phrases such as: customer focus, the involvement of all employees, continuous improvement, and the integration of quality management into the total organization.

Basic TQM supports:

- Line management ownership
- Employee involvement and empowerment
- Challenging quantified goals and benchmarking
- Focus on processes and improvement plans
- Specific incorporation in strategic planning
- Recognition and celebration

TQM has adopted several documents that are also used in other process improvement efforts to include the Lean Six Sigma program. Typically these documents are identified by the following titles:

- Deming's 14 Points
- Deming's 7 Deadly Diseases

- The Deming Cycle
- Joseph Juran's Roadmap for Quality Leadership
- The Triple Constraint Model

In general terms, TQM is a management approach to long-term success through customer satisfaction and is based on the participation of all members of an organization in improving processes, products, and services.

International Standards Organization (ISO)

International Standards Organization (ISO), founded in 1947, is an international standard-setting body composed of representatives from various national standards organizations. ISO has developed over 18,000 International Standards making it the largest standards-developing organization in the world. The ISO 9000 and ISO 14000 series are the most well known. However, up to 1100 new ISO standards are published every year.

The ISO 9000 family specifically addresses "Quality Management." This means what the organization does to fulfill:

- The customer's quality requirements, and
- Applicable regulatory requirements, while aiming to
- Enhance customer satisfaction, and
- Achieve continual improvement of its performance in pursuit of these objectives

The ISO 14000 family addresses "Environmental Management." This means what the organization does to:

- Minimize harmful effects on the environment caused by its activities, and to
- Achieve continual improvement of its environmental performance.

To be certified in an ISO standard, these steps are necessary:

- Locating and Selecting a Registrar—this is a company who is certified by ISO to make the initial assessment and provide suggestions for your ISO program
- Creating an application and conducting a document review
- Participating in an assessment

- Completing the ISO registration
- Participating in a recertification effort

ISO recertification efforts include gathering the proper measurements and articulating these measurements as well as identifying future opportunities for process improvement. There is also a time factor involved. Therefore, Lean Six Sigma often plays a primary role in ISO recertification.

Capability Maturity Model Integration (CMMI)

Capability Maturity Model Integration (CMMI) is another popular process improvement program. This integrated approach is intended to help an organization improve performance by recognizing certain levels of performance. CMMI can be used to guide process improvement across a project, a division, or an entire organization.

In CMMI models with a staged representation, there are five maturity levels designated by the numbers 1 through 5

1. Initial
2. Managed
3. Defined
4. Quantitatively Managed
5. Optimizing

CMMI was developed by the CMMI project, which was designed to improve the usability of maturity models by integrating many different models into one framework. The project consisted of members of industry, government and the Carnegie Mellon Software Engineering Institute (SEI). The main sponsors included the Office of the Secretary of Defense (OSD) and the National Defense Industrial Association.

Each level in the CMMI process requires detailed information gathering and analysis. The significance of Lean Six Sigma in CMMI is that often to move up one level, Lean Six Sigma practices need to be engaged.

Six Sigma

Defect Reduction

The Six Sigma problem-solving methodology is the most effective tool to quickly reduce and eliminate defects. It is a team-based methodology that works by systematically identifying and controlling the process variables that contribute to producing the defect or mistake.

DMAIC Model

Improvement of existing products or processes using the Six Sigma methodology is done in five steps:

- Define
- Measure
- Analyze
- Improve
- Control

Define

The purpose of the Define Phase is to make sure that everyone understands the project and the goals of the process improvement effort. The basic steps include:

- Create a process improvement charter and process map.
- Identify or define problems in the process that must be solved in order to meet or exceed the customer's specifications or expectations.
- Identify and quantify customer requirements.
- Identify and quantify the process output and defects that fall short of these requirements and create a problem statement.
- State the project goal, which also must be a clear and measurable goal, and include a time limit for the project's completion.
- Determine the few vital factors that are Critical to Quality that need to be measured, analyzed, improved, and controlled.

Measure

The purpose of the Measure Phase is to get a strong as-is snapshot of how the process is currently behaving. The basic steps include:

- Select the Critical to Quality characteristics in the process. These are the outputs of the given process that are important to the customer. How is the company doing now?

- Define what that process output should be, which is accomplished by looking at the customer requirements and the project goal.
- Define the defect for the process. Remember, a defect is an output that falls outside the limits of a customer's requirements or expectations and must be measurable.
- Find the inputs to the process that contribute to defects.
- Define the exact dollar impact of eliminating the defects in terms of increased profitability and/or cost savings.
- Measure the defects that affect the Critical to Quality characteristics as well as any related factors.
- Incorporate Measurement Systems Analysis—a method to make sure the defects are being measured properly.

Analyze

The purpose of the Analyze Phase is to review the measurements and information from the previous phase and determine, based on that information, what three to five solutions might be appropriate to solve the problem or roll out the activity.

- Determine root cause
- Identify variations that could be reduced
- Determine if correlation exists
- Do what-if scenarios
- Determine the timeline and cost of solutions
- Determine the sustainability of the solution

Improve

The purpose of the Improve Phase is to choose a solution, implement the solution, and be able to definitively prove that a process improvement has been accomplished. This is done by comparing the as-is state (Measure) with conditions after the process improvement has been rolled out. Basic steps include:

- Articulate the three to five possible solutions
- Gain consensus on the best solution
- Pilot

- Create an execution plan (Project Plan) if the solution is successful in the pilot
- Choose another one of the three to five solutions if the pilot is not successful
- Roll out

Control

The purpose of the Control Phase is to sustain the improvement. Basic steps include:

- Clearly articulating the process improvement achieved
- Creating a control plan to keep the process in place
- Designing a transition plan for the new owner

DFSS Model

Design for Six Sigma, also known as Design for Lean Six Sigma (DFSS or DFLSS), is applicable only in situations where a new product or service needs to be designed or re-designed from the very beginning. Many supporters of the DMAIC design believe that this is accomplished in the Analyze and Improve Phases of the DMAIC model. However, supporters of DFSS believe a design component is necessary. Recently models based on the DMAIC thinking process that do not have a design component are also referred to as DFSS or DFLSS models.

Today the most popular DFFS model is the Define–Measure–Analyze–Design–Verify (DMADV). The DMADV model contains the first three phases of the DMAIC model. The last two phases, Improve and Control, are replaced by Design and Verify.

Design

Design details, optimize the design, and plan for design verification. This phase may require simulations.

Verify

Verify the design, set up pilot runs, implement the production process, and hand it over to the process owner(s).

Statistical Thinking

Both the DMAIC and DMADV model are based on statistical thinking. The following principles form the basis for statistical thinking:

- All work occurs in a system of interconnected processes
- Inherent variation exists in all processes
- Reducing variation is the key to successfully improving a process

Recognizing Individual Tasks within the Process and Assigning Major Causes of Variability

To successfully analyze a process using statistical process control it is important to break things down into the smallest elements possible. All processes have inherent variability and that variability can be measured. Data is used to understand variability based on the type of variability. Deming used statistical quality control techniques to identify special and common cause conditions, in which common cause was the result of systematic variability, while special cause was erratic and unpredictable.

Common Cause

Common cause variability occurs naturally in every process. Common cause variation is fluctuation caused by unknown factors resulting in a steady but random distribution of output around the average of the data. Natural or random variation, that is inherent in a process over time, affects every outcome of the process. If a process is in-control, it has only common cause variation and can be said to be predictable. Common cause variations are due to the system itself and are somewhat expected. Examples of common cause of variability are:

- Variation in the weight of an extruded textile or plastic tubing
- Variation in moisture content of a resin
- Particle size distribution in a powder
- Poor training

Special Cause

Special cause variation is normally variation that cannot be controlled by the entity in charge.

Examples of special cause variation are:

- The first labels on a roll of self-adhesive labels are damaged, marred, or otherwise unusable.
- The cartons near the door of a warehouse are exposed to rain and ruined.

Stabilize Processes

Traditional tools for process stabilization include process capability studies and control charts. The Six Sigma methodology supports the concept that a process may be improved by simply stabilizing the process. Making a process stable means to bring the process within the upper and lower specification limits and as close to the norm as possible.

Lean Manufacturing/Lean Thinking

Whereas the Six Sigma model concentrates on defect and mistake reduction, Lean Manufacturing and Lean Thinking (service-related) concentrate on:

- Waste Reduction
- Speed
- Voice of the Customer/Employee/Business/Process

Waste Reduction

In Lean Manufacturing/Thinking other terms for waste are non-value, non-value added, and the Japanese term "muda." The misconception about the term is that when items are identified as waste it does not necessarily mean that the item will be reduced or eliminated. It simply means that it does not contribute directly to the process being studied. The reduction of waste concentrates on eight key areas: transportation, inventory, motion, waiting, over processing, over production, defects, and skills.

Speed

All process improvement programs are concerned with delivering a product or service that is cost-effective and has maintained a high degree of quality.

Speed is also important but not as apparent in other process improvement programs. Speed is highly recognized in Lean Manufacturing/Thinking. One avenue for speed is automation. The term automation, like the term waste, is often misunderstood. Automation simply means standardizing processes, which is also a goal of Six Sigma.

Lean introduced a number of philosophies and tools to help in the speed and automation process to include Just-in-Time thinking principles. Individually these efforts are sometimes known as concentration of assembly, Kanban cards, bar coding, visible record systems, production leveling, and work standardization.

Voice of the Customer/Employee/Business/Process

One of the unique things about the Lean methodology is an emphasis on how the customer, employee, business, and process are impacted by the process improvement. This is often referred to as VOC, VOE, VOB, and VOP.

Additional Methodologies and Bodies of Knowledge That Play a Role in Lean Six Sigma

Quality Body of Knowledge (Q-BoK™) is a collection of outlines and documents maintained by the American Society of Quality (ASQ). These outlines are used for general information, reference, and to study for a variety of ASQ certifications. The Q-BoK contains a Six Sigma Green Belt body of knowledge and a Black Belt Six Sigma body of knowledge. ASQ was the first to establish an industry-recognized body of knowledge for Six Sigma. ASQ currently does not have a Lean Six Sigma Body of Knowledge. However, the Lean Six Sigma Body of Knowledge (SSD Global Version 3.0) contains much of the industry-accepted documentation on Six Sigma.

Business Analysis Body of Knowledge (BABOK®) is maintained by the International Institute of Business Analysis. It supports six knowledge areas.

- Business Analysis Planning and monitoring is concerned with which business analysis activities are needed. This includes identifying the stakeholders.
- Elicitation is obtaining requirements from the stakeholders.
- Requirements Management and Communication deals with contradicting requirements and changes to requirements as well as communication to stakeholders.

- Enterprise analysis defines the business need and a solution scope.
- Requirements analysis is the progressive elaboration of requirements into something that can be implemented.
- Solution assessment and validation determine which solution is best, identify any modifications that need to be made to the solution, and an assessment of whether the solution meets the business needs.

The BABOK provides a framework that describes the areas of knowledge related to business analysis. The BABOK is intended to describe and define business analysis as a discipline, rather than define the responsibilities of a person. The Guide to the BABOK is not really a methodology, which makes it easy to partner with Lean Six Sigma.

In 2005, the International Institute of Business Analysis (IIBA) created the Certified Business Analysis Professional™ (CBAP®). This certification requires documenting hands-on work experience demonstrating an understanding of business analysis in addition to passing an exam.

Project Management Body of Knowledge (PMBOK® Guide) is maintained by the Project Management Institute (PMI). All process improvement programs recognize that basic project management must be in place before process improvement may begin. The PMBOK® Guide supports nine knowledge areas:

- Integration Management
- Scope Management
- Time Management
- Cost Management
- Quality Management
- Human Resource Management
- Communications Management
- Risk Management
- Procurement Management

The PMBOK® Guide also promotes that the following phases are necessary for a successful project:

- Initiating
- Planning
- Executing
- Monitoring and Controlling
- Closing

Business Process Reengineering (BPR) is an approach intended to elevate efficiency and effectiveness of an existing business process. BPR is also known as Business Process Redesign, Business Transformation, and Business Process Change Management. BPR supports the following methodologies for process improvement:

- Process Identification
- Review Update As-Is State
- Design To-Be
- Test and Implement To-Be

Change Management has a variety of meanings depending on the area. All areas of change management play a role in the New Lean Six Sigma. These areas include:

- Project Management refers to a project management process where changes are formally introduced and approved.
- Information Technology Service Management (ITSM) is a discipline used by IT professionals.
- People Change management is a structured approach to change individuals, teams, organizations, and societies.

Leadership Development traditionally has focused on developing leadership ability. In a Lean Six Sigma organization, these methods are imperative to the success of Lean Six Sigma Black Belts and Master Black Belts. Successful leadership development is generally linked to the following:

- Individual's ability to learn
- Quality and nature of the leadership development program
- Genuine support for the leader's supervisor

Leaders play a key role in building a successful Lean Six Sigma organization. There are four main areas of responsibility:

- Choosing the right projects
- Choosing the right people
- Following the right methodology
- Clearly defining roles and responsibility

Measurement Systems Analysis (MSA) is a science that considers selecting the right measurement. Studying the measurement interactions along with assessing the measurement device is also part of the mix. Are measures reliable and valid? What is the measurement uncertainty?

Statistics is the science of making effective use of numerical data relating to groups of individuals or experiments. Six Sigma and Lean have always included the field of statistics when measuring and analyzing data. The new International Lean Six Sigma Practitioner has to make these studies more digestible for the everyday person. A stronger emphasis is placed on choosing the right software and making sure that the statistic is valid.

Business Finance plays a stronger role for the new International Lean Six Sigma Practitioner. The buy-in and continued support of a project cannot be based solely on statistical data. Choosing the right Return on Investment formula and being able to measure project success using financial terms has become essential.

As we move forward as International Lean Six Sigma Practitioners it is important to remember that Lean Six Sigma is not just a matter of blending two highly successful process methodologies but rather encompassing a collection of bodies of knowledge.

Organizational Development is a body of knowledge and practice that enhances organizational performance and individual development. Today's organizations operate in a rapidly changing environment. One of the most important assets for an organization is the ability to manage change. Although there is not an industry-standard established document outlining the things necessary for successful organizational development, most professionals in this field rely on the works of William Bridges. Bridges is known as one of the foremost thinkers and speakers in the areas of change management and personal transition. Themes throughout Bridges's work encourage recognizing the various phases of change. The most popular being: Freezing, Changing, Re-freezing.

Section 2: Lean Six Sigma Knowledge

Systematic Approach to Eliminating/Reducing Waste and Eliminating Defects

The Internal Lean Six Sigma (ILSS) methodology foundation is Six Sigma. Six Sigma concentrates on eliminating defects using statistical thinking and is more fully described in Section 1. ILSS is strongly influenced by Lean Manufacturing/Thinking which supports a recognition of waste, speed, and considering things such as the Voice of the Customer, Voice of the Employee, Voice of the Business, and Voice of the Process.

Lean Six Sigma also recognizes a number of other bodies of knowledge, outlined in Section 1, that include:

- Total Quality Management (TQM)
- ISO
- CMMI
- Quality Body of Knowledge (Q-BoK)
- Business Analysis Body of Knowledge (BABOK)
- Project Management Body of Knowledge (PMBOK® Guide)
- Business Process Reengineering (BPR)
- Change Management
- Leadership Development
- Measurement Systems Analysis
- Statistics
- Business Finance
- Organizational Development

This makes Lean Six Sigma better, faster, and more cost-effective, which is the overall goal of any process improvement program.

Primarily Lean Six Sigma uses the DMAIC model, explained in Section 1, but does take advantage of the Plan–Do–Check–Act model and infrequently will use Design for Six Sigma (DFSS). The DFSS model is briefly discussed in Section 1, of this document. PDCA is as follows.

Plan–Do–Check–Act (PDCA)

The Plan–Do–Check–Act model (PDCA) is sometimes referred to as the Plan–Do–Study–Act model (PDSA). Checking would apply to an actual project whereas the term study would apply, in most cases, to a research project.

In ILSS, PDCA is most often used when the person already has a solid idea of how to solve the problem, or if they do not have time to use the DMAIC model. In some cases, a PDCA/PDSA may be used within the phases of the DMAIC. Any project management tools typically associated with PDCA/PDSA may be used; however, there is an additional set of ILSS tools that can work in partnership to make the PDCA/PDSA models more robust. Keep in mind that any project management tool, by default, is considered an ILSS tool. PDCA/PDSA is typically used for cheaper projects and takes less time to complete. PDCA was made popular by W. Edwards Deming, who is considered by many to be the father of modern quality control; however, it was always referred to by him as the "Shewhart Cycle." It was used by the US military during WWII.

The generally accepted steps in a PDCA/PDSA are as follows:

- **Plan:** Establish the objectives and processes necessary to deliver results in accordance with the expected output.
- **Do:** Implement the new process on a small scale if possible.
- **Check/Study:** Measure the new processes and compare the results against the expected results to ascertain any differences.
- **Act:** Act or abandon the project.

Important Names in Lean Six Sigma

There are many contributors to Lean Six Sigma and several were the original pioneers of the Total Quality Management movement. The names that International Lean Six Sigma Practitioners should know are in the following paragraphs. Further reading is encouraged on these contributors. International Lean Six Sigma Practitioners will greatly benefit from an understanding of the philosophy and spirit that created Lean Six Sigma and process improvement in general. Here are brief biographies:

Walter Shewhart

Walter Shewhart is often referred to as the grandfather of the quality movement. Both W. Edwards Deming and Joseph Juran were students of Shewhart. Dr. Shewhart believed that lack of information greatly hampered the efforts of control and management processes in a production environment. In order to aid a manager in making scientific, efficient, and economical decisions, he developed Statistical Process Control methods. Walter Shewhart was the first honorary member of the American Society of Quality in 1947.

W. Edwards Deming

The most popular name associated with quality remains W. Edwards Deming. Deming is credited with improving production in the United States during the cold war but is best known for his work in Japan. For his efforts he was awarded the Second Order of the Sacred Treasure by the former Emperor Hirohito. Japanese scientists and engineers named the famed Deming Prize after him. It is bestowed on organizations that apply and achieve stringent quality-performance criteria. The Deming Prize is still awarded today. Two documents still referenced frequently are the Deming's 14 Points and Deming's Seven Deadly Sins. Both of these documents refer to conditions and thoughts about business entities in general.

Joseph Juran

Joseph M. Juran helped establish the field of quality management and wrote the "Quality Control Handbook," which taught manufacturers worldwide how to be more efficient. This book is a textbook that is still used as foundational material in most quality engineering programs. His work in quality contributed to both Six Sigma and Lean Manufacturing. He created the Pareto principle, also known as the 80–20 rule. This rules states that 80 percent of consequences stem from 20 percent of causes. Today managers use the Pareto principle to help them separate what Mr. Juran called the "vital few" resources from the "useful many."

Malcolm Baldrige

Malcolm Baldrige was nominated to be Secretary of Commerce by President Ronald Reagan on December 11, 1980, and confirmed by the US Senate on January 22, 1981. During his tenure, Baldrige played a major role in bringing quality concepts to the government. Baldrige's award-winning managerial excellence contributed to long-term improvement in economy, efficiency, and effectiveness in government. Within the Commerce Department, Baldrige reduced the budget by more than 30% and administrative personnel by 25%.

The Malcolm Baldrige National Quality Improvement Act of 1987 established the Baldrige award which is given annually to companies showing the best quality approach and process improvement. Many of the basic criteria established for the award are built into the Lean Six Sigma process.

Genichi Taguchi

Genichi Taguchi contributed in several areas related to Six Sigma and Lean Manufacturing primarily in the area of statistics. Three of his major contributions included the Loss Function, where he devised an equation to quantify the decline of a customer's perceived value of the product. His other major contribution was of the concept of "noise," which meant distractions could interfere with process improvement. He also created Design of Experiment screening and factorial analysis models.

Eli Goldratt

Eli Goldratt in Lean Six Sigma is known for his work on Theory of Constraints, which is now called Constraint Management among most International Lean Six Sigma Practitioners. The Theory of Constraints states that we know before beginning a project that constraints will be contained within the process. Goldratt gives direction and ideas on how to handle those constraints. Goldratt is also the author of a book published in the early 1990s called *The Goal*. In this book, a novel about a businessman's view of his company, Goldratt brings out many concepts such as empowerment, win-win opportunities, and life balance that have been adopted philosophically by many textbooks on Lean Six Sigma.

Kaoru Ishikawa

Kaoru Ishikawa wanted to change the way people think about work. He urged managers to resist becoming content with merely improving a product's quality, insisting that quality improvement can always go one step further. He is best known for the Ishikawa diagram, a popular fishbone chart used in process improvement, and his thoughts that the job of quality belonged to everyone. This view was also supported by Joseph Juran.

Ishikawa also showed the importance of the seven quality tools: fishbone (Ishikawa diagram), control chart, run chart, histogram, scatter diagram, Pareto chart, and flowchart. Additionally, Ishikawa explored the concept of quality circles.

Basic Quality Concepts

ILSS supports basic quality concepts such as:

- Customer Satisfaction
- Supplier Satisfaction
- Continuous Improvement

Both customer and supplier satisfaction are based on the principle of the customer or supplier feeling that process improvement is in place and not based on return on investment or other revenue factors. In all quality efforts, making things better, faster, and more cost-effective (continuous improvement) is the key to success.

Quality Impact

Lean Six Sigma is a mistake-proofing program that believes prevention is always better than detection and is a primary belief in securing process improvement. Additionally recognizing all inputs and outputs and how the inputs ultimately impact each output is a constant consideration. How the inputs and outputs impact the customer is constantly assessed and reassessed. ILSS generally refers to Inputs as X and Outputs as Y. However, the terms Key Process Input Variables (KPIV) and Key Process Output Variables (KPOV) are also used as well as the Vital Few Xs and the Vital Few Ys—a term used often by Joseph Juran.

Section 3: Core Tools Used in Lean Six Sigma

Lean Six Sigma defines process improvement as making things better, faster, and more cost-effective. Better is another word for quality. Quality always comes with a cost. Faster, which means more efficient when used by ILSS practitioners, can only be achieved by eliminating or reducing a step in the process. Cost-effectiveness relates to profit, savings, or cost avoidance. A project that does not have the opportunity to make things better, faster, or more cost-effective may simply not be a process improvement project.

There are a number of methods used to measure process improvement. The most popular is return on investment. There are a number of formulas available to calculate both savings and profit. Financial terms commonly used in Lean Six Sigma are Return on Investment, Earned Value, and Net Present Value. Many industries like to use the Balance Scorecard technique. This technique measures improvement in the area of finance, process, training, and customer impact.

Another measure especially useful when presenting an idea about quality improvements is Cost of Poor Quality. In other words, what if we did not make this improvement? Would there be a ramification or penalty to pay?

Industry benchmarks and metrics are also an effective way to measure both the as-is state and the actual process improvement, once it is realized.

Lean Six Sigma Tools

The most popular tools used in Lean Six Sigma are the Seven Tools of Quality often referred to as the Seven Analytical Problem-Solving Tools or the Seven Tools of Process Improvement. Definitions of these tools are included in the SSD Global Lean Six Sigma Glossary available on line at www.SSDGlobal.net. They include:

- Fishbone
- Flowcharting
- Check Sheets
- Histogram/Frequency Diagram
- Pareto Chart
- Scatter Diagrams
- Control Charts

Additional Charts and Graphs that are commonly used in Lean Six Sigma include:

- Value Stream Mapping
- Gantt
- PERT
- Swim Lane Charts
- Spaghetti Diagrams
- Tim Woods or the Eight Areas of Waste
- SWOT Analysis
- FMEA Thinking Process

Less commonly used tools that may come in handy include:

- **3 Ps**
  - People
  - Product
  - Process
- **6 Ms**
  - Machines
  - Methods

  - Materials
  - Measure
  - Mother Nature
  - Manpower
- **6 Ws**
  - What
  - Where
  - Why
  - Who
  - When
  - Which
- **8 Ds—Short for the Eight Disciplines**
  - Establish the Team
  - Describe the Problem
  - Develop an Interim Containment Plan
  - Determine Root Cause
  - Choose Corrective Action
  - Implement Action
  - Prevent Recurrence
  - Recognize the Team

The Define–Measure–Analyze–Improve–Control Model (DMAIC)

As noted earlier, Lean Six Sigma concentrates on the DMAIC model for process improvement. Here are things to consider when working with the DMAIC model, also discussed in Section 1.

Define

- Core Activities include:
  - Gaining Consensus on the Statement of Work
  - Completing the Project Charter
  - Typical Project Charter Characteristics
    - Name/Title
    - Project Objectives
    - Scope
    - Deliverables

    - Assumptions/Constraints
    - Project ROI or Cost Savings
  - Forming a Team
  - Identifying the Major and Minor Stakeholders
- Key Tools in Define:
  - Project Charter Template
  - Process Map
  - Cost Benefit Analysis
  - Return on Investment and/or Cost Savings Calculations
  - Stakeholders Analysis
  - Supplier–Input–Process–Output–Customer (SIPOC) Diagram
  - Critical to Quality (CTQ) Definitions
  - DMAIC WBS
  - Quality Function Deployment/House of Quality

Measure

- Core Activities include:
  - Getting a Solid "As-Is" Picture of the Current Situation
  - Determining the Right Blend of Hard and Soft Metrics
  - Measuring the Measurement System/Measurement Systems Analysis
  - Avoiding Bias in Measurement by recognizing:
    - Linearity
    - Stability
    - Repeatability
    - Reproducibility
- Key Tools in Measure
  - Detailed Process Map
  - Benchmarking
    - Internal
    - Competitive
    - Functional
    - Collaborative
    - Generic
- Sigma Levels
- Return on Investment Calculations
- Failure Mode and Effects Analysis (FMEA)
- Industry Metrics
- Observation

- Gage R&R (repeatability and reproducibility)
- Data Collection Plans
- Scorecard

Analyze

- Core Activities in Analyze include:
  - Analyze Data
  - Determine Root Causes
  - Determine Correlations
  - Identify Variations
  - Determine Type of Data
    - Attribute
    - Variable
  - Determine Data Characteristics
  - Nominal
  - Ordinal
  - Interval
- Key Tools in Analyze
  - Basic Statistics
  - Measures of Central Tendency
    - Mean
    - Mode
    - Media
  - Range
  - Variance
  - Variation
  - Correlation
    - Positive
    - Negative
    - No Correlation
  - Confidence Levels
  - Confidence Intervals
    - Sample Size
    - Percentage
    - Population Size
  - Advanced Statistics
  - Process Capability

- Seven Tools of Quality
- The Five Whys
- Factorial Design

Improve

- Core Activities in Improve
  - List 3–5 Solutions
  - Gain Consensus on a Solution
  - Pilot Solution
  - Roll Out Solution
  - Evaluate for Process Improvement
- Key Tools in Improve
  - Decision Matrix/SWOT Analysis
  - Narrow Down List of Solutions
  - Project or Execution Plan
  - Failure Mode Effects Analysis (FMEA)
  - To Double Check Core Activities on Project Plan
  - Evaluation Tools

Control

- Core Activities in Control
  - Verify Benefits
  - Control Plan
  - Transition Plan
- Key Tools in Control
  - Measurement Tools
  - Control Charts
  - 5S Model

Pre-DMAIC Tools

There are a number of things that an International Lean Six Sigma Practitioner may elect to do prior to engaging in the DMAIC model. These include, but are not limited to, PDCA/PDSA, 5S Model, and SWOT analysis.

- Plan–Do–Check–Act (PDCA) Model (this model is discussed in Section 2)

- The Sort–Straighten–Shine–Standardize–Sustain (5S) Model
- Strengths–Weakness–Opportunity–Threats (SWOT) model

The 5S model is designed to physically organize an environment and consists of five phases: Sort, Straighten or Set-in-Order, Shine, Standardize, and Sustain. Each phase of the model has specific steps to be followed. In Sort, the first pass, all items that are obviously bad, broken, or not useful are discarded. In the Set-In-Order Phase sometimes referred to as Straighten, items are placed in piles or buckets according to pre-set criteria. For example: by colors, by seasons, by what items are used first, and so on. Shine means cleaning each pile of items but the purpose is to identify even more items that may be discarded. Standardize is developing a system of how to handle the various piles of items that have now been designated worthy to keep. Finally, the Sustain Phase, a system is developed and rolled out to keep everything in order.

A SWOT Analysis looks at quadrants to determine, via brainstorming, the Strengths, Weaknesses, Opportunities, and Threats of a project. Strengths and weaknesses can be thought of as pros and cons. A diagram that determines the pros and cons is called a Force Field Analysis. The SWOT diagram takes on additional factors such as threats to the project, or risks as well as opportunities, or possibilities. The SWOT Analysis is helpful in overall decision-making.

Constraint Management

As discussed earlier in the bio of Eli Goldratt, the Theory of Constraints is a program to allow project managers and International Lean Six Sigma Practitioners to recognize and handle various program constraints. Goldratt addresses exploiting the constraints which means making the constraints work and also the development of a constraints strategy. This is also known as Constraints Management. Types of constraints are:

- Market
- Capacity
- Resources
- Suppliers
- Finance
- Knowledge or Competence
- Policy

Section 4: Implementation

This section addresses implementing Lean Six Sigma. Lean Six Sigma is the only methodology that can be implemented as a grassroots effort. Generally speaking, all process improvement must occur from the top down. Whereas the top-down approach certainly makes ILSS easier, it is not required.

When implementing ILSS it is important to remember that Lean Six Sigma believes that basic project management must be in place in order for process improvement to take place. This includes basic project management knowledge with an understanding of financial management for the ILSS Black Belt role:

- Budget
- Earned Value
- Return on Investment

Other areas of knowledge necessary to be successful in the implementation process are as follows: Risk Management, which would include an understanding of Risk Analysis and Risk Mitigation as well as basic people management, which would include topics such as leadership, role definition, and project selections that are in alignment with the available human resources.

Basic project management activities include:

- Planning
- Assessing Risk
- Allocation of Resources
- Acquiring Human and Non-Human Resources

Primary tools used in project management include:

- Project Charter
- Process Map
- Stakeholder's Analysis
- Responsibility and Accountability Document
- Work Breakdown Structure
- Gantt Chart
- PERT Chart

Martial Art Designations Are Used to Denote Levels of Expertise

- **White Belt:** Understands terminology and program goals
- **Yellow Belt:** Understands DMAIC and tools
- **Green Belt:** Can apply to their job or area of expertise
  - Tactical Responsibilities
  - Applies Lean Six Sigma to Specific Job
- **Black Belt:** Can apply in all departments
  - Strategic Responsibilities
  - Can Make Process Improvement in Any Departments
  - Aligning Projects to Company Goals and Initiatives
  - Risk Analysis
  - Closed Loop Assessment
- **Master Black Belt:** Mentor, Coach, and Teacher/Facilitator

Arguments Supporting Lean Six Sigma Implementation

Although ILSS does not support radical change management and prefers that you work in tandem with the existing system, the argument that best supports ILSS implementation is that Lean Six Sigma is scalable, recognizes the importance of speed, and is a quality program that is also cost-effective.

Tools to express this message include:

- Voice of the Customer (VOC) Emphasis
- Collection of Data
- Analysis of Data
- Stakeholders
- Translating into Customer Requirements

Recognition of Waste as a Defect

To successfully implement Lean Six Sigma it is often necessary to help people understand the concept of waste. Mistakes are usually agreed upon but since waste or non-value is often subjective it is useful to break out the areas of waste for discussion. These include:

- Transportation and Motion
- Over Processing/Over Production

- Defects
- Skills
- Wait Time

In the implementation process it may be necessary to discuss the hidden areas of waste:

- Duplication of Reports
- Duplication of Duties

Finally, as far as buy-in is concerned in implementation, certain facts may be useful such as ILSS is inexpensive to implement and is used by many Fortune 500 companies.

Team Building

Lean Six Sigma is one of the very few methodologies that speak to the area of teams. When initiating a team it is important to explain roles and responsibilities. There are a number of team tools, primarily useful to ILSS Black Belts generally referred to as facilitation tools. However, it is important to remember various factors such as motivation.

Lean Six Sigma has adopted the popular paradigm that team development follows these phases:

- Forming
- Storming
- Norming
- Performing

This theory believes that successful activity in each phase is necessary to reach the next phase. Likewise International Lean Six Sigma Practitioners read and practice basic change management strategies to include:

- Win/Win
- Collaboration
- Agreement
- Empathy

Exploring these strategies is also helpful in conflict management and negotiation. ILSS recognizes the following situations as roadblocks to improvement:

- Lack of Critical Thinking
- Lack of Creative Thinking
- Lack of Basic Project Management Skills
- Poor Communication
- Lack of Motivation

Learning to recognize these conditions will give the International Lean Six Sigma Practitioner ideas on how to manage conflict and change management issues.

During the implementation process it is important to recognize the various voices mentioned throughout the body of knowledge that include:

- Voice of the Customer
- Voice of the Employee
- Voice of the Business (or Industry)
- Voice of the Process

Lean Six Sigma Black Belt Basic International Competency Model

Professional competency models are established to provide guidelines in determining expertise and knowledge in a particular area or subject.

The following criteria may be used for interview questions, testing, and practical application exercises.

Ability to Lead a DMAIC Project

- Complete understanding of the Define–Measure–Analyze–Improve–Control process
- Understand leadership responsibilities in deploying a Lean Six Sigma project
- Understand change management models
- Be able to communicate ideas

Ability to Describe and Identify Organizational Roadblocks and Overcome Barriers

- Lack of resources
- Management support
- Recovery techniques
- Change management techniques

Using Tools and Theories Such As

- Constraint management
- Team formation theory
- Team member selection
- Team launch
- Motivational management

Understand Benchmarking, Performance, and Financial Measures

- Best practice
- Competitive
- Collaborative
- Score cards
- Cost of Quality/Cost of Poor Quality (COQ/COPQ)
- Return on Investment (ROI)
- Net Present Value (NPV)

Use and Understand the Following Lean Six Sigma Tools

- Check Sheets
- Control Charts (line and run charts) and be able to analyze typical control chart patterns
- Critical Path
- Fishbone
- Flowcharting
- FMEA
- Gantt Chart
- Histogram
- Pareto Chart

- PERT Chart
- Scatter Diagrams
- Spaghetti Diagrams
- Swim Lane Charts
- SWOT Analysis
- Tim Woods or the Eight Areas of Waste
- Value Stream Mapping (Basic)

Define and distinguish between various types of benchmarking, including Best Practices, Competitive, and Collaborative.

Define various business performance measures, including Balanced Scorecard, Key Performance Indicators (KPI), and The Financial Impact Of Customer Loyalty.

Define financial measures, such as: Revenue Growth, Market Share, Margin, Cost of Quality (COQ)/Cost of Poor Quality (COPQ), Net Present Value (NPV), Return on Investment (ROI), and Cost Benefit Analysis.

***

SSD Global supports the concept that all process improvement programs are rooted in Total Quality Management (TQM) concepts and that process improvement first begins with a firm understanding of Project Management basics as outlined in the Project Management Body of Knowledge (PMBOK® Guide). Lean Six Sigma Black Belts and Master Black Belts should be well-versed in these areas. SSD Global suggests that International Lean Six Sigma Practitioners consider joining the Project Management Institute and/or the American Society of Quality.

SSD Global further supports that the newer and leaner Lean Six Sigma, which is based on Six Sigma with a heavy emphasis in Lean Manufacturing/Lean Thinking, has evolved to include other established bodies of knowledge. In addition to basic TQM and the PMBOK® Guide, successful Lean Six Sigma Black Belts and Master Black Belts should review, study, and monitor these additional bodies of knowledge:

- Business Analysis Body of Knowledge (BABOK)
- Business Process Reengineering (BPR)
- Change Management
- Leadership Development
- Measurement Systems Analysis

- Statistics
- Business Finance
- Organizational Development

Lean Six Sigma Body of Knowledge Narrative (SSD Global Version 5.0)

Narrative

This document expands the concepts as outlined in the Lean Six Sigma Body of Knowledge (SSD Global Version 4.0) summary outline. The following information is repeated from the summarized version.

The first entities attributed with blending Lean and Six Sigma were Allied Signal and Maytag, independently in 1999. At that time, it was referred to as "Lean and Six" as both Allied Signal and Maytag realized that the two methodologies complement one another. However, it was not until several years later that the term Lean Six Sigma became popular, and only since 2004 has been certified as an International Lean Six Sigma Practitioner gained recognition as a solid industry certification.

Over the past decade, Lean Six Sigma adopted many tools and ideologies that were not originally based on Lean or Six Sigma. In addition, the newer, leaner Lean Six Sigma has been improved to capitalize on any tools or thoughts contributing to process improvement. In other words, Lean Six Sigma has become better, faster, and more cost-effective as a methodology. It is the only methodology that works with different process improvement methodologies in its new form.

Although Six Sigma is the dominant methodology in Lean Six Sigma, which Lean Thinking heavily influences, the new, more powerful Lean Six Sigma comprises several bodies of knowledge.

This body of knowledge is presented in four parts:

- Major Process Improvement Programs That Contributed to Lean Six Sigma (Part I)
- Lean Six Sigma (Part II)
- Core Tools and Knowledge Used in Lean Six Sigma (Part III)
- Implementation (Part IV)

Part I: Major Process Improvement Programs That Contributed to Lean Six Sigma

The Primary Recognized Process Improvement Programs

Total Quality Management (TQM)

Total Quality Management (TQM) is the foundation of most process improvement programs. The core TQM strategy is to embed the awareness of quality throughout the entire organization. Both Six Sigma and Lean Manufacturing/Thinking promote concepts and tools first introduced by TQM. TQM also means continuously improving processes and products as well as reducing waste. This is why TQM aligns closely with Lean Six Sigma.

The significant difference between Lean Six Sigma and TQM is that the tools used in Lean Six Sigma are updated and less labor-intensive. Generally, the mission, goals, and philosophy of TQM are also represented in Lean Six Sigma.

Many TQM ideas and problem-solving tools can be traced back to the early 1920s when statistical theory was applied to product quality control. Using mathematical and statistical models to improve product quality was further developed in Japan in the 1940s. Americans like W. Edwards Deming and Joseph Juran led this effort. Deming popularized the idea, whereas Juran wrote much of the original literature.

Deming was a protégé of Dr. Walter Shewhart. Juran also studied with Shewhart. Shewhart is sometimes referred to as the father of statistical quality control. Shewhart's contribution to quality focuses on control charts, special/common cause variation, and analytical and statistical studies. Shewhart's work also concentrates on Statistical Process Control (SPC). Often SPC is studied as a sub-set of TQM. SPC examines various charts and graphs to determine and monitor process capability.

Beginning in the 1980s, a new phase of quality control and management began. The focus widened from the quality of products to the quality of all issues, including service opportunities within an organization. It was determined that many of the same mathematical and statistical models used to identify, monitor, and evaluate the quality of products could also be applied in the service industry.

In 1988, a significant step in quality management was made when the President of the United States established the Malcolm Baldrige Award.

This national award recognizes companies for their quality contributions. Malcolm Baldrige was responsible for bringing quality to the government during the Reagan Administration. The Baldrige Program's mission is to improve the competitiveness and performance related to quality.

The Baldrige Program was a direct result of the TQM movement and included the following:

- Raising the awareness of performance excellence
- Providing organizational assessment tools and criteria
- Educating business leaders
- Recognizing national role models in quality

TQM is a set of management practices throughout an organization to ensure that the organization consistently meets or exceeds customer requirements. In a TQM effort, all members of an organization participate in improving processes, products, and services. Quality initiatives are not limited to the Quality Department.

Modern definitions of TQM include phrases such as customer focus, the involvement of all employees, continuous improvement, and the integration of quality management into the entire organization.

Basic TQM supports:

- Line management ownership
- Employee involvement and empowerment
- Challenging quantified goals and benchmarking
- Focus on processes and improvement plans
- Specific incorporation in strategic planning
- Recognition and celebration

TQM has adopted several documents that are also used in other process improvement efforts, including the Lean Six Sigma program. Typically, these documents are identified by the following titles:

- Deming's 14 Points
- Deming's 7 Deadly Diseases
- The Deming Cycle
- Joseph Juran's Roadmap for Quality Leadership
- The Triple Constraint Model

Generally, TQM is a management approach to long-term success through customer satisfaction. It is based on the participation of all members of an organization in improving processes, products, and services.

International Standards Organization (ISO)

International Standards Organization (ISO), founded in 1947, is an international standard-setting body composed of representatives from various national standards organizations. ISO has developed over 18,000 International Standards, making it the largest standards-developing organization in the world. The ISO 9000 and ISO 14000 series are the most well-known. However, up to 1100 new ISO standards are published every year.

The ISO 9000 family explicitly addresses "Quality Management." This means what the organization does to fulfill the following:

- The customer's quality requirements, and
- Applicable regulatory requirements while aiming to
- Enhance customer satisfaction, and
- Achieve continual improvement of its performance in pursuit of these objectives

The ISO 14000 family addresses "Environmental Management." This means what the organization does to:

- Minimize harmful effects on the environment caused by its activities and to
- Achieve continual improvement of its environmental performance.

To be certified in an ISO standard, these steps are necessary:

- Locating and Selecting a Registrar—this is a company that is certified by ISO to make the initial assessment and provide suggestions for your ISO program
- Creating an application and conducting a document review
- Participating in an assessment
- Completing the ISO Registration
- Participating in a recertification effort

ISO recertification efforts include gathering the proper measurements and articulating these measurements, as well as identifying future opportunities for process improvement. There is also a time factor involved. Therefore, Lean Six Sigma often plays a primary role in ISO recertification.

Capability Maturity Model Integration (CMMI)

Capability Maturity Model Integration (CMMI) is another popular process improvement program. This integrated approach is intended to help an organization improve performance by recognizing certain performance levels. CMMI can guide process improvement across a project, a division, or an organization.

In CMMI models with a staged representation, there are five maturity levels designated by the numbers 1 through 5

6. Initial
7. Managed
8. Defined
9. Quantitatively Managed
10. Optimizing

CMMI was developed by the CMMI project, designed to improve the usability of maturity models by integrating many different models into one framework. The project consisted of members of industry, government, and the Carnegie Mellon Software Engineering Institute (SEI). The main sponsors included the Office of the Secretary of Defense (OSD) and the National Defense Industrial Association.

Each level in the CMMI process requires detailed information gathering and analysis. The significance of Lean Six Sigma in CMMI is that often, to move up one level, Lean Six Sigma practices need to be engaged.

Six Sigma

Defect Reduction

The Six Sigma problem-solving methodology is the most effective tool to reduce and eliminate defects quickly. It is a team-based methodology that systematically identifies and controls the process variables contributing to producing the fault or mistake.

DMAIC Model

Improvement of existing products or processes using the Six Sigma methodology is made in five steps:

- Define
- Measure
- Analyze
- Improve
- Control

Define

The Define Phase's purpose is to ensure that everyone understands the project and the goals of the process improvement effort. The basic steps include:

- Create a process improvement charter and process map.
- Identify or define problems that must be solved to meet or exceed the customer's specifications or expectations.
- Identify and quantify customer requirements.
- Identify and quantify the process output and defects that fall short of these requirements and create a problem statement.
- State the project goal, which must be clear and measurable, and include a time limit for completion.
- Determine the few vital factors that are Critical to Quality that need to be measured, analyzed, improved, and controlled.

Measure

The Measure Phase aims to get a solid as-is snapshot of how the process is currently behaving. The basic steps include:

- Select the Critical Quality characteristics in the process. These outputs of the given method are essential to the customer. How is the company doing now?
- Define the process output, which is accomplished by looking at the customer requirements and the project goal.
- Define the defect in the process. Remember, a defect is an output that falls outside the limits of a customer's requirements or expectations and must be measurable.

- Find the inputs to the process that contribute to defects.
- Define the exact dollar impact of eliminating the defects regarding increased profitability and cost savings.
- Measure the defects that affect the Critical to Quality characteristics and any related factors.
- Incorporate Measurement Systems Analysis—a method to make sure the defects are being measured correctly.

Analyze

The Analyze Phase aims to review the measurements and information from the previous step and determine, based on that information, what 3–5 solutions might be appropriate to solve the problem or roll out the activity.

- Determine the root cause
- Identify variations that could be reduced
- Determine if a correlation exists
- Do what-if scenarios
- Determine the timeline and cost of solutions
- Determine the sustainability of the solution

Improve

The Improve Phase aims to choose a solution, implement the solution, and be able to definitively prove that a process improvement has been accomplished definitively by comparing the as-is state (Measure) with conditions after the process improvement has been rolled out. Basic steps include:

- Articulate the three to five possible solutions
- Gain consensus on the best solution
- Pilot
- Create an execution plan (Project Plan) if the solution is successful in the pilot
- Choose another one of the three to five solutions if the pilot is not successful
- Roll out

Control

The purpose of the Control Phase is to sustain the improvement. Basic steps include:

- Clearly articulating the process improvement achieved
- Creating a control plan to keep the process in place
- Designing a transition plan for the new owner

DFSS Model

Design for Six Sigma, also known as Design for Lean Six Sigma (DFSS or DFLSS), applies only when a new product or service needs to be designed or re-designed from the very beginning. Many supporters of the DMAIC design believe this is accomplished in the Analyze and Improve Phases of the DMAIC model. However, supporters of DFSS believe a design component is necessary. Therefore, recent models based on the DMAIC thinking process that do not have a design component are also referred to as DFSS or DFLSS models.

Today the most popular DFFS model is the Define–Measure–Analyze–Design–Verify (DMADV). The DMADV model contains the first three phases of the DMAIC model. The last two phases, Improve and Control, are replaced by Design and Verify.

Design

Design details, optimize the design, and plan for design verification. This phase may require simulations.

Verify

Verify the design, set up pilot runs, implement the production process, and hand it over to the process owner(s).

Statistical Thinking

Both the DMAIC and DMADV models are based on statistical thinking. The following principles form the basis for statistical thinking:

- All work occurs in a system of interconnected processes
- Inherent variation exists in all processes
- Reducing variation is the key to successfully improving a process

Recognizing Individual Tasks within the Process and Assigning Major Causes of Variability

Breaking down into minor elements is essential to analyze a process using Statistical Process Control successfully. All methods have inherent variability, and that variability can be measured. Data is used to understand variability based on the type of variability. For example, Deming used statistical quality control techniques to identify special and common cause conditions, in which common cause resulted from systematic variability, while special reason was erratic and unpredictable.

Common Cause

Common cause variability occurs naturally in every process. Common cause variation is fluctuation caused by unknown factors resulting in a steady but random distribution of output around the average of the data. Natural or random variation, inherent in a process over time, affects every outcome. If a function is in control, it has only common cause variation and can be said to be predictable. Common cause variations are due to the system itself and are somewhat expected. Examples of common causes of variability are:

- Variation in the weight of an extruded textile or plastic tubing
- Variation in moisture content of a resin
- Particle size distribution in a powder
- Poor training

Special Cause

Special cause variation usually cannot be controlled by the entity in charge. Examples of particular cause variation are:

- The first labels on a roll of self-adhesive labels are damaged, marred, or otherwise unusable.
- The cartons near a warehouse door are exposed to rain and ruined.

Stabilize Processes

Traditional tools for process stabilization include process capability studies and control charts. The Six Sigma methodology supports the concept that a process may be improved by simply stabilizing the process. Making a process stable means bringing the process within the upper and lower specification limits and as close to the norm as possible.

Lean Manufacturing/Lean Thinking

Whereas the Six Sigma model concentrates on defect and mistake reduction, Lean Manufacturing and Lean Thinking (service-related) concentrate on:

- Waste Reduction
- Speed
- Voice of the Customer/Employee/Business/Process

Waste Reduction

In Lean Manufacturing/Thinking, other terms for waste are non-value, nonvalue added, and the Japanese term "muda." The misconception about time is that when items are identified as waste, it does not necessarily mean they will be reduced or eliminated. It simply means that it does not contribute directly to the studied process. The reduction of waste concentrates on eight key areas: transportation, inventory, motion, waiting, over-processing, overproduction, defects, and skills.

Speed

All process improvement programs are concerned with delivering a cost-effective product or service that has maintained a high degree of quality. Speed is also essential but not as apparent in other process improvement programs. Rate is universally recognized in Lean Manufacturing/Thinking. One avenue for speed is automation. The term automation, like the term waste, needs to be understood. Automation means standardizing processes, which is also a goal of Six Sigma.

Lean introduced several philosophies and tools to help in the speed and automation process, including Just-in-Time thinking principles. Individually these efforts are sometimes known as concentration of assembly, Kanban cards, bar coding, visible record systems, production leveling, and work standardization.

Voice of the Customer/Employee/Business/Process

One of the unique things about the Lean methodology is an emphasis on how the customer, employee, business, and process are impacted by the process improvement. This is often called VOC, VOE, VOB, and VOP.

Additional Methodologies and Bodies of Knowledge That Play a Role in Lean Six Sigma

Quality Body of Knowledge (Q-BoK™) is a collection of outlines and documents maintained by the American Society of Quality (ASQ). These outlines are used for general information, reference, and to study for various ASQ certifications. The Q-BoK contains a Six Sigma Green Belt body of knowledge and a Black Belt Six Sigma body of knowledge. ASQ was the first to establish an industry-recognized body of knowledge for Six Sigma. ASQ currently does not have a Lean Six Sigma Body of Knowledge. However, the Lean Six Sigma Body of Knowledge (SSD Global Version 3.0) contains much of the industry-accepted documentation on Six Sigma.

The International Institute of Business Analysis maintains a Business Analysis Body of Knowledge (BABOK®). It supports six knowledge areas.

- Business Analysis Planning and monitoring concerns which business analysis activities are needed. This includes identifying the stakeholders.
- Elicitation is obtaining requirements from the stakeholders.
- Requirements Management and Communication deal with contradicting requirements and changes to needs and communication with stakeholders.
- Enterprise analysis defines the business need and solution scope.
- Requirements analysis is the progressive elaboration of requirements into something that can be implemented.
- Solution assessment and validation determine which solution is best, identify any modifications that need to be made to the solution, and evaluate whether the solution meets the business needs.

The BABOK provides a framework that describes the areas of knowledge related to business analysis. The BABOK is intended to describe and define business analysis as a discipline rather than clarify the responsibilities of a person. As a result, the Guide to the BABOK is not a methodology, making it easy to partner with Lean Six Sigma.

In 2005, the International Institute of Business Analysis (IIBA) created the Certified Business Analysis Professional™ (CBAP®). This certification requires documenting hands-on work experience, demonstrating an understanding of business analysis and passing an exam.

Project Management Body of Knowledge (PMBOK® Guide) is maintained by the Project Management Institute (PMI). All process improvement programs recognize that essential project management must be in place before process improvement may begin. The PMBOK® Guide supports nine knowledge areas:

- Integration Management
- Scope Management
- Time Management
- Cost Management
- Quality Management
- Human Resource Management
- Communications Management
- Risk Management
- Procurement Management

The PMBOK® Guide also promotes that the following phases are necessary for a successful project:

- Initiating
- Planning
- Executing
- Monitoring and Controlling
- Closing

Business Process Reengineering (BPR) is an approach intended to elevate the efficiency and effectiveness of an existing business process. BPR is also known as Business Process Redesign, Business Transformation, and Business Process Change Management. BPR supports the following methodologies for process improvement:

- Process Identification
- Review Update As-Is State
- Design To-Be
- Test and Implement To-Be

Change Management has a variety of meanings depending on the area. However, all areas of change management play a role in the New Lean Six Sigma. These areas include:

- Project Management refers to a process of formally introducing and approving changes.
- Information Technology Service Management (ITSM) is a discipline used by IT professionals.
- People Change management is a structured approach to change individuals, teams, organizations, and societies.

Leadership Development traditionally has focused on developing leadership ability. In a Lean Six Sigma organization, these methods are imperative to the success of Lean Six Sigma Black Belts and Master Black Belts. Successful leadership development is generally linked to the following:

- Individual's ability to learn
- Quality and nature of the leadership development program
- Genuine support for the leader's supervisor

Leaders play a crucial role in building a successful Lean Six Sigma organization. There are four main areas of responsibility:

- Choosing the suitable projects
- Choosing the right people
- Following the proper methodology
- Clearly defining roles and responsibility

Measurement Systems Analysis (MSA) is a science that considers selecting the correct measurement. Studying the measurement interactions and assessing the measurement device is also part of the mix. Are measures reliable and valid? What is the measurement uncertainty?

Statistics is the science of effectively using numerical data relating to groups of individuals or experiments. Six Sigma and Lean have always included statistics when measuring and analyzing data. The new International Lean Six Sigma Practitioner has to make these studies more digestible for the everyday person. More emphasis is placed on choosing the right software and ensuring the statistic is valid.

Business Finance is more decisive for the new International Lean Six Sigma Practitioner. A project's buy-in and continued support cannot be based solely on statistical data. Choosing the right Return on Investment formula and measuring project success using financial terms has become essential.

As we move forward as International Lean Six Sigma Practitioners, it is crucial to remember that Lean Six Sigma is not just a matter of blending two phenomenally successful process methodologies but encompassing a collection of bodies of knowledge.

Organizational Development is a body of knowledge and practice that enhances organizational performance and individual development. Today's organizations operate in a rapidly changing environment. Therefore, one of the most critical assets for an organization is the ability to manage change. Although there is not an industry standard established document outlining the things necessary for successful organizational development, most professionals in this field rely on the works of William Bridges. Bridges is one of the foremost thinkers and speakers in change management and personal transition. Themes throughout Bridges' career encourage recognizing the various phases of change—the most popular are: Freezing, Changing, and Re-freezing.

Part II: Lean Six Sigma Knowledge

Systematic Approach to Eliminating/Reducing Waste and Eliminating Defects

The Internal Lean Six Sigma (ILSS) methodology foundation is Six Sigma. Six Sigma concentrates on eliminating defects using statistical thinking and is more fully described in Part I. ILSS is strongly influenced by Lean Manufacturing/Thinking, which supports recognizing waste and speed and considering things such as the Voice of the Customer, the Voice of the Employee, the Voice of the Business, and the Voice of the Process.

Lean Six Sigma also recognizes several other bodies of knowledge, outlined in Part I, that include:

- Total Quality Management (TQM)
- ISO
- CMMI
- Quality Body of Knowledge (Q-BoK)
- Business Analysis Body of Knowledge (BABOK)
- Project Management Body of Knowledge (PMBOK® Guide)

- Business Process Reengineering (BPR)
- Change Management
- Leadership Development
- Measurement Systems Analysis
- Statistics
- Business Finance
- Organizational Development

This makes Lean Six Sigma better, faster, and more cost-effective, which is the overall goal of any process improvement program.

Primarily Lean Six Sigma uses the DMAIC model, explained in Part I, but does take advantage of the Plan–Do–Check–Act model and infrequently will use Design for Six Sigma (DFSS). The DFSS model is briefly discussed in Part I of this document. PDCA is as follows.

Plan–Do–Check–Act (PDCA)

The Plan–Do–Check–Act model (PDCA) is sometimes called the Plan–Do–Study–Act model (PDSA). This is because checking would apply to an actual project, whereas the term study would apply, in most cases, to a research project.

In ILSS, PDCA is most often used when the person already has a solid idea of how to solve the problem or needs more time to use the DMAIC model. In some cases, a PDCA/PDSA may be used within the phases of the DMAIC. Any project management tools typically associated with PDCA/PDSA may be used; however, an additional set of ILSS tools can work in partnership to make the PDCA/PDSA models more robust. Keep in mind that any project management tool, by default, is considered an ILSS tool. PDCA/PDSA is typically used for cheaper projects and takes less time to complete. PDCA was made famous by W. Edwards Deming, who is considered by many to be the father of modern quality control; however, it was always referred to by him as the "Shewhart Cycle." The US military used it during WWII.

The generally accepted steps in a PDCA/PDSA are as follows:

- **Plan:** Establish the objectives and processes necessary to deliver results by the expected output.
- **Do:** Implement the new process on a small scale if possible.

- **Check/Study:** Measure the new processes and compare the results against the expected results to ascertain differences.
- **Act:** Act or abandon the project.

Important Names in Lean Six Sigma

There are many contributors to Lean Six Sigma; several were the original pioneers of the Total Quality Management movement. International Lean Six Sigma Practitioners should know the names in the following paragraphs. Further reading is encouraged on these contributors. In addition, International Lean Six Sigma Practitioners will significantly benefit from understanding the philosophy and spirit that created Lean Six Sigma and process improvement in general. Here are brief biographies:

Walter Shewhart

Walter Shewhart is often referred to as the grandfather of the quality movement. Both W. Edwards Deming and Joseph Juran were students of Shewhart. Dr. Shewhart believed that lack of information significantly hampered the efforts of control and management processes in a production environment. To aid a manager in making scientific, efficient, and economical decisions, he developed Statistical Process Control methods. Walter Shewhart was the first honorary member of the American Society of Quality in 1947.

W. Edwards Deming

The most famous name associated with quality remains W. Edwards Deming. Deming is credited with improving production in the United States during the cold war but is best known for his work in Japan. The former Emperor Hirohito awarded him the Second Order of the Sacred Treasure for his efforts. Japanese scientists and engineers named the famed Deming Prize after him. It is bestowed on organizations that apply and achieve stringent quality-performance criteria. The Deming Prize is still awarded today. Two documents still referenced frequently are Deming's 14 Points and Deming's Seven Deadly Sins. Both documents refer to conditions and thoughts about business entities in general.

Joseph Juran

Joseph M. Juran helped establish the field of quality management and wrote the "Quality Control Handbook," which taught manufacturers worldwide how to be more efficient. This book is a textbook that is still used as foundational material in most quality engineering programs. His work in quality contributed to both Six Sigma and Lean Manufacturing. In addition, he created the Pareto principle, also known as the 80–20 rule. This rule states that 80 percent of consequences stem from 20 percent of causes. Today managers use the Pareto principle to help them separate what Mr. Juran called the "vital few" resources from the "useful many."

Malcolm Baldrige

President Ronald Reagan nominated Malcolm Baldrige to be Secretary of Commerce on December 11, 1980 and confirmed by the US Senate on January 22, 1981. Baldrige played a significant role in bringing quality concepts to the government during his tenure. Baldrige's award-winning managerial excellence contributed to long-term economic improvement, efficiency, and effectiveness in government. Within the Commerce Department, Baldrige reduced the budget by more than 30% and administrative personnel by 25%.

The Malcolm Baldrige National Quality Improvement Act of 1987 established the Baldrige Award, which is given annually to companies showing the best quality approach and process improvement. Many of the primary criteria established for the award are built into the Lean Six Sigma process.

Genichi Taguchi

Genichi Taguchi contributed to several areas related to Six Sigma and Lean Manufacturing, primarily in statistics. Three of his significant contributions included the Loss Function, where he devised an equation to quantify the decline of a customer's perceived product value. His other notable contribution was the concept of "noise," which meant distractions could interfere with process improvement. He also created the Design of Experiment screening and factorial analysis models.

Eli Goldratt

Eli Goldratt in Lean Six Sigma is known for his work on the Theory of Constraints, now called Constraint Management among most International Lean Six Sigma Practitioners. The Theory of Constraints states that we know before beginning a project that constraints will be contained within the process. Goldratt gives direction and ideas on how to manage those constraints. Goldratt is also the author of a book published in the early 1990s called *The Goal.* In this book, a novel about a businessman's view of his company, Goldratt brings out many concepts such as empowerment, win-win opportunities, and life balance that have been adopted philosophically by many textbooks on Lean Six Sigma.

Kaoru Ishikawa

Kaoru Ishikawa wanted to change the way people think about work. He urged managers to resist becoming content with merely improving a product's quality, insisting that quality improvement can always go one step further. He is best known for the Ishikawa diagram, a famous fishbone chart used in process improvement, and his thoughts that the quality job belonged to everyone. Joseph Juran also supported this view.

Ishikawa also showed the importance of the seven quality tools: fishbone (Ishikawa diagram), control chart, run chart, histogram, scatter diagram, Pareto chart, and flowchart. Additionally, Ishikawa explored the concept of quality circles.

Basic Quality Concepts

ILSS supports basic quality concepts such as:

- Customer Satisfaction
- Supplier Satisfaction
- Continuous Improvement

Customer and supplier satisfaction is based on the customer or supplier's feeling that process improvement is in place, not on return on investment or other revenue factors. In all quality efforts, improving things faster and more cost-effectively (continuous improvement) is the key to success.

Quality Impact

Lean Six Sigma is a mistake-proofing program that believes prevention is always better than detection and is a primary belief in securing process improvement. Additionally, recognizing all inputs and outputs and how the inputs ultimately impact each work is a constant consideration. How the inputs and outputs affect the customer is constantly assessed and reassessed. ILSS generally refers to Inputs as X and Outputs as Y. However, the terms Key Process Input Variables (KPIV) and Key Process Output Variables (KPOV) are also used, as well as the Vital Few Xs and the Vital Few Ys—a term used often by Joseph Juran.

Part III: Core Tools Used in Lean Six Sigma

Lean Six Sigma defines process improvement as improving things faster and more cost-effectively. Better is another word for quality. Quality always comes with a cost. More quickly, which means more efficiency when ILSS practitioners use, can only be achieved by eliminating or reducing a step in the process. Cost-effectiveness relates to profit, savings, or cost avoidance. A project that does not have the opportunity to make things better, faster, or more cost-effective may not be a process improvement project.

There are several methods used to measure process improvement. The most popular is the return on investment. There are several formulas available to calculate both savings and profit. Financial terms commonly used in Lean Six Sigma are Return on Investment, Earned Value, and Net Present Value. In addition, many industries like to use the Balance Scorecard technique. This technique measures improvement in finance, process, training, and customer impact.

The Cost of Poor Quality is another measure handy when presenting an idea about quality improvements. In other words, what if we still need to make this improvement? Would there be a ramification or penalty to pay? Industry benchmarks and metrics are also an effective way to measure both the as-is state and the actual process improvement once it is realized.

Lean Six Sigma Tools

The most popular tools used in Lean Six Sigma are the Seven Tools of Quality, often called the Seven Analytical Problem-Solving Tools or the Seven Tools of Process Improvement. Definitions of these tools are included in the SSD Global Lean Six Sigma Glossary, available online at www.SSDGlobal.net. They include:

- Fishbone
- Flowcharting
- Check Sheets
- Histogram/Frequency Diagram
- Pareto Chart
- Scatter Diagrams
- Control Charts

Additional charts and graphs that are commonly used in Lean Six Sigma include:

- Value Stream Mapping
- Gantt
- PERT
- Swim Lane Charts
- Spaghetti Diagrams
- Tim Woods or the Eight Areas of Waste
- SWOT Analysis
- FMEA Thinking Process

Less commonly used tools that may come in handy include:

- **3 Ps**
  - People
  - Product
  - Process
- **6 Ms**
  - Machines
  - Methods
  - Materials
  - Measure
  - Mother Nature
  - Workforce
- **6 Ws**
  - What
  - Where
  - Why

- Who
- When
- Which

- **8 Ds—Short for the Eight Disciplines**
  - Establish the Team
  - Describe the Problem
  - Develop an Interim Containment Plan
  - Determine the Root Cause
  - Choose Corrective Action
  - Implement Action
  - Prevent Recurrence
  - Recognize the Team

The Define–Measure–Analyze–Improve–Control

As noted earlier, Lean Six Sigma concentrates on the DMAIC model for process improvement. Here are things to consider when working with the DMAIC model, also discussed in Part I.

Define

- Core Activities include:
  - Gaining Consensus on the Statement of Work
  - Completing the Project Charter
  - Typical Project Charter Characteristics
    - Name/Title
    - Project Objectives
    - Scope
    - Deliverables
    - Assumptions/Constraints
    - Project ROI or Cost Savings
  - Forming a Team
  - Identifying the Major and Minor Stakeholders
- Key Tools in Define:
  - Project Charter Template
  - Process Map
  - Cost Benefit Analysis
  - Return on Investment and Cost Savings Calculations

  - Stakeholders Analysis
  - Supplier–Input–Process–Output–Customer (SIPOC) Diagram
  - Critical to Quality (CTQ) Definitions
  - DMAIC WBS
  - Quality Function Deployment/House of Quality

Measure

- Core Activities Include:
  - Getting a Solid "As-Is" Picture of the Current Situation
  - Determining the Right Blend of Hard and Soft Metrics
  - Measuring the Measurement System/Measurement Systems Analysis
  - Avoiding Bias in Measurement by recognizing:
    - Linearity
    - Stability
    - Repeatability
    - Reproducibility
- Key Tools in Measure
  - Detailed Process Map
  - Benchmarking
    - Internal
    - Competitive
    - Functional
    - Collaborative
    - Generic
- Sigma Levels
- Return on Investment Calculations
- Failure Mode and Effects Analysis (FMEA)
- Industry Metrics
- Observation
- Gage R&R (repeatability and reproducibility)
- Data Collection Plans
- Scorecard

Analyze

- Core Activities in Analyze include:
  - Analyze Data
  - Determine Root Causes

  - Determine Correlations
  - Identify Variations
  - Determine the Type of Data
    - Attribute
    - Variable
  - Determine Data Characteristics
  - Nominal
  - Ordinal
  - Interval
- Key Tools in Analyze
  - Basic Statistics
  - Measures of Central Tendency
    - Mean
    - Mode
    - Media
  - Range
  - Variance
  - Variation
  - Correlation
    - Positive
    - Negative
    - No Correlation
  - Confidence Levels
  - Confidence Intervals
    - Sample Size
    - Percentage
    - Population Size
  - Advanced Statistics
  - Process Capability
- Seven Tools of Quality
- The Five Whys
- Factorial Design

Improve

- Core Activities to Improve
  - List 3–5 Solutions
  - Gain Consensus on a Solution
  - Pilot Solution

- Roll Out Solution
- Evaluate for Process Improvement
- Key Tools to Improve
  - Decision Matrix/SWOT Analysis
  - Narrow Down the List of Solutions
  - Project or Execution Plan
  - Failure Mode Effects Analysis (FMEA)
  - To Double Check Core Activities on Project Plan
  - Evaluation Tools

Control

- Core Activities in Control
  - Verify Benefits
  - Control Plan
  - Transition Plan
- Key Tools in Control
  - Measurement Tools
  - Control Charts
  - 5S Model

Pre-DMAIC Tools

There are several things that an International Lean Six Sigma Practitioner may elect to do before engaging in the DMAIC model. These include but are not limited to PDCA/PDSA, 5S Model, and SWOT analysis.

- Plan–Do–Check–Act (PDCA) Model (this model is discussed in Part II)
- The Sort–Straighten–Shine–Standardize–Sustain (5S) Model
- Strengths–Weakness–Opportunity–Threats (SWOT) model

The 5S model is designed to organize an environment physically and consists of five phases: Sort, Straighten or Set-in-Order, Shine, Standardize, and Sustain. Each stage of the model has specific steps to be followed. In Sort, the first pass, all harmful, broken, or useless items are discarded. In the Set-In-Order Phase, sometimes referred to as straightening, items are placed in piles or buckets according to a pre-set criterion. For example: by colors, by seasons, by what items are used first, and so on. Shine means cleaning each pile of items, but the purpose is to identify even more things that may be discarded. Standardize is developing a system of overseeing the various banks of items that are now designated worthy of keeping. Finally, a method is developed and rolled out in the Sustain Phase to keep everything in order.

A SWOT Analysis looks at quadrants to determine, via brainstorming, the project's Strengths, Weaknesses, Opportunities, and Threats. Strengths and weaknesses can be thought of as pros and cons. A diagram that determines the pros and cons is called a Force Field Analysis. The SWOT diagram takes on additional factors such as threats to the project, risks, opportunities, or possibilities. The SWOT Analysis is helpful in overall decision-making.

Constraint Management

As discussed earlier in the bio of Eli Goldratt, the Theory of Constraints is a program to allow project managers and International Lean Six Sigma Practitioners to recognize and manage various program constraints. Goldratt addresses exploiting the rules, which means making the rules work and developing a constraint strategy. This is also known as Constraints Management. Types of conditions are:

- Market
- Capacity
- Resources
- Suppliers
- Finance
- Knowledge or Competence
- Policy

Part IV: Implementation

This part addresses implementing Lean Six Sigma. Lean Six Sigma is the only methodology that can be implemented as a grassroots effort. Generally speaking, all process improvement must occur from the top down. Whereas the top-down approach certainly makes ILSS easier, it is not required.

When implementing ILSS, it is essential to remember that Lean Six Sigma believes critical project management must be in place for process improvement. This includes basic project management knowledge with an understanding of financial management for the ILSS Black Belt role:

- Budget
- Earned Value
- Return on Investment

Other areas of knowledge necessary to be successful in the implementation process are as follows: Risk Management, which would include an understanding of Risk Analysis and Risk Mitigation as well as essential people management, which would consist of topics such as leadership, role definition, and project selections that are in alignment with the available human resources.

Basic project management activities include:

- Planning
- Assessing Risk
- Allocation of Resources
- Acquiring Human and Non-Human Resources

Primary tools used in project management include:

- Project Charter
- Process Map
- Stakeholder's Analysis
- Responsibility and Accountability Document
- Work Breakdown Structure
- Gantt Chart
- PERT Chart

Martial Art Designations Are Used to Denote Levels of Expertise

- **White Belt:** Understands terminology and program goals
- **Yellow Belt:** Understands DMAIC and tools
- **Green Belt:** Can apply to their job or area of expertise
  - Tactical Responsibilities
  - Applies Lean Six Sigma to Specific Job
- **Black Belt:** Can apply in all departments
  - Strategic Responsibilities

- Can Make Process Improvements in any Department
- Aligning Projects to Company Goals and Initiatives
- Risk Analysis
- Closed Loop Assessment

- **Master Black Belt:** Mentor, Coach, and Teacher/Facilitator

Arguments Supporting Lean Six Sigma Implementation

Although ILSS does not support radical change management and prefers that you work in tandem with the existing system, the argument that best supports ILSS implementation is that Lean Six Sigma is scalable, recognizes the importance of speed, and is a quality program that is also cost-effective.

Tools to express this message include:

- Voice of the Customer (VOC) Emphasis
- Collection of Data
- Analysis of Data
- Stakeholders
- Translating into Customer Requirements

Recognition of Waste as a Defect

To successfully implement Lean Six Sigma, it is often necessary to help people understand the concept of waste. Mistakes are usually agreed upon, but since waste or non-value is often subjective, it is helpful to break out the waste areas for discussion. These include:

- Transportation and Motion
- Over-Processing/Over Production
- Defects
- Skills
- Wait Time

In the implementation process, it may be necessary to discuss the hidden areas of waste:

- Duplication of Reports
- Duplication of Duties

Finally, regarding buy-in in implementation, specific facts may be helpful, such as ILSS being inexpensive to implement and used by many Fortune 500 companies.

Team Building

Lean Six Sigma is one of the few methodologies that speak to teams. When initiating a group, it is essential to explain roles and responsibilities. Several team tools are valuable for ILSS Black Belts, generally called facilitation tools. However, it is vital to remember various factors, such as motivation.

Lean Six Sigma has adopted the popular paradigm that team development follows these phases:

- Forming
- Storming
- Norming
- Performing

This theory believes that successful activity in each phase is necessary to reach the next step. Likewise, International Lean Six Sigma Practitioners read and practice fundamental change management strategies, including:

- Win/Win
- Collaboration
- Agreement
- Empathy

Exploring these strategies is also helpful in conflict management and negotiation. ILSS recognizes the following situations as roadblocks to improvement:

- Lack of Critical Thinking
- Lack of Creative Thinking
- Lack of Basic Project Management Skills
- Poor Communication
- Lack of Motivation

Recognizing these conditions will give the International Lean Six Sigma Practitioner ideas on managing conflict and change management issues.

During the implementation process, it is essential to recognize the various voices mentioned throughout the body of knowledge that includes:

- Voice of the Customer
- Voice of the Employee
- Voice of the Business (or Industry)
- Voice of the Process

SSD Global Solutions Model for International Innovative Design Watermark–Creation–Enhancement–Application (WCEA©)

Many sophisticated design innovation models are industry-specific. The International Lean Six Sigma (ILSS) practitioner should always attempt to work within the parameters of the company model. However, the ILSS practitioner could be asked to build a model to facilitate innovative design or assess an existing model. For this reason, the ILSS practitioner should be prepared. Fully understanding the Design–Measure–Analyze–Improve–Control (DMAIC) model will provide the ILSS with the most core activities.

SSD Global created the Watermark–Creation–Enhancement–Application (WCEA) model for two purposes. The first is to provide a framework for the ILSS practitioner, new to innovative design. In this case, the WCEA model may be considered a template for building a model. Once the basic framework is filled in with the industry specifics, the ILSS practitioner can begin to mistake-proof and modify the model by conducting interviews with staff involved in the use of the model. The second purpose is to provide the ILSS practitioner with a quick education on terms and processes typically used in innovative design environments.

Throughout projects dealing with innovation, many activities reflect those used within the Define Phase of the DMAIC model. Likewise, metrics that facilitate these activities are used in the Measure, Analyze, and Control Phases.

The four phases of the WCEA model include:

- Watermark
- Creation
- Enhancement
- Application

Watermark

Think of the Watermark Phase as the big picture. The first step is simply getting a broad view or perspective of the innovation. What will the innovation accomplish? What resources would be needed? Who is the audience? Is it marketable? Watermark is managed by discussion and illustration. No attempt is made to create any business plan. People would describe this phase as agile, meaning that if someone introduces another idea, the conversation may take a different direction.

Attention should be focused on the user. What will the user gain? What type of training, if any, will the user need? When the Watermark Phase is concluded, is there a clear understanding of what product will be built? Although many of the activities in Watermark are similar to those performed in the Define Phase of the DMAIC model, the next step at the end of this phase is to complete the design and build.

Naturally, designers would be included in this session. Much of the go or no-go decision will depend on how well the designer can convert thought into simple visuals. Someone from marketing can help create an engaging narrative. Engineering or Information Technology (IT) should be included to help with any reality checks needed. A strong facilitator is required to manage this meeting. Design, in general, is a highly collaborative activity.

Business Process Modeling (BPM) in systems engineering represents an enterprise's processes so that the current process may be analyzed and improved. BPM is typically performed by business analysts and managers seeking to improve process efficiency and quality. It is remarkably similar to a Value Stream Map (VSM). In general, VSM tends to concentrate on speed and waste. BPM focuses slightly more on the impact on other departments and often incorporates IT or other processes in the background. Although BPM differs from innovative design, many of the core tools used in the BPM practice can be applied in the Watermark Phase of this model.

Much of BPM is now computerized and available in software packages. For the ILSS practitioner, the challenge is to think about the psychology and logic behind creating these electronic tools. Considering the individual building blocks addressed in BPM will help finalize the Watermark Phase. These components include:

- Company
- Client (Consumer)

- Flow from Company to Client
- Flow from Client to Company

Creation

In the WCEA model, the Creation Phase is where the design is completed and the product is built. This would encompass several steps in the DMAIC or Design for Six Sigma (DFSS) model. The most common DFSS model is the Define–Measure–Analyze–Design–Verify (DMADV). Creation would take place in the DMADV model in the Design Phase.

The basic blueprint for the Creation Phase has already been recorded in Watermark. Now, engineering must solidify the design and build the product. This is typically the most labor-intensive part of the process. This is where recording, writing, or videotaping information is done. Some products are easier to create than others. In this Phase of this model, attention is given primarily to the prototype. Mass manufacturing is considered at a later date. Therefore, the possibility of applying Lean Manufacturing concepts should be addressed. Another area crucial to the success of the Creation Phase is Time Management. Producing and keeping a schedule, and recognizing when resources are available, is essential.

In this phase, it is essential to incorporate any compliance or regulation issues that might impact the product.

Enhancement

The Enhancement Phase is about optimizing the product before the rollout. Optimizing is modifying or adjusting a process or product for the best performance. This means minimizing variation and eliminating defects.

Six Sigma offers a variety of tools to do this since variation reduction and a focus on defect elimination are the heart of the methodology. Usually, engineering is still involved in this phase; however, the dynamics and the objectives change. Many of the tools used in the Measure Phase of the DMAIC model are used since the first step to optimization would be getting a clear picture of where the product stands. Where the possible variables exist must be recorded before an attempt to reduce variation can begin. Once a clear picture is available, tools typically used in the Analyze Phase of the DMAIC model are valuable.

Sometimes this phase requires scientific testing such as a Design of Experiment (DOE) or Hypothesis testing. However, this phase may be completed quickly by simply engaging focus groups or having the end user try out the product.

In innovative design projects, optimizing is just as important as creating the product.

Application

The application represents the product rollout and marketing strategy. In a typical Lean Six Sigma project, the ILSS practitioner is not responsible for hyping the product. However, the ILSS practitioner knows that securing buy-in is essential. Therefore, managing the rollout is usually part of the assignment. Marketing is overseen by a different department altogether. However, in innovative design projects, marketing is considered part of the project.

A market emphasis on design innovation is placed on branding. Branding is creating a unique name and image for a product. There are several things to remember when marketing a product. For example, the product title should be kept clear and short. In addition, the title should be practical as well as descriptive.

Product images should be high-quality with appropriate captions. Product descriptions should offer an overview with the essential information in the first sentence. This sentence should include the benefit of the product. Marketing uses the term "Call to Action." A Call to Action is a word or phrase that allows the product to be purchased. The most common Call to Action on the Internet would be to Add to the Cart. In print ads, it might be Buy Now.

Today, the types of media to be used are an essential topic. How the advertisements will appear in the different forms of media should be considered, along with the costs for production and implementation. For low-priced products, some rich-media features are not profitable.

In summary, the SSD Global Model for International Innovative Design was explicitly developed for the ILSS practitioner who has yet to have the opportunity to work in this type of environment. The model is intended to provide enough foundation information to allow the ILSS practitioner to engage in critical-thinking skills necessary to contribute to the design effort. WCEA also highlights the main methodological differences between innovative design models and typical LSS methods. For example, creating a solution and building the prototype happens much earlier in innovative design models than in the DMAIC process. In addition, external marketing, which is typically not a part of a Lean Six Sigma effort, is a significant component of innovative design models.

The WCEA model may also be a stand-alone model for an ILSS practitioner charged with creating a process for innovative design. In this case, WCEA would be the outline and industry-specific tools, and compliance would be built into each model phase.

A recap of the WCEA model shows that the Watermark Phase forms the big picture. The Creation Phase is where the product is built. The Enhance Phase is where the product is optimized. Finally, the Application Phase is where the product is rolled out to the public (perhaps only as a pilot) with an effective marketing strategy.

Index

Pages in *italics* refer to figures and pages in **bold** refer to tables.

A

Accreditation Association for Ambulatory Health Care, 192
Accreditation Commission for Health Care, 192
Activity Network Diagram, 142
ADDIE model, 178–180, 185
adult learners, 182–183
affinity diagram, 81
Agile, 16, 22, 233–234
Allied Signal, 227, 247, 259, 290
American Academy of Project Managers, 25
American National Standard (ANSI/PMI99-001–2008), 19
American National Standards Institute (ANSI), 19
American Society of Quality (ASQ), 8, 51
  ASQ-SSBOK, 8–11, 13–14
Analysis-Design-Development-Implementation-Evaluation, *see* ADDIE model
analytical problem-solving tools, *see* Seven Tools of Quality
Analyze Phase, 72, 265, 281–282, 296, 311–312
  activities, 69, 98–99
  ANOVA, 109–110
  correlation analysis, 100
  Design of Experiments (DOE), 108–109
  5 Whys, 100
  objective, 97
  outcome, 131
  Seven Tools, 101
  Statistical Process Control (SPC), 103–106
  statistical thinking, 101–103
  Stem-and-Leaf Diagram, 106–107
  tools, 99, 131
  Type I or Type II errors, 107
analyze phase of ADDIE Model, 178
ANOVA, 103, 109–110
Application Phase of WCEA Model, 321
artificial intelligence (AI), 199–206
  concept, 199–200
  decision-making, 205–206
  increasing efficiency, 203
  Lean Six Sigma and, 200–201
  quality control, 204–205
  reducing waste, 203
  streamlining processes, 201–202
ASQ, *see* American Society of Quality
Australia, Lean Government in, 37
Australian Institute of Project Management, 25
autocratic leaders/leadership, 156
Automotive Industry Action Group (AIAG), 94

B

Baldrige, Malcolm, 261, 275, 292, 306
benchmarking, 87–88
  internal, 171

BIM, *see* Building Information Modeling
Black Belt, 52, 229–230, 239–242, 269, 284–290, 315–316
box plots, 143, *144*
brainstorming, 41–42
Bridges model, 175; *see also* change management
Brown, Mike, 159
Building Information Modeling (BIM), 140
Business Analysis Body of Knowledge (BABOK®), 214, 269–270, 300–301
business finance, 27, 216, 272, 302–303
Business Process Reengineering (BPR), 215, 271, 301

C

Canada, Lean Government in, 37
Capability Analysis, 92
Capability Maturity Model Integration (CMMI), 263, 294
CAPM, *see* Certified Associate in Project Management
cause-and-effect diagram, 58–59, *59*
CBAP®, *see* Certified Business Analysis Professional™
c chart, 105; *see also* control charts
Certified Associate in Project Management (CAPM), 24–25
Certified Business Analysis Professional™ (CBAP®), 270
CGMP, *see* Current Good Manufacturing Practice
change management, 26, 156, 163–176, 271, 302
  Bridges model, 175
  DMAIC model as, 168–174
  GSS model, 167–168
  internal benchmarking, 171
  Kotter's 8-Step, 166
  Kübler-Ross model, 176
  Lewin's 3-Stage model, 166
  models, 163
  Nudge Theory, 174–175
  primarily people-centric model, 174
  primarily process-centric model, 164–174
  resistance, 173
  scorecards, 172
chatbots, 202
check sheet, 56–57, *58*
Class I medical devices, 194
Class II medical devices, 194
Class III medical devices, 195
closed-loop system, 122–123
Close-out activities, 125–126
CMMI, *see* Capability Maturity Model Integration
common cause variation, 267, 298
communication, 5, 233
Community Health Accreditation Program, 192
competency models, 236–246
  Black Belt, 239–242, 287–290
  Green Belt, 237–239
  Master Black Belt, 243–245
Compliance Team, Inc., 192
CompUSA, 159
Constraint Management, *see* Theory of Constraints
continuous improvement (CI), 31, 37–38, 40–42, 155, 160, 173, 193, 218, 223, 227–228
continuous learning, 6–7
Continuous Process Improvement (CPI), 7, 39–42
control charts, 63, *65*
  c chart, 105
  healthcare organizations, 191
  np chart, 105
  p chart, 104
  SPC and, 103–105, 108–109
  u chart, 105
  X-bar/R chart, 104
Control Phase, 72, 119–129, 134, 266, 282, 297, 313
  activities, 70, 119–120
  close-out activities, 125–126
  documentation, 121–123
  ROI calculations, 121
  5S plans, 123–125
  standardization, 122
  sustainability, 121–123, 126–129

tools, 132
transition plan, 121–123
COPQ, *see* Cost of Poor Quality
Correlation analysis, 100
Cost of Poor Quality (COPQ), 10–11, 147
COVID-19 pandemic, 223, 231–233
Cp and Pp indexes, 91–92
CPM, *see* Critical Path Method
creation phase of WCEA model, 320
crisis management, 232–235
root cause analysis, 234–235
Critical Path Method (CPM), 142–143, *143*
Critical-to-Quality (CTQ), 10, 36, 51, 69, 77–79, *80*, 88, 92
CTQ, *see* Critical-to-Quality
cultures, training, 183–184
current Good Manufacturing Practice (cGMP), 196
customer focus, 7
customer satisfaction, 277, 307

D

data collection plan, 94–96
decision-making, AI and, 205–206
decisiveness, 5
Defects per Million Opportunities (DPMO), 225
Define-Measure-Analyze-Develop-Verify (DMADV), *see* DMADV
Define-Measure-Analyze-Improve-Control (DMAIC), *see* DMAIC model
Define Phase, 71, 73–83, 133, 264, 279–280, 295, 310–311
activities, 68
affinity diagram, 81
CTQ, 77–80, *80*
Kano model, 81–82, *82*
objective, 74
outcome, 130
process mapping, 75
project charter, 75–77
QFD, 79–80
SIPOC, 78–79, *79*
SWOT analysis, 76–77
tools, 74, 130
WBS, 80–81
delegation, 5
Delphi technique, 144–145
Deming, W. Edwards, 11, 55, 85, 164, 184–185, 209, 230, 260, 267, 274–275, 291, 298, 304–305
Department of Defense (DoD), 33
Department of Health and Human Services, 34–36
Department of Homeland Security (DHS), 33–34
Department of Veterans Affairs (VA), 32
Design for Lean Six Sigma (DFLSS), 44–46
Design for Six Sigma (DFSS), 44–46, 212, 266, 297
design innovation, 208–209
Design of Experiments (DOE), 108–109, 114
Design phase of ADDIE Model, 178
design thinking, 207–220
BPR, *see* Business Process Reengineering
business finance, 216
innovation, 207–210
ISO 9000, 217
ISO 12500, 217
ISO 13053, 217
ITIL, 217–218
leadership development, 216
Lean Six Sigma and, 220
MBNQA, 218–219
MSA, *see* Measurement Systems Analysis
organizational development, 216–217
PMBOK® Guide, 214–215
PRINCE2, 217
TRIZ, 209–212, 218
Development phase of ADDIE Model, 178
DFLSS, *see* Design for Lean Six Sigma
DHS, *see* Department of Homeland Security
DMADV, 13, 45, 212, 266–267, 297
DMAIC model, 17, 23, 35, 229, 264–266, 279–282, 295–297, 310–313
Analyze Phase, *see* Analyze Phase
benefits, 132
as change management, 168–174
Control Phase, *see* Control Phase
Define Phase, *see* Define Phase

implementation, 134–135
Improve Phase, *see* Improve Phase
Measure Phase, *see* Measure Phase
summary, 130–136
toll gate, *see* toll gate
value stream mapping (VSM), 70
work breakdown structure (WBS), 68, 80–81
DMEPOS (durable medical equipment, prosthetics, orthotics, and supplies), 197
documentation, 121–123
Documented Information, 7
document retention program, 123
DoD, *see* Department of Defense
DOE, *see* Design of Experiments
DSS, *see* Design for Six Sigma
durable medical equipment (DME), 197

E

efficiency, AI and, 203
Egypt, 41
8D method, 139–140, 279, 310
E-learning, 181–182
engagement, leaders/leadership, 157–159
enhancement phase of WCEA model, 320–321
Enron financial fiasco, 159
evaluation phase of ADDIE Model, 179
expectations, 6

F

fact-based decision making, 7
Failure Mode and Effects Analysis, *see* FMEA (Failure Mode and Effects Analysis)
Five Ps, 28–29
5S plans, 36, 123–125, 283, 313–314
5 Whys, 100
flowcharting, 55–56, *56*
FMEA (Failure Mode and Effects Analysis)
Improve Phase, 114–115
Measure Phase, 89–91, *90*
formative evaluation, 179
Frequency Diagram, 106
F-test, 103

G

Gantt chart, 145
General Electric, 224, 229
Goldratt, Eliyahu M., 22, 276, 307
Governance, Structure, and Systems (GSS), *see* GSS (Governance, Structure, and Systems) model
Government, Lean, 30–38; *see also* specific country
Green Belts, 51–52, 229–230, 237–239, 269, 285, 300, 315
GSS (Governance, Structure, and Systems) model, 167–168; *see also* change management

H

healthcare organizations, 189–193
Healthcare Quality Association on Accreditation, 192
Health Facilities Accreditation Program (HFAP), 191–192
Hickenlooper, John, 34
hiring managers, 238–239, 242, 245
histogram, 59–60, *60*
Hungary, Lean Government in, 37
hypothesis testing, 102–103

I

implementation of Lean Six Sigma, 314–318
arguments supporting, 316
implementation phase of ADDIE Model, 179
Improve Phase, 72, 134, 265–266, 282, 296, 312–313
activities, 69, 112
Design of Experiments (DOE), 114
FMEA, 114–115
mistake-proofing, 111–113, 115, 117
project plan, 115–117
risk management, 116–117
time management, 113
toll gates, 115
tools, 112, 131–132
WBS, 114–116

Information Technology Infrastructure Library (ITIL), 16, 217–218
innovation, 207–210; *see also* design thinking
Institute of Electrical and Electronics Engineers, 19
Instructional Systems Design (ISD), 178
internal benchmarking, 171; *see also* benchmarking; change management
International Institute of Business Analysis (IIBA), 214, 270, 300
International Lean Six Sigma (ILSS), 3
  quality concepts, 276–277
International Organization for Standardization (ISO), 262–263
  certification, 3–4, 262–263, 293–294
  ISO 16, 4, 7
  ISO 9000, 3–4, 8, 217, 262, 292–293
  ISO 9000:2015, 4
  ISO 9001, 4, 195
  ISO 9001:2015, 8, 13
  ISO 12500, 217
  ISO 13053, *see* ISO 13053
  ISO 13485, 195–196, 198
  ISO 14000, 8, 262, 293
  ISO 14001, 8
  key terms, 7
  overview, 3
  project management, 18
Ishikawa, Kaoru, 55, 230, 276, 307
ISO 16, 4, 7
ISO 9000, 3–4, 8, 217, 262, 292–293
ISO 9001, 4, 195
ISO 12500, 217
ISO 13053, 8–15, 217
  benefits, 14–15
  ISO 13053–1, 9–12
  ISO 13053–2, 12–13
ISO 13053–1, 9–12
ISO 13053–2, 12–13
ISO 13485, 195–196, 198
ISO 14000, 8, 262, 293
ISO 14001, 8
ISO 21500, 18, 20
  goal, 21
  ISO 21500:2015, 18
  ISO 21500:2021, 19

J

Joint Commission, 189–190, 192–193
Juran, Joseph, 55, 184–185, 230, 260, 274–277, 291, 305–306

K

Kaizen Events, 35, 46–47
Kano model, 81–82, *82*
Key Process Input Variables (KPIV), 98, 277
Key Process Output Variables (KPOV), 98, 277
Kotter's 8-Step, 166; *see also* change management
KPIV/KPOV (Key Process Input or Output Variables), 98
Kübler-Ross model, 176; *see also* change management

L

Laissez-faire leaders/leadership, 156
"Leaders Asleep at the Wheel", 158
leaders/leadership, 7, 22, 26, 216, 271, 302
  activities, 160–161
  autocratic, 156
  building team, *see* team building
  challenge, 152–162
  change management, *see* change management
  creating project plan, 153–154
  defining project scope, 152
  engagement, 157–159
  evaluating project, 155
  laissez-faire, 156
  models, 41
  participative, 156
  PMO functions, 162
  project execution, 154–155
  relation-oriented, 157
  self-assessment, 159–160
  servant, 157
  styles, 156–157
  task-oriented, 157
  transformational, 157
  Western corporate models, 161

leading by example, 6
Lean Manufacturing, 43, 70, 226–227, 232, 241, 268–269, 299
Lean Six Sigma
  artificial intelligence (AI) and, 200–201
  COVID-19 and, 223, 231–233
  design thinking and, 220
  healthcare organizations, 189–193
  history, 223–231
  medical devices, 195–198
  tools, 139–146, 240–241, 278–279, 288–289, 308–310
  see also specific tool
Lean Thinking, 35, 268, 299
Lewin, Kurt, 156–157
Lewin's 3-Stage model, 166; *see also* change management

M

Malcolm Baldrige National Quality Award (MBNQA), 218–219, 261, 291–292
management principals, 4–7
manuals, training, 182
Master Black Belt, 52, 229–230, 243–245, 285, 289, 302, 316
matrix diagram, 145
Maytag, 227, 247, 259, 290
Measurement Systems Analysis (MSA), 26–27, 94, 215–216, 272, 302–303
Measure Phase, 72, 133, 264–265, 280–281, 295–296, 311
  activities, 68–69
  benchmarking, 87–88
  Cp and Pp indexes, 91–92
  data collection plan, 94–96
  FMEA, 89–91, *90*
  MSA, 94
  outcome, 130–131
  process map, 87
  purpose, 86
  reliability, 93
  scorecards, 88–89, *89*
  Sigma calculations, 91
  toll gate, 92–93
  tools, 86–87, 131
  validity, 93
medical devices, 195–198
  Class I, 194
  Class II, 194
  Class III, 195
  durable, 197
  ISO 13485, 195–196, 198
  RFIDs, 196
mistake-proofing, 111–113, 115, 117
Motorola, 224, 229
MSA, *see* Measurement Systems Analysis
Mutually Beneficial Supplier Relationships, 7

N

National Committee for Quality Assurance, 192
Non-US-based governmental entities, 36–38
non–value added, 41
np chart, 105; *see also* Control charts
Nudge Theory, 174–175

O

Operational Excellence (OE), 7, 39–42
organizational development, 216–217, 272, 303

P

Pareto chart, 61, *61–62*
participative leaders/leadership, 156
p chart, 104; *see also* Control charts
PEMDAS (Parenthesis, Exponents, Multiplication, Division, Addition, and Subtraction), 105
Plan–Do–Check–Act (PDCA), 17, 23, 35, 45–46, 228, 273–274, 282, 304–305
plans, training, 180–181
PMBOK® Guide, *see* Project Management Body of Knowledge
PMI-ACP (Agile Certified Practitioner), 24
PMI Risk Management Practitioner (PMI-RMP), 25
PMI Scheduling Practitioner (PMI-SP), 25
Portfolio Management Professional (PfMP), 24
Pp index, *see* Cp and Pp indexes

Primarily people-centric model, 174; *see also* Change management
Primarily process-centric model, 164–174; *see also* Change management
PRINCE2, 18–20, 217
  certifications, 25
  PMBOK® Guide *vs.*, **21**
  revisions, 21
Prioritization Matrix, 145
proactivity, 5
process approach, 7
process-based project management methodology, 21–22
process map, 87
process mapping, 75
  healthcare organizations, 191
Program Evaluation and Review Technique (PERT), 140, 142–143, *143*, 145
Program Management Practitioner (PgMP), 25
project charter, 75–77
project execution, 154–155
project management, 16–29
  ANSI, 19
  benefits, 28
  business finance, 27
  change management, 26
  documents outlining approach to, 18–19
  Five Ps, 28–29
  ISO standard, 18
  leadership development, 26
  MSA, 26–27
  self-study program, 26–29
  WBS method, 17–18
Project Management Association, 25
Project Management Body of Knowledge *(PMBOK® Guide)*, 18–21, 23–24, 48–49, 71, 214–215, 241–242, 270, 301
Project Management Institute (PMI), 16, 18, 21, 270, 301
  certifications, 24–25
Project Management Practitioner (PMP), 25
Project Management Professional (PMP), 24
project plan, 115–117, 153–154
P-value, 103

Q

QFD, *see* Quality Function Deployment/Design
Quality Body of Knowledge (Q-BoK™), 214, 269, 300
quality control, AI and, 204–205
Quality Function Deployment/Design (QFD), 79–80, 146
quality impact, 277, 308
Quality Management System (QMS), 7
Quality System Regulations (QSR), 196
Quick Start Guide, 147–151

R

radio-frequency identification (RFID), 196
RAND Corporation, 144
Rapid Improvement Events, *see* Kaizen Events
regression analysis, 108–109
relation-oriented leaders/leadership, 157
relationship building, 6
reliability, 93; *see also* Validity
resistance to change management, 173
RFID, *see* Radio-frequency identification
risk-based Thinking, 7
risk management, 24, 116–117
ROI calculations, 121
root cause analysis
  crisis management, 234–235
  healthcare organizations, 191

S

scatterplots, 62–63, *63*
scope creep, 24
SCORE®, 47
scorecards, 88–89, *89*, 174
self-assessment, leaders/leadership, 159–160
self-study program, 26–29; *see also* project management
servant leaders/leadership, 157
Seven Tools of Quality, 43–66, 101, 141, 278
  cause-and-effect diagram, 58–59, *59*
  check sheet, 56–57, *58*
  control charts, 63, *65*

flowcharting, 55–56, *56*
histogram, 59–60, *60*
Pareto chart, 61, *61–62*
scatterplots, 62–63, *63*
Shewhart, Walter, 55, 274, 305
Sigma calculations, 91
6 Ws, 141–142, 279, 309–310
SIPOC, 78–79, *79*
6 Ms, 141, 278–279, 309
Six Sigma, 224–225
Six Sigma Black Belt Body of Knowledge (ASQ-SSBOK), 8–11, 13–14; *see also* American Society of Quality
special cause variation, 267–268, 298
speed, 268–269, 299
stabilization processes, 268, 298–300
standardization, 122
statistical hypothesis test, 102–103
Statistical Process Control (SPC), 103–106, 108–109, 140; *see also* control charts
statistical thinking, 49, 101–103, 267, 297
statistics, 216, 272, 302
Stem-and-Leaf Diagram, 106–107, 146
streamlining processes, 201–202; *see also* artificial intelligence
summative evaluation, 179
supplier satisfaction, 277, 307
SurgiChip tag, 196
sustainability, 121–123, 126–129
conserving resources, 126–127
improving employee morale, 127
increasing efficiency, 128–129
reducing costs, 126
reducing waste, 128
SWOT analysis, 76–77, 283, 314
System Approach to Management, 7

T

Taguchi, Genichi, 275–276, 306
Taguchi method, 114
Taiwan, 41
task-oriented leaders/leadership, 157
team building, 22, 153, 286–287, 317–318
Telemedicine, 189
Theory of Constraints (TOC), 22, 283, 314
Theory of Inventive Problems Solving (TRIZ), 22, 209–212, 218
3 Ps, 141, 278, 309
time management, 113
TOC, *see* Theory of Constraints
toll gate, 67, 92–93, 115; *see also* DMAIC model
Total Quality Management (TQM), 23, 183–184, 230, 260–262, 291–293
traditional project management, 21
training
cultures, 183–184
manuals, 182
plans, 180–181
transfer of ownership, 122
transformational leaders/leadership, 157
transition plan, 121–123
TRIZ, *see* Theory of Inventive Problems Solving
T-test, 103, 109
Type I or Type II errors, 107

U

u chart, 105; *see also* Control charts
United Kingdom, Lean Government in, 37
United States, Lean Government in, 30–36
Department of Defense (DoD), 33
Department of Health and Human Services, 34–36
Department of Homeland Security (DHS), 33–34
Department of Veterans Affairs (VA), 32
U.S. Food and Drug Administration (FDA), 194, 196–197

V

VA, *see* Department of Veterans Affairs
validity, 93; *see also* reliability
Value Stream Mapping (VSM), 35, 50, 70
healthcare organizations, 191
variability, 267–268, 298
common cause, 267, 298
special cause, 267–268, 298
video conferencing, 231
virtual collaboration, 231

Vital Few Xs, 98, 277
Vital Few Ys, 98, 277
VOC, *see* voice of the customer
voice of customer/employee/business/process, 269, 299
voice of the customer (VOC), 36, 269, 299
VSM, *see* value stream mapping

W

Wall Street Journal, 158–159
waste, 41, 49–50
  AI and, 203
  as a defect, 285–286, 316–317
  misconception, 268
  necessary, 49
  reduction, 49–50, 268, 294, 299
Watermark Phase of WCEA Model, 319–320
WBS, *see* Work Breakdown Structure
WCEA (Watermark-Creation-Enhancement-Application) Model, 219, 318–322
  application, 321
  creation, 320
  enhancement, 320–321
  watermark, 319–320
White Belts, 229, 285, 315
Work Breakdown Structure (WBS), 17–18, 68, 80–81, 114–116

X

X-bar/R chart, 104

Y

Yellow Belt, 51–52, 229, 285, 315

Printed in the United States
by Baker & Taylor Publisher Services